The Live Longer Now Cookbook

for Joyful Health & Long Life

by Jon N. Leonard and Elaine A. Taylor

Publishers · GROSSET & DUNLAP · New York

A FILMWAYS COMPANY

Dedication

This book is affectionately dedicated to Nathan and Ilene Pritikin and to the many devoted workers in the Longevity Institute in Santa Barbara, California.

The authors and publishers wish to remind you that it is sound practice to consult your doctor before beginning any new dietary program.

Contents

iv

Foreword

The Live Longer Now Cookbook is a prescription for a life free of the degenerative diseases that afflict most Americans in their middle or later years. While the hundreds of excellent recipes it contains will add zip and zest to your daily diet, that is not the book's real importance. The real importance of this cookbook lies in the fact that it places within your hands the means to effect a change in dietary lifestyle largely ensuring that you will never develop heart disease or other degenerative diseases that stem from dietary causes.

Heart disease is responsible for one out of every two deaths in our country. We now know from mounting evidence that, with the proper diet, it is largely within our personal control to avoid becoming a fatal statistic.

Our daily diet is responsible for diminishing our enjoyment of life in many ways. As we age, we exhibit a gradual loss of sensory functions. Our hearing, visual acuity, and even our sense of touch diminish. This progressive encroachment on our sensory functions is so universal a phenomenon in our culture as to be accepted as normal and inevitable; yet it too is largely a result of diet.

Worldwide epidemiological studies have shown that there are native populations that are virtually free of both cardiovascular disease and the tendency to lose sensory functions with age. The dietary patterns of these populations tend to be similar but are markedly different from those in the Western developed nations.

Native populations consume only about 10% of their total calories in fat while the average American diet is made up of 40–50% of total calories in fat. The large quantity of animal protein eaten by Americans and others in affluent nations results in an average daily cholesterol intake of 600 milligrams; the small amount of animal protein eaten by the native populations studied provides negligible dietary cholesterol. The mainstay of the native population diets is carbohydrate food (in the form of cereal grains, vegetables and fruits) that has not been processed or refined. The American diet minimizes carbohydrates, and usually these carbohydrates have been processed and refined.

These intriguing dietary clues have been researched in laboratory experiments with animals whose circulatory systems very closely resemble man's. The results have confirmed the evidence from the population studies: high-fat diets promote cardiovascular disease; low-fat diets help prevent heart disease and can also cause heart disease to regress.

Recent clinical data in studies by Professor David Blankenhorn and his associates at the University of Southern California, and at the Longevity Rehabilitation Center in Santa Barbara, California, of which I am the director, is corroborating the relationship between diet and heart disease. Several hundred patients have now completed the Longevity Rehab Center 30 day live-in session program, in which a 10% fat diet and exercise are the primary therapies; evidence of reversal of heart disease symptoms, as determined by treadmill electrocardiograph testing, is mounting.

Ultimately, dietary treatment is the salvation for almost all heart disease patients. The use of drugs to lower cholesterol level does not save the heart disease patient, as has been demonstrated by the massive federally-funded Coronary Drug Project. The patients at the Longevity Rehab Center whose heart disease symptoms vanish as a result of dietary therapy come to us armed with dozens of drugs; 80% leave drug-free. Many of them have had bypass surgery but are now fighting to keep their new grafts from closing. Diet therapy offers the only practical way of stopping the process of artery disease that caused their original artery blockage.

Generalized artery blockage is the key characteristic in heart disease. In almost all cases of heart disease, the heart itself is not diseased. It is the arteries feeding the heart, which have gradually become blocked by lesions or plaques that effectively reduce the area in which blood may flow. The lesion-forming process, known as atherosclerosis (replacing the old term, arteriosclerosis), is at work all over the body, in the smaller as well as the larger arteries.

Progressive reduction of the area in which blood may flow in the body arteries deprives the body tissues of the oxygen it normally receives from the flowing blood. As a consequence, we eventually fall victim to a host of problems, including the decline in performance of our sensory organs. We may develop high blood pressure—the body's method of compensating for the reduced blood flow in the arteries, and this may lead to strokes. We may find it difficult or painful to walk, due to inadequate circulation to the limbs. We may have insufficient circulation to the heart, producing the terrible pain of angina. Other systems of the body may also be affected.

None of these conditions need occur if our diet is directed against the formation of the arterial lesions or plaques. Some recognition of the need for lowering our fat intake has resulted in the advocation of compromise diets. These diets, which only slightly lower the percent of dietary fat consumed, have been demonstrated to be insufficiently effective in helping the heart disease patient. Nor do they avoid the ultimate blocking of arteries by lesions. What does work is a diet based on a food composition similar to that consumed by native populations found to be remarkably free of cardiovascular disease, a diet that has been confirmed in laboratory studies as a successful means for preventing and treating heart disease, and one which has been further confirmed in clinical experience conducted at the Longevity Rehab Center and other research centers.

The Live Longer Now Cookbook answers a great need, providing hundreds of palate-pleasing recipes based on a plan for a 10% fat intake and a safe maximum cholesterol intake of 100 milligrams daily (about 3-4 ounces of animal protein per day). This is a diet plan that has been demonstrated to be effective in preventing heart disease and in promoting the regression of its symptoms. If you follow this diet, you can add many healthy years to your life.

Nathan Pritikin
Director
Longevity Research Institute

Preface

A wise and loving cook has two goals. The first is to provide eating pleasure for all who taste his or her meals. The second is to provide, in these meals, a foundation for good health and long life.

But does the wise cook, the cook whose goal it is to provide both eating pleasure and healthful food, usually attain this goal? We emphatically think not. For the past forty years, heart disease, hypertension, and other equally serious maladies that are directly related to the food we eat have been on the increase in Western culture. The "delicious dishes" that are endlessly presented in cookbook literature almost always violate the simplest principles for avoiding these ailments. Thus it is nearly impossible to use today's cookbooks (as even the wisest cook must do at times) and still achieve the goal of producing healthful meals.

The purpose of this book, therefore, is to give the wise cook an alternative. All the recipes within these pages are specifically designed to avoid the diet-related maladies of modern society and thereby to pave the way to longer, healthier living.

We suggest that you read the introductory chapters before you begin using the recipes. This material will provide a thumbnail sketch of the health principles used throughout, and will show how you, as the cook, may begin putting them into practice.

We wish you and your family the best of health and culinary satisfaction as you start on the road to achieving the wise cook's central goal: fine taste together with fine health and a long life.

Acknowledgments

The authors wish to acknowledge the deep-felt debt that is owed the many people who contributed in an important way to the making of this cookbook. Recipe contributions and suggestions literally came from all over the world.

For their efforts in recipe preparation, manuscript review, or manuscript preparation, our thanks go to: Betty Joseph, Nadine and Jerry Davis, Beth Reynolds, Renay Coyne, C. C. Morris, Calista Leonard, the Pritikin family, Doris Taylor, Darlene Taylor, Inge Stupak, Dorothy MacArthur, Carl Marsch, Janet Lindner, John Van Uden, Sylvia Gilbar, and Donna Caruthers.

For their patience and understanding, our special thanks go to the publishing people at Grosset & Dunlap.

And finally, to those in our personal lives who have experienced with us the pleasure and pain of writing this cookbook, we offer a mixture of thanks and apologies.

Guide to the Use of This Book

This book is a general cookbook. It is designed primarily for the health-conscious cook, but it may be used just as easily by the cook who is not particularly concerned about health matters. The dabbler will find it quite easy to use these recipes from time to time when the urge for a "shot of health" or a little variety strikes. The purist, on the other hand, will find it possible to prepare every meal from the principles and recipes contained herein. Naturally we, the authors, like to encourage purism in longevity cookery, because we are so very aware of the health benefits that accrue. But we don't discourage the dabbler. Dabbling can be a lot of fun, and may eventually lead to full-time longevity cookery. But whether you are a purist or a dabbler, the information that follows will be quite important for the easy use of this book.

CONVENTIONS USED

Parentheses are used in the ingredients list of the recipes to flag optional ingredients: these may be used or omitted at the cook's discretion.

Temperatures are always in Fahrenheit degrees.

Measurements are always level.

Commercial Products Whenever a commercial product is called for (e.g., a 15-ounce can of tomatoes), it is always assumed that the cook has selected a product that is free of fat, sugar, salt, and other gremlins (see Shopping Guide, page 30).

Use the liquid in the can, whenever a can of something is called for, unless otherwise stated.

When dried foods like pastas, beans, and rice are called for, they should be uncooked, unless otherwise stated.

Vegetables are always raw, unless otherwise stated.

Ingredient-Naming Conventions When a recipe calls for flour, it means unbleached white wheat flour, not whole wheat flour or rye flour. When it calls for peas, it means green peas, not chick-peas. These and many other naming conventions are used in this book. How is the cook supposed to know these conventions? Table 1 summarizes all the naming conventions used in the book, so the reader need only refer to it to resolve any ambiguity.

Composition of Foods Be sure to read page 29 about learning the composition of the foods we eat.

Use of Boldface Type Boldface type is used in two ways in this book. Throughout the main portion of the text, boldface type indicates a recipe that exists in the book. If **Sour Cream** is mentioned, it refers to the sour cream recipe on page 334. It does *not* refer to the kind of sour cream one buys at the market. Such sour cream is always high in fat, whereas the recipe on page 334 is 100% fat free. In the index, however, boldface type serves a different purpose: it is used to indicate all recipes, instructions, and citations that pertain to vegetarian eating. Thus, a vegetarian using the index would simply look only for entries in boldface.

TABLE 1
Naming Conventions Used

Allspice: ground allspice

Apples: red apples

Arrowroot: arrowroot flour

Basil: basil leaves (same as sweet basil leaves)

Bread crumbs: dried bread crumbs

Cardamom: ground cardamom

Cinnamon: ground cinnamon

Cumin: ground cumin

Curry powder: mild curry powder

Dry mustard: mild dry mustard

Egg white: uncooked, fresh egg white

Flakes: Dehydrated minced vegetables are always referred to as "flakes." Thus, for example, *onion flakes* always mean dried minced onions, and anything at the market that matches this description can be used.

Flour: unbleached white wheat flour

Ginger: ground ginger

Green beans: same as snap beans or string beans

Green cheese: hard green skim cheese; a strong Swiss-style cheese, often sold in the shape of a little cone (2 inches) under the name Sapsago cheese.

Green pepper: green bell pepper

Horseradish: ground dried horseradish

Junket: Junket brand rennet tablets

Mace: ground mace

Marjoram: marjoram flakes

Nutmeg: ground nutmeg

Onion: Spanish onion

Oregano: ground oregano

Paprika: mild paprika

Peas: green peas

Pepper: ground black pepper

Peppercorns: black peppercorns

Red pepper: cayenne pepper or ground red chili peppers

Rosemary needles: dried rosemary needles

Saffron: ground saffron

Sage: ground sage

Skim milk: fresh liquid skim milk

Tamarind: dried tamarind pods, including shell, flesh, and seeds. Medium tamarind = tamarind pod containing 2 seeds. (See also page 35.)

Tarragon: dried tarragon leaves

Thyme: ground thyme

Vermouth: dry, white vermouth

CHAPTER 1

Introduction

ABOUT THIS BOOK

This is a book about the art of *longevity cookery*. Health and long life are what this cookbook is all about. The heart of longevity cookery is cooking without certain substances that we call "food-gremlins." These food-gremlins are fat, sugar, salt, caffeine, and cholesterol. Indeed, there are specific health reasons for eliminating these substances from our diet, and we shall discuss them in the pages that follow. For the moment, let us simply state that eliminating food-gremlins is most beneficial to health and longevity, and something every conscientious cook should strive for.

Longevity cookery, therefore, means gremlin-free cooking, which is an unusual kind of cooking to be sure. Indeed, most international cooking literature tends to rely rather heavily on the use of gremlin foods. The extent to which ordinary cooking depends on fats, sugars, and salt can be seen by scanning the recipes of any cookbook; recipe after recipe will call for one or more of these substances, in unfortunately large quantities.

The reader who has not yet experienced the pleasure of low-gremlin cookery is in for a pleasant education. Fat, sugar, and salt, used so abundantly in cooking everywhere, are *taste-maskers.* While adding their own flavor and texture, they usually hide much of the flavor and texture of the foods to which they are added. When these substances are omitted, the subtle and delicate natural food flavors are no longer hidden. The longer one experiences gremlin-free cookery, the more sensitive one becomes to actual food flavors and textures.

In a sense this cookbook is a result of a recent advance in our knowledge of health and long life and their relationship to what we eat. In 1974 a group of scientists published the results of their findings on the subject of food and health, in a book for the layman.[1] These findings, the most up-to-date and authoritative in the field, demonstrated the remarkable effects that a low-gremlin diet has on longevity and general health. The logical next step was to get this longevity cookery information into the hands of the homemaker so that these health benefits could actually be put to practice. This cookbook is an attempt to do that.

ABOUT GOOD HEALTH

Nearly everyone has the potential to have a long and healthy existence. The body is *supposed* to work well; it was designed that way. Its sixty trillion cells, if properly treated, will work in perfect synchrony throughout an individual's life.

In a way, good health is the absence of illness; that is, the absence of breakdown in the body's complex machinery. But more than the absence of illness, *good* health is the body's state of peak

1. *Live Longer Now* by Jon N. Leonard, Jack L. Hofer, and Nathan Pritikin; Grosset & Dunlap, Inc., New York (1974). If the reader does not already have this book, it would be an excellent idea to get it. It will add greatly to the reader's understanding of food and nutrition.

performance; doing not only what it's supposed to do, but doing it well with capacity to spare.

The lack of *good* health is everywhere apparent in our culture: obesity, degenerative disease, and fatigue are hallmarks of today's society. Sadder even than the fact that the lack of good health shortens our life is the fact that it deprives us of much of the joy and satisfaction that life offers.

A foundation of good health makes our tasks easier and our rewards more enjoyable. On the job, tip-top health facilitates tip-top performance and imagination. The quality of our health at home may spell the difference between a smooth-running, robust household and a disorganized, depressed one. Even the pleasure of our party times is increased by peak health. Good health puts us in harmony with our world. Every moment and every thing takes on new freshness and beauty when our body is operating at maximum efficiency.

ABOUT NOT-SO-GOOD HEALTH

Illness in today's society comes mostly in the form of the *degenerative diseases:* heart disease (the number-one killer), atherosclerosis, diabetes, high blood pressure, and stroke. These diseases account for most of the deaths each year (over a million in the United States alone) and most of the need for health care. Thus the eradication of these degenerative diseases would virtually wipe out the largest segment of ill health in modern society.

The thrust of the recent findings regarding degenerative diseases is that they are caused by improper eating habits[2] and can be both prevented and reversed by the adoption of longevity (low-gremlin) cookery. It has been estimated that a nationwide adoption of new eating habits would, by itself, increase the national lifespan by

---

2. And improper exercise habits. (See *Live Longer Now*, cited in previous footnote.)

about twenty years. Therefore, by adopting these new eating habits the *individual* can achieve better health and an increased lifespan.

GETTING LOST HEALTH BACK AGAIN

In our society, when health is lost it is usually lost to one or another of the degenerative diseases. To the best of our knowledge, there is nothing that will return this sort of lost health so quickly and so reliably as low-gremlin eating. An example of its effectiveness is illustrated by the Long Beach Veterans Study, recently completed.[3]

The study involved thirty-eight veterans between the ages of 45 and 70, who were living in the vicinity of Long Beach, California. All participating veterans suffered extensively from degenerative disease. Nineteen veterans were selected first and were examined to determine precisely the extent and severity of their various illnesses.[4] These people were designated the experimental group—the group that would begin eating low-gremlin foods in an attempt to reverse their degenerative conditions.

Next, nineteen more veterans, matched as closely as possible in age and physical condition to the first group, were selected. These were designated the control group; they would continue on whatever diet and under whatever medical care they were presently receiving.

The study took six months. During this period the experimental group ate as many meals as possible at the study headquarters,

3. The study involved exercise (walking) as well as low-gremlin eating. Detailed results of the study may be obtained by writing: Longevity Research Institute, 627 Lilac Drive, Santa Barbara, Calif., 93108. Ask for a copy of "1975 Long Beach Veterans Study." Enclose $1.00 to defray printing, mailing, and handling costs.

4. Examinations were exhaustive, requiring a full day of each participant's time, and included, among many other things, X-ray angiography and four-color thermography as a means of measuring the extent of artery damage due to degenerative disease.

where low-gremlin meals were provided nine hours a day, seven days a week. Participants were encouraged to take all meals there and spend as much time there as practicable.

For those in the experimental group who complied with the dietary regimen, health improvements were phenomenal. Blood pressure levels dropped immediately to normal or near-normal levels. The blood cholesterol level and the blood triglyceride level (measures of heart attack risk) dropped 33 percent in the average participant. The distance a participant could walk without developing claudication or angina pains increased typically from blocks to miles. Most meaningfully, there was a suggestion in many of the participants of a reopening of arteries that had been significantly closed by degenerative disease. Such a reversal in arterial closure under controlled study conditions had never before been obtained in humans. By the study's end, most participants in the experimental group were off all drugs, walking miles each day, and feeling better than they had felt in years.

Participants in the control group, however, did not fare so well. None showed significant improvement in blood pressure, cholesterol level, triglyceride level, walking ability, or arterial closure. And none was off drugs.

Advanced age need not be a limiting factor in recovering good health. Consider the case of Mrs. Eula Weaver. Mrs. Weaver, a great-grandmother in her eighties, began a program of exercise and low-gremlin longevity cookery as a last-ditch effort to regain lost health. At that time she was taking numerous drugs for her arthritis and her atherosclerosis symptoms (angina and high blood pressure). Fifty feet (indoors around the living room) was the limit of her walking ability. In six months, Mrs. Weaver's walking had expanded to several city blocks. By the end of the second year, Mrs. Weaver was jogging more than a mile a day and was off all drugs. By the summer of her third year, Mrs. Weaver, by then 86 years old, surprised even her closest friends by entering the Senior Olympics held in Irvine, California. And she brought home gold medals in both the half-mile and the one-mile run.

Mrs. Weaver's successes have startled and pleased many, including a number in the medical profession. The American Medical Association published an enthusiastic story about her, along with a photo of her competing at the Senior Olympics.[5]

The point of all this is that longevity cookery works and works well in the restoration of good health.

ABOUT WEIGHT CONTROL

We all know that our weight is controlled by the caloric value of the food we eat. But few people realize that *how much* food we eat is controlled by something else: the appestat mechanism. The purpose of the body's appestat is to regulate the amount of food we take in so that our weight does not fluctuate too rapidly. It is like the thermostat in a room, which regulates the amount of heat taken into the room so that the room's temperature remains constant. For many individuals the appestat mechanism is amazingly reliable; despite large variations in the kind and quantity of food available, a person's weight may fluctuate within a narrow range of only a few pounds over twenty or thirty years.

The kind of food we eat affects the functioning of the appestat. But the average American diet, with its high fats and concentrated sweets, creates an appestat malfunction that will cause the appestat to call continually for a larger quantity of these foods than the body needs. The result? Steady weight increase. Efforts to reverse this increase will fail unless the appestat returns to normal functioning. The dieter usually fights his appestat with all the will power he can muster. Unfortunately, however, will power is no match for a malfunctioning appestat.

Longevity cookery helps to reestablish a properly functioning appestat, one that serves to control weight. By eliminating high gremlin foods and concentrated sweets, and replacing them with complex carbohydrates, we give the appestat the materials it needs to function properly. No more food will be called for than is necessary to maintain a healthy and proper body weight.

Longevity cookery is an excellent way for one who is overweight to reduce, and an excellent way for one who is not overweight to maintain a constant weight. Use the calorie table on the following pages to estimate caloric intake if weight reduction is in order. This is the world's first longevity cookery calorie table. It contains calorie counts for most common longevity foods, as well as calorie counts for the basic recipes in this book (those recipes for things like sauces, breads, cheeses, etc., that might well be used as basic ingredients in meal after meal).

TABLE 2
Calorie Table for Common Foods and Selected Recipes in This Book (When computing calories for the recipes in this book, optional ingredients were *always* omitted.)

BREADS

FOOD	AMOUNT	CALORIES
Corn Pitas	1 pita (2⅔ ounces)	173
Dinner Rolls	1 roll (2 ounces)	136
Lefse	1 lefse (2¼ ounces)	80
Pita Bread	1 pita (2⅔ ounces)	173
Sourdough Biscuits	1 biscuit (1 ounce)	58
Sourdough Bread	1 slice (1 ounce)	85
Water Bagels	1 bagel (1¼ ounces)	75
White Bread	1 slice (1 ounce)	75
Yeast Corn Muffins	1 muffin (2 ounces)	122

DAIRY PRODUCTS

FOOD	AMOUNT	CALORIES
Buttermilk	1 cup	81
Cottage Cheese	1 cup	125
Cream Cheese	1 cup	188
Egg white	1 medium egg	15
Fresh Cheese	1 pound	376
	1 cup (grated)	60
Hoop Cheese	1 pound (2 cups)	376
Instant Cheese	½ cup	94
Skim milk	1 cup	81
Sour Cheese	1 cup	188
Sour Cream	1 cup	125
Whey	1 cup	54
Yogurt	1 cup	101

FRUIT JUICES, VEGETABLE JUICES, AND OTHER NONDAIRY BEVERAGES

FOOD	AMOUNT	CALORIES
Apple juice	1 cup	106
Apple Milk	1 cup	93
Apricot Cooler	1 cup	100
Apricot nectar	1 cup	130
Banana Shake	1 shake (1½ cups)	218
Blackberry juice	1 cup	84
Coffee, decaffeinated	1 cup	0
Grapefruit juice	1 cup	85
Grape Juice	1 cup	150
Half-Whey Orangeade	1 cup	78
Herb tea	1 cup	0
Hot Alfalfa Tea	1 cup	0
Lemon juice	1 tablespoon	3
Lime juice	1 tablespoon	4
Orange juice	1 cup	102
Peach nectar	1 cup	109
Pear nectar	1 cup	118
Pineapple juice	1 cup	125

Pineapple-Orange Whey	1 cup	87
Pink Lemonlessade	1 cup	91
Tangerine juice	1 cup	97
Tomato juice	1 cup	43
Vegetable juice	1 cup	48
Whey Lemonade	1 cup	90

FRUIT

FOOD	AMOUNT	CALORIES
Apples	1 medium (¼ pound)	60
Apricots	1 medium (2 ounces)	27
Bananas	1 medium (⅓ pound)	87
Blackberries	1 cup	93
Blueberries	1 cup	95
Cantaloupe	1 medium (1 pound)	68
Cherries	1 pound (about 60 large cherries)	242
	1 large cherry	4
Figs, fresh	1 pound (about 10 large figs)	363
	1 large fig	36
Fruit cocktail	1 cup, water-packed, canned	84
Grapefruit	1 small (1 pound)	90
Grapes, green seedless	1 pound (275 grapes)	275
	1 grape	1
Guavas	1 medium (¼ pound)	68
Honeydew melon	1 medium (1 pound)	94
Lemons	1 large (⅓ pound)	30
Mangos	1 large (⅓ pound)	67
Nectarines	1 small (2 ounces)	34
Oranges	1 medium (½ pound)	85
Papayas	1 small (1 pound)	118
Peaches	1 large (½ pound)	75
Pears	1 medium (¼ pound)	63
Pineapple	1 medium (2 pounds)	250
	1 cup diced, fresh	90
	1 cup diced, canned (water-packed)	90
	1 cup diced, canned (juice-packed)	130
Plums	1 pound (10 medium)	300
	1 medium	30

Raisins	1 tablespoon	27
Raspberries	1 cup	80
Strawberries	1 cup	60
Tangerines	1 large (¼ pound)	50
Watermelon	1 melon ball (¾ inch)	3
	1 pie-shaped wedge (¾ inch thick, 6 inches wide)	50

MEAT, FISH, AND POULTRY[1]

FOOD	AMOUNT	CALORIES
Bluefish (filets)	1 pound	531
Bonito (filets)	1 pound	762
Bullhead (filets)	1 pound	381
Butterfish (Gulf; filets)	1 pound	431
Chicken (whole)	1 pound	229
(breast)	1 pound	295
(thigh)	1 pound	304
(leg)	1 pound	175
(back)	1 pound	187
(wing)	1 pound	143
Chuck steak (boneless arm cut)	1 pound	521
Cod (filets)	1 pound	354
Flank steak (boneless, no visible fat)	1 pound	631
Flounder (filets)	1 pound	358
Grouper (filets)	1 pound	395
Haddock (filets)	1 pound	358

1. Calorie figures for beef assume the beef is "good" grade (see page 34). For all meats, the amount column shows the amount of meat as purchased, including any bone and fat. Calories are for the edible portion of the meat, *after all visible fat has been trimmed off at home.* Unless otherwise stated, calories are computed for the uncooked meat. (Cooked meat may contain fewer calories if fat is rendered and discarded during cooking. Each tablespoon of discarded fat reduces the calorie count by 100 calories.) Don't be fooled into thinking that some meats are less caloric than others just because we show a pound of some cuts having fewer calories than a pound of others. Remember, fewer calories in the cut of meat very often comes because the cut has more inedible bone or trimmable fat (wasted poundage).

Hake (filets)	1 pound	336
Halibut (filets; Atlantic, Pacific, California)	1 pound	445
Hamburger, leanest (30% fat, maximum)	1 pound	812
Lamb leg	1 pound	403
Ocean perch (filets)	1 pound	415
Pike (filets)	1 pound	410
Pork chop (loin chop, thin class pork)	1 pound	574
Red snapper (filets)	1 pound	422
Rockfish (filets)	1 pound	440
Round steak (boneless)	1 pound	545
Salmon, pink[2] (filets)	1 pound	540
(steak with bone)	1 pound	475
(canned, water-packed)	One 7-ounce can	280
Sea bass (filets)	1 pound	422
Short loin (T-bone steak)	1 pound	360
(club steak)	1 pound	416
(porterhouse steak)	1 pound	371
Sirloin steak	1 pound	385
Sole (filets)	1 pound	358
Squid	1 small (¼ pound)	95
Trout (Brook; flesh only)	1 pound	458
Tuna (Yellowfin filets)	1 pound	603
(canned, water-packed)	One 6½-ounce can	234
Turkey, cooked		
(light meat)	One ¾-inch cube	6
(light meat)	1 cup of ¾-inch cubes	180
(dark meat)	One ¾-inch cube	7
(dark meat)	1 cup of ¾-inch cubes	210

2. Avoid salmon (other than pink salmon) because of its high fat content.

SAUCES AND DRESSINGS

FOOD	AMOUNT	CALORIES
Autumn Bean Dressing	1 cup	217
Bean-Thickened Gravy	1 cup	128
Blue Cheese Dressing	1 cup	188
Boiled Dressing	1 cup	147
Buttermilk Mock Sour Cream	1 cup	162
Buttermilk Spring Dressing	1 cup	95
Cheese Sauce	1 cup	152
Chili Salsa	1 cup	83
Compromise White Sauce	1 cup	200
Creamy Salad Dressing	1 cup	141
Curried Pea Sauce	1 cup	147
Enchilada Sauce	1 cup	43
French Dressing	1 cup	82
Fresh Cheese Sauce	1 cup	130
Garlic and Vinegar Dressing	1 cup	74
Green Dressing	1 cup	133
Green Dressing, Yogurt-Style	1 cup	130
Green Molé Sauce	1 cup	117
Hamburger Sauce	1 cup	130
Herbed Yogurt	1 cup	103
Hot Sauce	1 cup	95
Lemon-Dill Marinade	1 cup	25
Lemon Mock Sour Cream	1 cup	115
Mediterranean Sauce	1 cup	90
Mexican Mock Sour Cream	1 cup	166
Mild Pepper Sauce	1 cup	43
Mrs. Marsch's Sauce for Squid	1 cup	100
Mushroom Sauce	1 cup	170
Pimiento Dressing	1 cup	166

Red Chili Liquid	1 cup	30
Red Molé Sauce	1 cup	88
Red Molé Sauce with Tomato	1 cup	81
Richer Mediterranean Sauce	1 cup	164
Sour Cream and Curry Dressing	1 cup	124
Sour Cream and Garlic Dressing	1 cup	126
Sour Cream and Onion Dressing	1 cup	129
Spaghetti Sauce #1	1 cup	67
Spaghetti Sauce #2	1 cup	53
Spaghetti Sauce #3	1 cup	93
Spaghetti Sauce #4	1 cup	60
Spaghetti Sauce #5	1 cup	122
Spaghetti Sauce #6	1 cup	60
Spiced Vinegar Dressing	1 cup	58
Steak Sauce	1 cup	50
Taco Salsa	1 cup	120
Thousand Island Dressing	1 cup	106
Tomato Sauce	1 cup	62
Tuna Mushroom Sauce	1 cup	223
Versatility Sauce	1 cup	107
White Sauce	1 cup	175
Tangy Salad Dressing	1 cup	46

STAPLES
(All uncooked)

FOOD	AMOUNT	CALORIES
Active dry yeast	1 envelope (¼ ounce)	20
Barley, pearl	1 cup	745
Cornmeal (whole ground)	1 cup	575
Cornstarch	1 cup	528
	1 tablespoon	33

Cream of Wheat	1 cup	700
Flour (unbleached, white, wheat)	1 cup	403
(whole wheat)	1 cup	414
Gelatin (Knox unflavored)	1 envelope (¼ ounce)	24
Grape-Nuts	1 cup	400
Junket (rennet)	1 tablet (1½ grams)	1
Kasha (buckwheat groats)	1 cup	600
Macaroni	1 cup	335
Malto Meal	1 cup	600
Milk, nonfat dry	1 cup	224
Millet	1 cup	660
Noodles	1 cup	279
Oats, rolled	1 cup	354
Onion flakes	1 tablespoon	15
Parsley flakes	1 tablespoon	2
Rice	1 cup	726
Rice flour	1 cup	432
Rye flour	1 cup	457
Spaghetti, broken	1 cup	335
Shredded Wheat	1 biscuit (⅚ ounce)	75
Tamarind	1 medium (See page 00)	4
Vegetable Powder	1 tablespoon	30
Vinegar	1 cup	30
Wheat Heart Cereal	1 cup	605
Wheat, whole grain	1 cup	706
Wild rice	1 cup	600
Wine	1 cup	200

VEGETABLES

FOOD	AMOUNT	CALORIES
Artichokes	1 large	50
Asparagus	1 stalk	3
Beans[3], dried (cooked)	1 cup	250

3. Includes red, Mexican red, pinto, black, brown, white (navy), calico, Bayo beans, and some other varieties. Look for green beans, limas, kidney beans, peas, lentils, and black-eyed peas under their own headings.

Beets	1 cup diced, cooked	80
Black-eyed peas, dried		
(cooked)	1 cup	160
Broccoli, raw	1 medium stalk (⅓ pound)	30
cooked	1 cup (flowerets plus chopped stem)	45
Brussels sprouts	1 sprout	6
Cabbage, cooked	1 cup shredded	40
raw	1 cup shredded	20
Carrots	1 medium (3 ounces)	30
	1 cup diced, cooked	60
Cauliflower	1 cup cooked flowerets	30
Celery	1 stalk (2 ounces)	10
	1 cup diced	30
	1 small bunch (½ pound)	30
Chili peppers	1 can (4 ounces)	30
	1 large fresh chile (2 ounces)	15
Corn, on cob	1 medium ear (6 ounces)	90
kernels	1 cup	140
Cucumbers	1 slice (silver-dollar size)	1
	1 large (1 pound)	65
Eggplant	1 medium (1 pound), pared	90
Garlic	1 tablespoon garlic juice	20
	1 clove	10
Green beans	1 cup cooked, sliced	30
Green pepper	1 medium (¼ pound)	20
	1 cup chopped	33
Kidney beans, dried		
(cooked)	1 cup	170
Lentils, dried (cooked)	1 cup	240
Lettuce	1 large leaf	3
Lima beans (cooked):		
dried	1 cup	160
fresh	1 cup	150
Mushrooms	1 cup fresh, sliced	25
	1 cup canned	28
Onions	1 medium (⅓ pound)	58
	1 cup chopped	115

Peas, green (cooked):

dried whole	1 cup	200
split	1 cup	260
fresh	1 cup	110
Potatoes[4], boiled	1 medium (⅓ pound)	90
baked	1 medium (⅓ pound)	90
mashed	1 cup	140
diced, cooked	1 cup	110
Spinach, cooked	1 cup chopped	46
uncooked	1 bunch (1 pound)	85

Squash (cooked):

winter	1 cup mashed	80
summer	1 cup sliced	34
Sweet potatoes (or yams)	1 medium (⅓ pound)	140
Tomatoes	1 medium (¼ pound)	25
	1 cup chopped, fresh	50
	1 cup chopped, canned	50
Tomato paste	One 6-ounce can	140

4. Sweet potatoes listed under own heading.

CHAPTER 2

Cooking for Good Health

FIVE COMMANDMENTS FOR HEALTHFUL EATING

1. DON'T USE FATS OR OILS

    Avoid fatty meats: fatty hamburgers, fatty steak, bacon, sausage, etc.

    Avoid oils: cooking oils, salad oils, vegetable oils, shortening.

    Avoid oily plants: olives, avocados, and nuts.

    Avoid all dairy products except nonfat ones.

2. DON'T USE SUGAR

    Avoid sugar, honey, molasses, syrup, and other simple carbohydrates like them.

    Avoid pies, cakes, and pastries.

    Avoid breads and cereals that are made with sugar, honey, etc.

3. DON'T USE SALT

    Don't salt the plate or the cook pot.

    Avoid obviously salty products such as salted crackers or salted herrings.

4. DON'T USE CHOLESTEROL

Limit total meat and fish intake to ¼ pound daily.

Avoid animal organs (liver, brains, heart, etc.), animal skin, shellfish, egg yolks.

5. DON'T USE COFFEE OR TEA

You may drink decaffeinated coffee or herb teas.

These commandments cover 90 percent of what we need to know to reduce the gremlin level in our cooking. Most of the remaining 10 percent is contained in Table 3 below. This use-and-avoid list supplements the Five Commandments.

The commandments are all negative. They all begin with *Don't*. Much as we all like a positive approach to life, the commandments are best stated in this negative way, because they deal with substances that are poisonous when taken in excess. The best advice with poisons is *always* negative: don't use them in food.

Of course one can't completely avoid salt, because some salt occurs naturally in every food product. In fact, it would not be wise to avoid all salt even if one could, because a little salt is needed for health (about what one would get naturally from vegetables). The point of the commandment about salt is to avoid contaminating one's food with large amounts of it, as happens when one adds salt to the pot or the plate, or when one eats obviously salty food products. Thus if one reasonably and conscientiously avoids salt in his diet, the commandment will be satisfied and salt intake will drop dramatically.

The commandment to avoid fat also bears comment. The body needs some fat. How much is needed? Only a few grams a day: one can almost get one's daily fat requirement from a few leaves of lettuce, so little is needed. What kind of fat is needed? Only the fat from linoleic acid (or one of its close relatives). This fat, termed "essential fat," is found in abundance in all vegetable products. The body can *manufacture*, from carbohydrates and proteins, any additional fat needed: fat for fat-soluble vitamins, fat for linings around the organs, fat for fatty supports around the eye muscles, and so forth.

TABLE 3

	FOODS TO USE	FOODS TO AVOID
MEAT*	Chicken and turkey (white meat preferred; do not eat skin)	Duck, goose, ground turkey
	Veal, lean beef, lean pork, and lean leg of lamb (trim all visible fat before cooking; remove any rendered fat after cooking)	Lamb (except lean leg of lamb), mutton, ham
		Organ meats—liver, kidney, heart, sweetbeads
		Marbled and fatty meats—spareribs, frankfurters, sausages, bacon, luncheon meats, fatty hamburgers, etc.
FISH* & SHELLFISH	Leaner varieties of fish preferred (whitefish, halibut, etc.)	All shellfish
EGGS	Whites only	No egg yolks
VEGETABLES	All vegetables (except olives & avocados)	Olives; avocados
DRIED LEGUMES	Dried peas and beans of all kinds	Limit soybeans to not more than twice a week—they are high in fat.
NUTS & SEEDS	None (sprouted seeds excepted)	All

*Total meat and/or fish intake to be limited to 4 oz. per day.

	FOODS TO USE	FOODS TO AVOID
FRUIT	Fresh fruit (maximum 3–4 pieces per day) Canned fruit in water pack (maximum 4 oz. per day) Raisins and/or prunes (maximum 1½ oz. per day)	Canned fruit packed in syrup Figs, dates
FRUIT JUICES	Limit fruit juices to 6 oz. per day	Fruit juices with added sugar
SWEETENERS	None	Sugar, honey, molasses, etc.
FATS & OILS		Butter, margarine, all cooking oils, lard, meat fat, drippings, vegetable oils, etc.
MILK PRODUCTS	Nonfat (skim) milk **Buttermilk, Cottage Cheese, Sour Cream, Yogurt,** or any of the other homemade products discussed in Chapter 13 Commercial cheese made from nonfat (skim) milk such as hoop cheese, or farmer's or baker's cheese	Whole or low-fat milk (including powdered and canned forms) Creams and nondairy cream substitutes Chocolate milk Yogurt made from whole or low-fat milk All cheeses (except *100% nonfat cheeses*)
BREADS,	Breads or crackers made without oil	Any baked goods with shortening, oil,

CRACKERS & BAKERY FOODS	or shortening, sugar or sweeteners, such as sourdough bread, Scandinavian-type crackers	sugar, or sweeteners, such as cakes, pies, crackers, donuts, sweet rolls, commercial mixes with dried eggs and whole milk
CEREALS	Cold cereals without shortening or sugar, such as Shredded Wheat, Grape-Nuts; hot cereals without shortening or sugar such as oatmeal	Any grain that is not whole, natural, and unbleached.
RICE & GRAINS	Brown rice preferred / Any whole grain	Non-whole grain products are suggested only for occasional use if whole-grain products are not obtainable, as in restaurants.
PASTA	Spaghetti, macaroni, noodles (preferably whole wheat)	Egg noodles or spinach noodles (if made with eggs)
DESSERTS	See Chapter 9	Ice cream, sherbet, puddings, canned fruit in syrup, gelatin desserts with sugar, baked goods with sugar and fats
SNACKS	See Chapter 3	Candy; fried foods such as potato chips
BEVERAGES	Herb teas, decaffeinated coffee, nonfat milk	Soft, hard, and caffeine drinks
CONDIMENTS	Spices of all kinds	Do not add salt to cooking pot or serving dish

The Five Commandments tell us what not to eat. What, then, is left that we *can* eat after we've excluded the things listed there? Plenty. Practically the entire plant kingdom is available for our culinary enjoyment: vegetables, fruits, legumes, grains, etc. We can enjoy dishes containing lean meats: beef, fish, chicken, turkey, and so on, provided we also follow the other recommendations regarding meats listed in the Five Commandments. We can eat pasta dishes such as lasagna and ravioli. We can eat breads (properly made) such as wheat breads, rye breads, and corn breads. We can even partake of delicious desserts that don't violate the Five Commandments. The fact is that we can eat any dish that is made in accordance with the commandments, without fat, sugar, salt, cholesterol, or caffeine. What *can* be eaten is just about everything, but with a change in how it is prepared.

ABOUT NUTRITION

Nutritionally speaking, the food we eat may be divided into five categories: carbohydrates, fats, protein, vitamins and minerals, and bulk.

Carbohydrates are the body's preferred energy source, for they burn with 100-percent efficiency and create no by-products to be disposed of other than water and carbon dioxide. Fats and protein may also be used for energy, but not with the same efficiency. When fats and proteins provide energy, complex by-products are produced that place a strain on the body's handling and disposal systems.

The body prefers to use protein in maintaining old body tissues and constructing new ones. Growing children, lactating or menstruating women, and people recuperating from injury will all have an increased demand for protein.

But, as mentioned earlier, we require very little dietary fat. Except for the daily requirement of a few grams of essential fats, abundantly provided in a minimal amount of vegetables or grains, the body will manufacture all the fat it needs by itself.

Daily percentages of fat, protein, and carbohydrates should be kept within the following limits:

1. fat, 10 to 15 percent of total calories;
2. protein, 10 to 15 percent of total calories;
3. carbohydrates, 70 to 80 percent of total calories.

The percentage of protein suggested is more than adequate to meet the needs of a human being, male or female, under the most demanding conditions of life, including growth, menses, and recovery from injury.[1] The relatively high percentage of carbohydrates recommended will insure that the daily need for calories is met in the most efficient manner, and will eliminate the bodily stresses caused by the consumption of larger percentages of protein or fat. Vegetables, fruits, cereals, breads, and legumes are the main sources of our carbohydrates,[2] and can in fact also supply us with both the protein and the fats we need. Of course meat, fish, and dairy products provide less in the way of carbohydrates, much more in the way of fats, and much protein.

Vitamins and essential minerals are chemicals that are needed for health but which our human bodies cannot make. When we

1. Recent studies indicate that high-protein diets are associated with a leaching of minerals from bones. See, for instance, Morgen, S., *et al.*, *American Journal of Clinical Nutrition*, 27: 584–9, 1974. Other studies suggest that high-protein diets accelerate the aging process. See, for instance, Mazess, R. B., *et al.*, *American Journal of Clinical Nutrition*, 27: 916–25, 1974.

2. It is necessary to draw a distinction between two kinds of carbohydrates: complex carbohydrates and simple carbohydrates. Complex carbohydrates are to be eaten and enjoyed; simple carbohydrates are to be avoided. The difference between the two is a chemical one. Complex carbohydrates are composed of molecules that are large and complex. The human body is accustomed to handling them effectively. Vegetables, cereals, fruit, breads, and legumes are all examples of complex carbohydrates. Sugar, syrup, and honey are examples of simple carbohydrates. The human body is *not* (in an evolutionary sense) accustomed to handling these simple carbohydrates (or foods like pies, cakes, and pastries that are made from them). The simple molecules that make them up are capable of entering the bloodstream directly; no digestion is required. Thus when we eat them, they enter our bloodstream at a much higher rate than the body needs or can handle. The result is rapid fluctuations in blood sugar (first too high, then too low) and a sustained increase in blood fat. Over the long term, these factors influence the development of heart diseases, diabetes, and other degenerative diseases.

TABLE 4

FOOD AND NUTRITION BOARD, NATIONAL ACADEMY

RECOMMENDED DAILY DIETARY

	(years) From Up to		Weight (kg)	(lbs)	Height (cm)	(in)	Energy (kcal)[2]	Protein (g)	Vitamin A Activity (RE)[3]	(IU)	Vitamin B₁ (Thiamin) (mg)
INFANTS	0.0–0.5		6	14	60	24	kg × 117	kg × 2.2	420[4]	1400	0.3
	0.5–1.0		9	20	71	28	kg × 108	kg × 2.0	400	2000	0.5
CHILDREN	1–3		13	28	86	34	1300	23	400	2000	0.7
	4–6		20	44	110	44	1800	30	500	2500	0.9
	7–10		30	66	135	54	2400	36	700	3300	1.2
MALES	11–14		44	97	158	63	2800	44	1000	5000	1.4
	15–18		61	134	172	69	3000	54	1000	5000	1.5
	19–22		67	147	172	69	3000	54	1000	5000	1.5
	23–50		70	154	172	69	2700	56	1000	5000	1.4
	51+		70	154	172	69	2400	56	1000	5000	1.2
FEMALES	11–14		44	97	155	62	2400	44	800	4000	1.2
	15–18		54	119	162	65	2100	48	800	4000	1.1
	19–22		58	128	162	65	2100	46	800	4000	1.1
	23–50		58	128	162	65	2000	46	800	4000	1.0
	51+		58	128	162	65	1800	46	800	4000	1.0
PREGNANT							+300	+30	1000	5000	+0.3
LACTATING							+500	+20	1200	6000	+0.3

1. The allowances are intended to provide for individual variations among most normal persons as they live in the United States under usual environmental stresses. Diets should be based on a variety of common foods in order to provide other nutrients for which human requirements have been less well defined.

2. Kilojoules (KJ) = 4.2 × kcal

3. Retinol equivalents

4. Assumed to be all as retinol in milk during the first six months of life. All subsequent intakes are assumed to be one-half as retinol and one-half as β-carotene when calculated from international units. As retinol equivalents, three-fourths are as retinol and one-fourth as β-carotene.

VITAMINS								MINERALS					
Vitamin B2 (Riboflavin)	Vitamin B6	Vitamin B12	Vitamin C (Ascorbic Acid)	Vitamin D	Vitamin E Activity[5]	Folacin[6]	Niacin[7]	Calcium	Phosphorus	Iodine	Iron	Magnesium	Zinc
(mg)	(mg)	(μg)	(mg)	(IU)	(IU)	(μg)	(mg)	(mg)	(mg)	(μg)	(mg)	(mg)	(mg)
0.4	0.3	0.3	35	400	4	50	5	360	240	35	10	60	3
0.6	0.4	0.3	35	400	5	50	8	540	400	45	15	70	5
0.8	0.6	1.0	40	400	7	100	9	800	800	60	15	150	10
1.1	0.9	1.5	40	400	9	200	12	800	800	80	10	200	10
1.2	1.2	2.0	40	400	10	300	16	800	800	110	10	250	10
1.5	1.6	3.0	45	400	12	400	18	1200	1200	130	18	350	15
1.8	1.8	3.0	45	400	15	400	20	1200	1200	150	18	400	15
1.8	2.0	3.0	45	400	15	400	20	800	800	140	10	350	15
1.6	2.0	3.0	45	—	15	400	18	800	800	130	10	350	15
1.5	2.0	3.0	45	—	15	400	16	800	800	110	10	350	15
1.3	1.6	3.0	45	400	10	400	16	1200	1200	115	18	300	15
1.4	2.0	3.0	45	400	11	400	14	1200	1200	115	18	300	15
1.4	2.0	3.0	45	400	12	400	14	800	800	100	18	300	15
1.2	2.0	3.0	45	—	12	400	13	800	800	100	18	300	15
1.1	2.0	3.0	45	—	12	400	12	800	800	80	10	300	15
+0.3	2.5	4.0	60	400	15	800	+2	1200	1200	125	18+[8]	450	20
+0.5	2.5	4.0	60	400	15	600	+4	1200	1200	150	18	450	25

5. Total vitamin E activity, estimated to be 80 percent as α-tocopherol and 20 percent other tocopherols.

6. The folacin allowances refer to dietary sources as determined by *Lactobacillus casei* assay. Pure forms of folacin may be effective in doses less than one-fourth of the RDA.

7. Although allowances are expressed as niacin, it is recognized that on the average 1 mg of niacin is derived from each 60 mg of dietary tryptophan.

8. This increased requirement cannot be met by ordinary diets; therefore, the use of supplemental iron is recommended.

consistently miss a particular kind of vitamin in our diet we develop one of the vitamin-deficiency diseases—scurvy, pellagra, etc. Vitamins are organic chemicals—chemicals that are made by living things. Plants make vitamins, many animals make human vitamins; microorganisms make them too. A vitamin usually plays the role of a *coenzyme* in the body, acting as the key that enables an enzyme to function. The body has literally thousands of different types of enzymes, each doing its separate job. Taken as a whole, the body's enzymes are the tools responsible for building all the body's complex structures during growth, repair, and maintenance. They are also responsible for disassembling food, and removing worn-out tissue. One can easily imagine that the body would quickly weaken if an entire class of enzymes were made inoperable. A vitamin deficiency very often has precisely this effect: because the particular vitamin is the *co*enzyme for a particular class of the body's enzymes, its absence renders the entire class inoperable and so causes general breakdown in the body's function.

Except for the fact that essential minerals are inorganic (that is, not made by living things), they are like vitamins. They are sometimes found as coenzymes for bodily enzymes, and without them in our diet we develop specific deficiency illnesses.

The best way to get the vitamins and minerals we need is in a broad and balanced diet: plenty of fruit, vegetables, and grain products; a regulated amount of lean meats; and nonfat dairy products. We do not recommend vitamin or mineral supplements for the normal individual on such a healthy diet. For such a person there is no benefit from taking a supplement, yet there is always the danger of serious bodily damage caused by a vitamin or mineral overdose. If you *are* taking supplements (and plan to continue), please see Table 4 on recommended vitamin and mineral dosages. This table has been compiled by the Food and Nutrition Board of the National Academy of Sciences, and we recommend that the dosages indicated not be exceeded.[3] The next table, Table 5, shows

---

3. Not all of the vitamins and minerals are equally dangerous if taken excessively. Vitamins A and D are the most toxic. However, all vitamins show some toxicity in overdose.

the main food sources for the vitamins and minerals recommended by the Food and Nutrition Board. More than anything else, this table illustrates how easy it is to obtain all recommended nutrients simply by eating a wide selection of vegetables, grains, fruits, legumes, dairy products, and meats (in small amounts).

Bulk is just as important in the diet as the nutrients we've discussed. Yet its importance is quite different. It does not provide nutrients directly to the body's cells as the other dietary components do. It simply aids the process of digestion by providing a handy medium for carrying the other materials through the digestive tract during their absorption or elimination. Cellulose, which provides this needed bulk, comes primarily from the fruit and vegetables we eat. It is indigestible because our bodies don't manufacture the enzyme needed to break it down. But it is ideally suited as an intestinal carrying medium, and in this way facilitates our digestion and elimination.

TABLE 5

SOURCES OF NUTRIENTS

Carbohydrates	Fruits and vegetables Milk products, especially whey Grains, breads, cereals, and pastas
Protein	Legumes: beans, lentils, etc. Whole grains, cereals, breads Meat, fish, poultry Milk, yogurt, buttermilk, cheese
Essential fats (linoleic acid)	Vegetables Whole grains, cereals, breads
Vitamin A	Dark green vegetables Swordfish, squid Winter squash, sweet potatoes

Vitamin B₁ (thiamin)	Legumes: beans, lentils, etc. Fish, yeast Chard, kale, corn, potatoes
Vitamin B₂ (riboflavin)	Legumes: beans, lentils, etc. Whole grains, cereals, breads Meat, fish, poultry Milk, cheese, yogurt, buttermilk Dark green vegetables
Vitamin B₆	Legumes: beans, lentils, etc. Whole grains, cereals, breads Meat, fish, poultry Starchy vegetables Dark leafy green vegetables
Vitamin B₁₂	Milk, cheese, buttermilk, yogurt Meat, fish, poultry
Vitamin C (ascorbic acid)	Citrus fruit Pineapple, strawberries Tomatoes, potatoes Other fruits and vegetables
Vitamin D	Sunlight Saltwater fish Fortified skim milk
Vitamin E	Legumes: beans, lentils, etc. Whole grains, cereals, breads Green vegetables
Niacin	Legumes: beans, lentils, etc. Whole grains, cereals, breads Meat, poultry, fish Greens
Folacin	Legumes: beans, lentils, etc. Dark green vegetables Fruit
Calcium	Legumes: beans, lentils, etc. Milk, cheese, buttermilk, yogurt Meat, fish, poultry Whole grains, breads, cereals Green vegetables, salad greens

Phosphorus	Legumes: beans, lentils, etc.
	Milk, cheese, buttermilk, yogurt
	Meat, fish, poultry
	Whole grains, breads, cereals
Iodine	Vegetables grown in iodine-rich soils
	Seafood
Iron	Legumes: beans, lentils, etc.
	Meat, fish, poultry
	Whole grains, breads, cereals
	Green vegetables
Magnesium	Legumes: beans, lentils, etc.
	Milk, cheese, buttermilk, yogurt
	Whole grains, breads, cereals
	Most dark green leafy vegetables
Zinc	Whole grains, breads, cereals
	Meat, fish, poultry
	Milk, cheese, buttermilk, yogurt

COMPOSITION OF FOODS

T-bone steak is a food, a delicious, mouth-watering, old-fashioned, down-home-in-the-country food. We think of steak sauce, lettuce and tomatoes, hot bricks of charcoal for broiling, and baked potato with sour cream and chives when we think about T-bone steak. The same is true of any other food that may cross our minds; foods usually evoke thoughts such as how to make it, how we like it, what to serve with it, how it tastes, and how it smells.

But as we become concerned with the other part of cooking, the part that involves our health, our thoughts of food take on added dimensions. For then our main concern is what foods are made of—their nutritional composition. Just as a good cook must become familiar with how different foods look, taste, smell, and react to heat, so he must become familiar with how much fat, salt, and cholesterol they contain. How does he do this? By obtaining the latest, most up-to-date handbook on the composition of foods, spending time looking up common foods in it, and selecting those with nutritional superiority.

The best handbook in existence on the subject is undoubtedly *Composition of Foods* by B. K. Watt and A. L. Merrill. Everyone interested in health should have a copy of this classic, 190-page book. It gives the vitamin, mineral, caloric, fat, protein, and carbohydrate content of thousands of common kitchen foods. It's not only informative, it's easy to use and it's fun to browse in. The handbook can be obtained from the U. S. Department of Agriculture, or by sending $5.00 to Composition of Foods, P.O. Box 17873, Tucson, Arizona 85731.

SHOPPING GUIDE

Longevity cookery calls for longevity shopping. Shopping for low-gremlin foods is a challenge in today's supermarket, overflowing as it is with thousands upon thousands of sugary, fatty, chemically treated products in every category. The list below will help to identify those products the shopper should look for, and those to avoid. Before shopping, read the list over. It will help you develop a "nose" for low-gremlin foods.

In addition, you will be pleased to discover that longevity cooking will reduce grocery costs significantly. We estimate that the food costs of the average household will shrink by about 25 percent. A large part of this decrease comes from a reduced emphasis on meats, especially the expensive (and fattier) cuts of meat.

Remember the cardinal rule in longevity shopping: read the labels before buying. If the list of ingredients on the label shows that the product contains gremlins, don't buy it. In this book we talk only about the gremlin content of foods; we don't talk about other additives, such as chemical flavors, colors, conditioners, and preservatives. The shopper who hasn't paid much attention to the ingredients on labels may well be shocked to see the long list of chemicals contained in many products. Evidence for the harmfulness of these additives, though plentiful, is not so convincing as the evidence against gremlins. Nevertheless, we feel that a product should be avoided if it contains artificial additives, especially if it contains lots of them.

STAPLES:

Unbleached white flour	Arrowroot flour
Whole-grain flours	Tapioca
Potato flour	Active dry yeast
Rice flour	Unflavored gelatin
Cornmeal	Junket
Cornstarch	

Powdered pectin (often in home canning department of supermarket; made by MCP)
Powdered cultured buttermilk (made by Darigold, Seattle, Wash.)
Vinegar (wine, cider, distilled)
Soups (Acceptable commercial soups exist, but are rare. Avoid bouillon cubes.)

DRIED FOODS:
Beans (red, black, navy, pinto, kidney, lima, etc.)
Mung beans and alfalfa seeds for sprouting
Peas (split peas, garbanzos, lentils, etc.)
Barley
Brown rice
Wild rice
Bulgur wheat (fast-cooking Middle Eastern rice substitute)
Dried wheat berries (whole dried wheat kernels)
Dried chopped vegetables (onions, green peppers, etc.)

SPICES:
Spices play a more important role in longevity cookery than in ordinary cooking, partly because to some extent spices make up for

the loss in flavor that results from omitting salt, fat, and sweeteners, and partly because omitting gremlin substances allows the subtle effects of spices to shine through in a way that is impossible if these substances are present. Table 6 (p. 35) lists all the spices used in this cookbook. Because spices are much more expensive, pound for pound, than other foods, it may be tempting to skimp a bit on them. But they are used only in small (and therefore inexpensive) amounts and can make or break any dish. So have a well-stocked spice cabinet, and make sure that the spices in it are all fresh. In the long run the result will be better-tasting dishes and less food waste. One caution: avoid spice *mixes* containing gremlins as ingredients.

CEREALS AND GRAINS:
Hot Cereals

Wheatena

Cream of Wheat (regular only)

Roman meal

Wheat Hearts

Zoom

Molina brand unprocessed bran flakes

Cold Cereals

Shredded Wheat

Grape-Nuts

Wheat, rye, and oat flakes

Grains

Wheat berries

Oats (rolled oats, steel-cut oats)

Other whole grains (a good selection can often be found in health-food stores.)

BREADS:

Fresh breads: Read ingredients on label before buying. A bread may be used even if salt is indicated on the label, provided the bread does not taste salty (see page 272). Avoid breads containing other gremlins. Sourdough bread, rolls, or biscuits are usually gremlin-free. Whole-grain bread or rolls (whole wheat, rye, pumpernickel) are sometimes free of gremlins.

Specialty breads: Use corn tortillas (avoid flour tortillas) for making tacos, enchiladas, and other Mexican dishes. Use **Pita Bread** (sometimes called Bible bread or Armenian pita) for stuffing sandwich-style.

Crackers:
Norwegian flatbread ⎫
Matzo   ⎪
Rice cakes   ⎬   May not be widely available
Whole wheat waferettes ⎪
Cold water crackers   ⎭

PASTAS:
Macaroni   Manicotti
Spaghetti   Grandini
Ravioli   Noodles (avoid egg noodles)
Lasagna

PRODUCE:
Vegetables: Use fresh, dried, frozen, or canned vegetables. Avoid fatty vegetables, primarily avocados, olives, and nuts. Avoid canned vegetables packed in sugar, fat, or salt. Avoid frozen vegetables in sauces.
Fruits: Subject to the limitations shown in Table 3, use fresh, frozen, canned, or dried fruit.

DAIRY FOODS:
Milk: Use fresh, dry, or condensed nonfat milk. Avoid whole or low-fat milk products.

Buttermilk: Use homemade nonfat **Buttermilk** or find a brand with a fat content less than 1½ percent.[4]

---

4. That is, the percentage of fat, when computed on a weight basis using the fully moisturized product, should be less than 1½ percent. The advertised fat content is usually computed on this basis, and is what the shopper should go by.

Cheeses: Use cheeses that have a fat content of less than 8 percent (on a *dry-weight* basis; see page 327). Hoop cheese, dry curd cottage cheese, farmer's cheese, and pot cheese are often found commercially with such a low fat content. It is quite difficult to find sliceable, meltable, commercial cheeses with a low fat content. If in doubt about the content of a commercial cheese, avoid it. Use any of the homemade cheese in Chapter 13.

Eggs: Use fresh or dried egg whites freely. Avoid the yolks.

JUICE:
Use fresh, canned, or frozen fruit or vegetable juices. Limit fruit juices to 6 ounces per day.

MEAT:
Red meats (beef, pork, lamb): Use fresh, frozen, or canned. Use lean, unsalted cuts. Choose good or standard grades rather than choice or prime. Avoid organ meats (liver, heart, kidney, sweetbreads). Because of their high levels of fat, avoid spareribs, bacon, hot dogs, sausage, luncheon meats, hamburger (other than leanest hamburger[5]), and lamb cuts (other than leg of lamb).

Fish: Use fresh, frozen, or canned. Use the leaner varieties of fish (sole, halibut, snapper, etc.). Avoid the especially fatty varieties (herring, kipper, sardine, shad, smelt, and eel). Use canned fish only if water-packed. Avoid shellfish.

Poultry: Use fresh, frozen, or canned. Use chicken or turkey, avoiding skin and organs. Avoid duck and goose.

---

5. Federal regulations prohibit the sale of hamburger that exceeds 30 percent fat. Within this general limitation, hamburger is sold at all degrees of leanness. Shop around to find a market that sells hamburger that is as lean as possible. (Look for hamburgers that render very little fat when fried.)

TABLE 6
Spices Used in Longevity Cookery

Allspice, ground
Almond extract
Angostura Bitters
Anise seeds

Basil (also called sweet basil leaves)
Bay leaves

Cardamom, ground
Caraway seeds
Cayenne pepper
Celery, seeds and powder
Chervil
Chili powder (avoid salted brands)
Cilantro (also called coriander)
Cinnamon, ground
Cloves, whole and ground
Coriander seeds (also called cilantro)
Cumin seeds, whole and ground
Curry powder, mild

Dill, seed and weed

Fenugreek

Garlic flakes
Garlic powder
Ginger, ground

Herb Seasoning
Horseradish, powdered (use both Schilling and Hime Japanese brands)

Italian Seasoning (blend of dried, minced spices)

Juniper berries, dried

Mace, ground
Marjoram, ground
Mint flakes
Mushroom powder
Mustard, seeds and dry ground

Nutmeg, whole and ground

Onion flakes
Onion powder (see toasted onions)
Oregano, flakes (leaves) and ground

Paprika, mild
Parsley flakes
Pepper, ground (black and white)
Peppercorns (black)

Rosemary, dried needles (leaves)

Saffron, whole and ground
Sage, ground
Savory

Tamarind pods (If not available, substitute 1 tablespoon **Bean Thickened Gravy** plus 1 drop Angostura Bitters for each tamarind.)
Tarragon
Thyme, dried leaves and ground
Toasted onions
Turmeric

Vanilla
Vegetable flakes

THE WELL-STOCKED
LONGEVITY KITCHEN

Let's face it. There's no such thing as the "properly" stocked kitchen. What's proper for one family will not necessarily be proper for another. Individual food preferences, family size, budgetary limitations, and many other factors will influence what ought to be in any kitchen. But just so that you can see what a longevity kitchen *might* contain, we present the following lists. For recipes in bold-faced letters, see Index.

IN THE REFRIGERATOR:
Dairy Products
    Skim milk
    Buttermilk
    Fresh Cheeses
    Cottage Cheeses
    Cream Cheese
    Sour Cream
    Yogurt
    Miscellaneous cheeses: Echtarharkäse cheese, green cheese, moldy blue cheese (used in small quantity to flavor **Blue Cheese Dressing**)
    Fresh and hard-boiled eggs (only the whites are used)

Vegetables
    Fresh lettuce, tomatoes, onions, green peppers, and mushrooms
    Other vegetables in season
    Leftover cooked vegetables

Beverages and Fruits
    Lemons and limes
    Orange juice, apple juice, tomato juice, **Whey Lemonade,** etc.

Grain Foods
> **Sourdough Starter**
> Fresh cornmeal, fresh wheat berries
> Leftover pancakes
> Leftover cooked rice and beans

Condiments
> **Hamburger Sauce**
> **Chili Salsa**
> **Taco Salsa**
> Leftover canned California green chilies
> Pimientos

IN THE FREEZER:
Meats
> Beef steaks (sirloin, round, etc.)
> Leanest ground beef
> fish filets
> Chicken and turkey breasts
> Lamb bones
> **Beef Sausage**
> **Mock Pork Sausage**

Fruits and Vegetables
> Bags and cartons of frozen vegetables: corn, limas, peas,
> broccoli, etc.
> Bags and cartons of frozen berries: blueberries, blackberries,
> strawberries, etc.

Soups, Stocks, Sauces
> Bags of ice cubes of frozen **Bean-Thickened Gravy**, beef stock,
> chicken stock, etc.
> Jars of **spaghetti sauces, soups, stocks, salsas,** etc.

Cheeses
> **Cottage Cheese**
> **Homemade Hoop Cheese**
> **Fresh Cheese**

Breads
> **Pita Bread**
> **Sourdough Bread** and **Biscuits**
> Corn tortillas

Miscellaneous Items in Baggies
> Chopped onions
> Chopped green peppers
> Lemon peels

IN THE CUPBOARDS
Spices

Dried Chilies

Canned Goods (packed without gremlins)
> Condensed skim milk
> Tomatotes, tomato paste, tomato juice
> Canned California green chilies
> Juices (fruit and vegetable)
> Canned fruits (mandarin oranges, pineapple, peaches, etc.)
> Vegetables (beans, green beans, corn, potatoes, etc.)
> Meats (tuna, salmon)

Crackers
> (Norwegian flatbread, matzo crackers, etc.)

Pasta
> (Macaroni, spaghetti, noodles, etc.)

Cereals
> Hot cereals (Wheat Hearts, Quaker Oats, etc.)
> Cold Cereals (Shredded Wheat, Grape-Nuts, etc.)
> Grains (oats, wheat berries, etc.)

Staples
> Flours and starches (all kinds)
> Special staples (yeast, junket, pectin, gelatin)
> Vinegar

Dried Foods
> Beans (red, black, navy, pinto, kidney, etc.)
> Rice (brown rice, wild rice)
> Barley

SITTING OUT
> Bowls of Ripening Fruit
> Bag of Potatoes
> Bag of Onions
> Garlic

EQUIPMENT FOR THE LONGEVITY KITCHEN

No specialized equipment is required for longevity cooking. Equipment we have found especially useful include the following:

Asbestos pad. Put it between the pot and the flame to slow down the heating up of milk when making cheese, and to stabilize the simmer when making stocks.

Blender. The blender is terribly convenient, and an absolute necessity for many recipes. A variable-speed blender with both continuous blending and burst, or chop, blending is quite handy. Some blender manufacturers make minicontainers (about 1-cup capacity) that can be interchanged with the standard 5-cup capacity container. Minicontainers make it easy to make small quantities (1 cup or less) of sauces and dressings, which would be nearly impossible to make with the larger-capacity container. (Small amounts don't always blend well in the large container because the ingredients won't stay close enough to the chopping blades to be chopped up.)

Bowl. Be sure to have a large (10-quart) bowl for making bread.

Bulb baster. Great for removing unwanted grease as well as for basting.

Cake-cooling racks. These little wire beauties come in handy for pizza cooking, chalupa baking, tortilla chip toasting, and even cheese draining.

Cheesecloth. Have plenty on hand. The automotive department of the supermarket is often the place to find it these days.

Chopping board. Can't get along without it.

Colanders. Large colanders, both the legless kind with a handle and the kind with legs that can sit up by itself, are needed.

Containers. Since so much of longevity cookery involves creating basic ingredients at home (stocks, soups, sauces, dressings, etc.), lots and lots of plastic containers are needed in which to store these ingredients until needed. Have all sizes and shapes handy. Be sure to have tight-fitting lids. Containers must be useful for both freezer and cupboard. Plastic zip-lock bags come in handy too.

Electric Mixer.

Grinder. A meat grinder or food mill is needed for grinding cooked and raw meats and poultry.

Ice cube trays. Extra trays are handy for freezing stocks and sauces into cubes that can be bagged and stored until needed.

Knives. All sizes, very sharp, are needed.

Nonstick cookware. Cooking without oil demands an assortment of nonstick cookware. Have Teflon or other nonstick skillet (heavy flat frying surface), frying pan (heavy), cookie sheets, and loaf pans (large, medium, and small).

Pastry brush with natural fibers.

Pastry cloth and stockinette rolling pin cover. Needed for rolling out delicate or hard-to handle pastries. Essential for **Lefse.**

Pots. Large pots for stock making.

Pressure cooker. Nice to have.

Ramekins. These delightful individual casserole dishes, used so often in Italian restaurants, can make many a casserole dish more elegant and easier to serve.

Rolling pin.

Rubber spatula. Can't beat it for scraping blender contents off the sides of the blender and back into the blades.

Scale. A kitchen scale is needed for several reasons: for keeping track of daily meat intake; for measuring yield when making cheese; and for keeping track of calories for the weight watcher.

Steaming basket. A vegetable steaming basket is inexpensive and perfect for steaming vegetables to just the right degree.

Strainers. Both large and small (tea strainer) are essential.

Thermometer. For cheese making, a thermometer that is accurate between 75° and 150° is necessary.

Timer. Have at least one mechanical timer available. Hang it where it is convenient to use (over the stove, for example).

Waterless cookware. Excellent for cooking vegetables with small amounts of water. It leaves them crisp, delicious, and not waterlogged.

Wire whisk. Have an assortment of wire whisks for blending batters, sauces, and egg whites.

Wooden spoons.

Yogurt maker. Yogurt can be made without a commercial yogurt maker, but it sure is handy to have one. It controls temperature for a long period of time. Without it, temperature control is a constant battle.

MENU SELECTION AND MEAL PLANNING

The planning of any meal starts with the selection of a menu, the list of dishes that will be served. What makes a workable menu is influenced by cultural eating customs, family likes, the appetites of those eating, and nutritional considerations. Just imagine the menu differences that would exist between two families, one used to the Oriental custom of taking many small meals throughout the day, and the other used to the American custom of three square meals a day, the largest in the evening. Therefore, selecting a menu must of necessity be a specialized process: whatever menus work for family and friends are good menus.

Dinner menus sometimes pose a special problem. Many of us are accustomed to a dinner with a large meat dish on center stage, which leads us to exceed our daily allowance of ¼ pound of meat. In addition we may be accustomed to accompaniments that tend to violate various of the Five Commandments for Healthy Eating. So here are some helpful ideas for dinner planning.

1. Start the meal with a hearty soup, which can be completely fat- and cholesterol-free but still quite satisfying. Prepare soups in large batches and freeze quantities for future meals.

2. Routinely include a large salad of mixed lettuce combined

with other vegetables, raw or cooked. (Try adding cooked pinto or garbanzo beans to a green salad. Delicious!) The salad helps fill the plate, satisfies the need to chew, and provides needed bulk and nourishment.

3. Serve several cooked vegetable and carbohydrate courses. Have a green and a yellow vegetable and one—maybe two— carbohydrate courses such as a lasagna or spaghetti. The leftover vegetables and the liquid in which they are cooked can be used in the next night's soup or frozen for a future soup. Be sure to offer plenty of bread with the meal, too.

4. The meat, poultry, or fish dish now has been removed from center stage to a position of lesser importance, thanks to putting more emphasis on other meal elements. For the meat, poultry, or fish dish, cultivate recipes in which these foods are used in combination with many other ingredients, such as stews or chop-suey-type dishes. One can cheat on the amounts of the meat, poultry, or fish by using smaller amounts in proportion to the other required ingredients. Even then the dish will be adequately flavored. Or, as a nice change, substitute a vegetable entree for the meat, poultry, or fish dish. A beneficial practice is to cook up enough meat for several meals when using the leaner cuts that require long slow cooking, and to freeze the surplus. The vegetables can be added when the actual meal is prepared. This is a big time-saver. It also helps to reduce meat intake because each cut of meat will need to be budgeted for more than one meal.

5. Dessert, if desired, can be fruit or fruit salad, or any of the satisfying specialties in the desserts chapter.

Planning meals a week ahead can be a real cost-saver. Work for menus that will take advantage of current bargains at the supermarket, and be sure to make plans for using up the leftovers that are bound to accumulate. The menus on the following pages may help in weekly meal planning. Follow these menu suggestions verbatim or use them just as idea starters, whichever works best. (See Index for page numbers.)

MIX AND MATCH DINNER MENU IDEAS

MAIN DISH	ACCOMPANIMENTS	SOUP	SALAD	DESSERT	NICE EXTRAS
Tuna Noodle Casserole	French-Cut Green Beans Chili Baked Squash	Cream of Celery Soup	Garden Green Salad	Junket	Raw Zucchini Spears
Pasta e Fagioli	Cauliflower in Bloom Barrego-Style Beans	Vegetable Soup	Cabbage Salad	Refrigerator Cheese Pie	Savory Tomato Juice Cocktail
Chicken Enchiladas	Pimiento Green Beans Zucchini in Mediterranean Sauce	Filipini Consommé	Mushroom Salad	Ice Cream Pie	Fresh Cheese slices Lefse Bread
Potato-Salmon Bake	Artichokes Mashed Squash	Love Soup	Chrysanthemum Salad	Bernice's Fruit Pie	Sourdough Bread
Chili Corn Pie	Green Peas with Vegetable Flakes Glazed Yams	Minestrone	Zesty Green Salad	Whipped Fruit Mold	Pita Bread
Beefaroni	Broccoli with Cheese Mashed Yams	Leek Soup	International Salad	Grape Gelatin	Sour Cheese Sourdough Biscuits

Main Dish	Vegetables	Soup	Salad	Dessert	Bread
Arroz con Pollo	Asparagus / Baked Acorn Squash	Asparagus Soup	Saturday Tossed Salad	Apple Bake	Corn Pitas
Beef Shepherd's Pie	Cauliflower in Sour Cream / Armenian Stuffed Zucchini	Onion Soup	Rainy Day Salad	Strawberry Yogurt	Buttermilk Herb Bread
Eggplant Enchilada Pie	Fresh Black-Eyed Peas / Mashed Potatoes	Split Pea Soup	Green Bean Salad	Orange Sherbet	Antipasti Misti
Ratatouille sans Oil	Baked Beans / Company Potatoes	Julienne Soup	Pea Salad	Buttermilk Chiffon Cheesecake	Antipasti Misti
Broiled Fish Filets	Lentil and Spinach Loaf / Squash Gourmet	Louisiana Soup	Stuffed Tomato Salad	Junket	Large-Curd Cottage Cheese
Fish in Cheese Sauce	Garden Casserole / Baked Cherry Tomatoes	Cream of Potato Soup	Holiday Salad	Rice Pudding	Dinner Rolls
Salmon-Stuffed Fish Filet Rolls	Vegetable Casserole / Carrots with Pineapple	Pink Soup	Danish Cucumbers	Ice Cream Pie	Sourdough Bread

MAIN DISH	ACCOMPANIMENTS	SOUP	SALAD	DESSERT	NICE EXTRAS
Chicken Cacciatore	Millet and Vegetables Mixed Greens	Barley Soup	Cucumber Salad	Rice Mold	Fresh Cheese
Stuffed Chicken Supreme	Stuffed Potatoes Continental Zucchini	Gazpacho	Zucchini Salad	Refrigerator Cheese Pie	Sourdough Biscuits
Turkey Fricassee	Tomatoed Potatoes Stuffed Yams	Asparagus Soup	Asparagus Tip Salad	Whipped Fruit Mold	Brussels Hors d'oeuvre
Beef Roast	Cabbage and Peppers Farmer's Onion-Cheese Pie	French Onion Soup	Garden Squash Salad	Apple Bake	Dinner Rolls
Swiss Steak	Chili Steamed Corn Spinach and Onions	Tomato and Onion Soup	Buttermilk Coleslaw	Buttermilk Chiffon Cheesecake	White Bread
Hamburger-Macaroni Skillet Dinner	Rice and Onions with Curry Green Beans with Nutmeg	Tomato-Rice Soup	Potato Salad	Rice Pudding	Buttermilk Water Bagels
Everyday Meat Loaf	Corn Pudding Teflon-Fried Zucchini	Potato Chowder	Zesty Green Salad	Apple Pie	Yeast Corn Muffins

PUT ON "STRICTLY VEGETARIAN" DINNERS

MAIN DISH	ACCOMPANIMENTS	SOUP	SALAD	DESSERT	NICE EXTRAS
Green Bean Casserole	Scalloped Potatoes Stuffed Yams	Asparagus and Cream Cheese Soup	Fruit and Cottage Cheese Salad	Noodle Pudding Supreme	Yogurt Sourdough Bread
Mushroom and Potato Garden	Lentil Loaf with Spinach Topping Grated Beets with Orange	Lentil Soup	Pineapple Sour Cream Salad	Fresh Fruit Dessert	Herb Bread Buttermilk (with Orange Juice)
Skillet Corn and Peppers	Appled Rice Chili Beans	Rice and Yogurt Soup	Cloved Peach Salad	Spiced Applesauce	Corn Tortillas
Corn and Pepper Noodle Bake	Eggplant and Chickpeas Stove Potatoes	Quick Vegetable Soup	Carrot and Pea Aspic	Apple Pie	Dinner Rolls
Vegetarian Stuffed Peppers	Yogurt Scalloped Potatoes Macaroni and Cheese	Lima Bean Soup	Savory Cottage Cheese Salad	Orange Fluff	Ricotta Cheese
Nada's Vegetarian Cabbage Rolls	Zucchini Lasagna Kasha	Tomato Bouillon	Green Bean Aspic	Yam and Apple Pudding	Nachos

MAIN DISH	ACCOMPANIMENTS	SOUP	SALAD	DESSERT	NICE EXTRAS
Vegetable Pot Pies	Macaroni Custard Lima Bean Patties	Alphabet Soup	Cottage Cheese and Tomato Salad	Hawaiian Ambrosia	Zippy Tom
Enchiladas	Scalloped Potatoes with Vegetables Squash Empanada	Fresh Tomato Rice Soup	Pineapple and Grapefruit Salad	Orange Gel	Tortilla Chips
Manicotti	Refried Beans Creole Corn	Red Lentil Soup	Pineapple Cottage Cheese Salad	Strawberry Crepes	Corn Tortillas
Spinach Lasagna	A Whey to Cook Rice Company Potatoes	Minestrone with Rice	Green Bean Mold	Stewed Fruit Sauce	Sourdough Bread

TRY SIMPLE LUNCHEON MENUS

MAIN DISH	SALAD	BEVERAGE	EXTRAS
Pita Meat Loaf Burger	Saturday Tossed Salad	Whey Lemonade	Fruit Cups
Pita Pizzas	Zesty Green Salad	Buttermilk	Junket

L.A. Chalupas	Cottage Cheese and Tomato Salad	Banana Shake	Dog Bone Cookies
Pita Burritos	Lettuce and Tomatoes	Apple Milk	Tortilla Chips
Garbanzo Burgers	Danish Cucumbers	Apricot Cooler	Sourdough Biscuits Hamburger Sauce
Macaroni and Beans	Zucchini Salad	Iced Coffee (decaffeinated)	Sourdough Bread
Senate Bean Soup	Garden Green Salad	Zippy Tom	Lefse
Alphabet Soup	Green Been Salad	Pineapple-Orange Whey	Pita Bread
Chili con Carne	Cucumber Salad	Iced Camomile Tea	Yeast Corn Muffins

PLAN ZIPPY BREAKFASTS

MAIN DISH	BEVERAGE/FRUIT	EXTRAS
Dorothy's Spanish Omelet	Tomato Juice Orange Segments	Sourdough Toast
Country-Style Oats	Half Grapefruit Hot Coffee (decaffeinated)	Sourdough Biscuits
Breakfast Bagels Hot Wheat Hearts Cereal	Buttermilk mixed with Orange Juice	Hard-Cooked Egg White Slices with Apple Slices

MAIN DISH

Eggs à la Buckingham

Sourdough Pancakes

Breakfast Spaghetti

French Toast

Toasted Wheat Berry Cereal

BEVERAGE/FRUIT

Half-Whey Orangeade
Apple slices

Hot Coffee (decaffeinated)
Half Grapefruit

Buttermilk

Apple Milk

Orange Juice
Grapefruit

EXTRAS

Fresh Cheese Slices

Blueberry Sauce

Sourdough Toast

Wild Blueberry Sauce

White Bread Toast

COOKING TIPS

Longevity cooking is, in some ways, quite simple. Everyday meals can require minimum preparation. Rice, simple whole-grain cereals, a few basic breads, a few lean-meat casserole dishes, and a wide variety of fresh and cooked vegetables are key items in longevity cookery and are easily prepared. In some ways, however, longevity cooking can be quite involved. If, for example, we want to enjoy old favorites like cheesecake or pizza, we will have some work to do. The supermarket sells neither longevity cheesecake nor longevity pizza. If these are what we want, we'll have to make them from scratch, using special techniques. The recipes explain the special techniques needed, when they are needed. A few general tips that may also prove useful are presented in the paragraphs below.

The nonstick cooking surfaces (Teflon, Teflon II, Baker's Secret, etc.) will be most useful for cooking without fats or oil. Use nonstick pots, pans, cookie sheets, muffin tins, casseroles, etc.

In common usage, *sauté* means to fry rapidly in fat. In longevity cookery, however, *sauté* means to cook rapidly in water or other permissible liquid (like garlic juice plus water). Chopped vegetables sautéed the longevity way are actually more flavorsome and more useful as cooking ingredients than vegetables sautéed in fat or oil.

Fat is a word one encounters often in this cookbook. Some people mean only *animal fat* when they use the word *fat*. But we mean much more. We mean all substances that, chemically, are fats. This includes animal fats, of course. But it also includes oils, like cooking oils that are liquid at room temperature. It includes solid shortenings: hydrogenated vegetable shortenings, all-purpose shortenings, lard, butter, and margarine. It includes the vegetable oils: olive oil, corn oil, safflower oil, etc. And naturally it includes the fatty drippings from cooked meats. Chemically, all these items are fats. Avoid them all in longevity cookery.

Skim fat from soups, stocks, and many other dishes by refrigerating (or even placing in freezer) for several hours. Fat will rise to the top and congeal for easy removal.

Ground meat can be browned directly—without adding fat, in a preheated heavy pan (or Teflon utensil). As the meat sticks, loosen it with a spatula and stir. Slow-brown leaner meats. Place meat plus a tablespoon or two of liquid (water, broth, tomato juice) into a cold Teflon skillet. Heat over a moderate flame and stir occasionally. Continue heating until meat is well browned, after which onions, garlic, green pepper, and so on may also be added. The process takes a bit of time, but results are good. Another method is to place the meat under the broiler for quick browning, then remove it to continue preparation on top of the stove or in the oven. This method works well with such foods as pot roasts, stew meat, and chicken. (To broil chicken, strip the skin from all of the pieces before placing on the broiler pan.) Baste if required with rendered juices.

To fry lean steaks, try slicing very thin while still partially frozen and then frying immediately in a Teflon skillet.

To make fatless gravies, begin with a cold stock (beef, chicken, etc.) that has been skimmed of fat. Use 1 tablespoon of cornstarch or arrowroot per cup of stock. Mix cornstarch or arrowroot with a little of the stock and make a paste. Add a little more stock to make a thinner paste. Heat remaining stock over moderate flame, stir in paste, and cook until thickened.

Making breaded chicken, fish, eggplant, and so forth is done in three steps. First, moisten each piece in a suitable liquid (stock, skim milk, water, tomato juice, etc.). Second, dip each piece in a suitable breading mixture (matzo meal, dried sourdough bread crumbs, seasoned cornmeal, flour, etc.). Third, place on a Teflon baking surface and bake in a 350° oven. (Baste with liquid if desired.)

Follow these rules when reheating foods:

- Reheat white-sauced foods in a double boiler over water.
- To reheat a roast, either reheat the whole roast by allowing it to return to room temperature and then heating it in a 350°

oven, or slice the roast paper-thin and then pour boiling gravy over the slices.

- Bring casseroles to room temperature, then reheat in a 325° oven.
- Reheat soups by bringing to a boil and serving quickly.

To make broiler-pan cleaning a lot easier, don't leave the pan in the oven while the oven is preheating. Keep it cool. Put the meat to be broiled into the hot oven on a cool pan, and cleaning will be a snap.

To hard-boil eggs, cover with cold water, bring to a boil, cover, remove from heat, and let stand 20 to 25 minutes. The eggs will cook by standing in the hot water, and the shell will peel off easily.

When egg whites are called for in a recipe for cooking, powdered egg white may be used. (If the egg whites will not be cooked at some point, use only fresh egg whites.) Egg whites prepared from the powder should be stored in the refrigerator in a nonmetallic, well-sealed container. Discard after one week. Sniff for freshness before using. If in doubt, throw them out.

Sometimes recipes from other cookbooks can be converted to longevity cookery by appropriate substitutions. Here are some that will often work:

- If the recipe calls for whole eggs, use the white of 2 eggs for each whole egg called for.
- If the recipe calls for a cheese, a sour cream, a sauce, a dressing, etc., for which there is an identically named recipe in this book, substitute the ingredient prepared from the recipe in this book for the ingredient called for. (Thus, if the recipe calls for a cottage cheese, use the appropriate cottage cheese recipe in this book.)
- If the recipe calls for a fat, and the fat is to be used only for sautéing, substitute an equal amount of garlic juice and water.
- If the recipe calls for whole milk, use skim milk.
- If the recipe calls for salt, omit it. (This *rarely* affects the chemistry of the recipe, only the taste. Sometimes added gar-

lic or red or black pepper is needed to put zip back in the taste.)

- If the recipe needs to be sweet to be good, and calls for sugar, honey, etc., it will be hard to convert. It can be sweetened with mashed fruits or fruit juices, but these ingredients can involve problems of their own (see page 283).

Regular nonfat dry milk tastes much different than instant nonfat dry milk, and is called for in several recipes. The instant nonfat dry milk is not an appropriate substitute. The regular dry milk is considerably harder to mix up than the instant dry milk. A blender is helpful in this task.

Corn tortillas keep well in the freezer. To use them after they have been frozen, simply warm them in the oven or in the microwave. They easily become quite manageable again.

Bean sprouts and sprouts from seeds like alfalfa seeds and wheat seeds make truly delightful ingredients and garnishes for salads, Oriental dishes, and rice dishes. So lovely and healthful, these simple sprouts are fun to prepare at home. Follow these directions.

- Use untreated mung, soy, lentil, wheat, or alfalfa seeds or beans. Have ready a strainer and a nonmetallic container. Ideal containers are crocks, bean pots, cookie jars, and mixing bowls covered with dinner plates. A Mason jar placed inside a can will do just fine.

- *First Day.* Rinse ½ cup beans (⅛ cup seeds) several times in strainer. Place in warm water (4 parts water to 1 part beans) and let stand in warm place 8 hours or overnight.

- *Second Day.* Rinse beans in strainer and clean container out. Size of beans will now have doubled. Place beans in a container that has room for 8 times the amount of swelled beans (1 cup swelled beans in a 2-quart container). Cover and put in cupboard. Rinse beans in strainer with warm water about 3 times a day, cleaning or changing container each time. Do not permit any standing water in the container.

- *Third Day.* Often, sprouts are ready on the third day. (Commercially available sprouts are often past their prime.)

- Beans are ready to serve when sprout is about 1 inch long. The whole sprout is edible. For green sprouts, keep the beans or seeds in the light from the second day on. Sprouts kept out of the light will be white. When sprouts reach desired length, refrigerate in a sealed container. Sprouts will keep in refrigerator for 8 to 10 days.

There are a number of different vinegars on the market, most of which are permissible in longevity cookery. They differ in taste, and affect foods differently. Wine, malt, and cider vinegars are all made by natural organisms. Distilled (or white) vinegar is simply acetic acid, made in the laboratory. If a particular vinegar is called for in a recipe, be sure to use it. If the kind of vinegar is not specified, use distilled vinegar.

Spices are quite important in longevity cookery. Be sure that spices on hand are fresh. Replace ground spices and dried-flake spices on a yearly basis. Store tightly covered in a cool, dark place in the kitchen. Use the information in the Vegetable Cooking and Spicing Chart on page 344 as a guide to the seasoning of vegetables. Remember that strong-flavored vegetables need more spicing than mild-flavored ones. Follow the directions in the recipes for the spicing of meats and other dishes.

To peel tomatoes, plunge them briefly into boiling water. Skin will then peel off easily.

Tamarinds are used as a spice for steak sauces, curry sauces, and other well-seasoned sauces. In this book, when we call for tamarinds, we mean dried tamarinds. The dried, discardable shell peels off easily, revealing a fleshy inside, which in turn contains hard seeds. (Like peanuts, tamarind pods can contain 1, 2, 3, or even more seeds per shell, and also like peanuts, the tamarind shell has a nodule for each seed. When we call for a medium tamarind, we mean one with 2 nodules, that is, 2 seeds.) Use the flesh and seeds for spicing. The flesh softens and can be dissolved in the cooking liquid when cooked. The seeds have to be fished out and put aside. (May be reused for other dishes at a future time.) A workable substitute for 1 medium tamarind is: 1 tablespoon **Bean-Thickened Gravy** plus 1 drop Angostura Bitters.

Kelp is used in several recipes. Since kelp is seaweed, it is salty. We don't expect the reader to use it unless it is desalted first. To desalt kelp, boil a few minutes, then drain and discard the water.

CHAPTER 3

Appetizers

The appetizer has a single purpose: to whet the appetite for the meal to follow. It may be a first course served at the table, or it may be served hors d'oeuvre fashion in the living room. At the table it is usually presented in individual dishes, whereas in the living room it is usually adapted for finger eating. One can be totally imaginative in creating appetizers that are decorative, appetite stimulating, and complementary to the meal.

GREEN PEPPER CASKS

Use a large green pepper as a cask for holding an appetizer dip. Cut the top off the pepper in an attractive fashion, saving the top for a lid. Remove seeds and ribs from the pepper, fill it with **Sour Cream** or other appropriate dip, and place it at the center of a serving dish that has been covered with a bed of lettuce. Arrange a selection of vegetables, such as radish rosettes, cucumber slices, cauliflower slices, zucchini slices, carrot sticks, celery sticks, etc., around the dip-filled pepper. For added decoration, make several bundles of **Raw Zucchini Spears;** hold the spears together with onion ring bands or orange rind bands. Distribute the bundles around the plate. For variety, use additional green pepper casks on the same platter to hold such dippables as bread cubes, cheese cubes, or meat cubes. Provide toothpicks or little forks to facilitate dipping.

GARDEN BASKET

Served without a dip, this appetizer is light as Spring and deliciously attractive. Make a spray arrangement of long carrot and celery sticks (leaves remaining on some of the celery sticks) in an attractive napkin-lined bread basket. Place radish rosettes over the carrots and celery to give the impression of a radish mound from which the celery and carrots emanate. Place carrot curls over and around the radish mound and in other nooks and crannies. Keep covered with a slightly damp towel in the refrigerator until ready to serve. Serve with a beverage and a basket of **Sourdough Bread** slices if desired.

FRUIT CUPS

Fruit cups make a delightful light appetizer for the table. Every variety of fruit and every conceivable combination is fair game for a fruit cup appetizer. For fun, use a halved and hollowed melon or orange as the cup. Garnish the cup with mint or berries.
Some favorite combinations:
- Grapes, orange wedges, and freshly thawed frozen blackberries. Dash of lemon juice over the top.
- Honeydew melon balls, banana slices, and apples slices. Deliciously mellow.

- Pineapple chunks and banana slices served with orange juice over the top.
- Watermelon balls and berries heaped into the center of 1-inch thick rings sliced from honeydew melon or cantaloupe.

PINEAPPLE BRISTLE

Slice top from pineapple, close to the leaves. Save top. Pare rind from pineapple deep enough so that eyes are removed from pineapple meat. With a long-bladed knife, cut out a cylinder close around the core. Cut the meat to the core in parallel slices about an inch apart all around the pineapple. Hold slices in place with toothpicks fastening them to the core. These slices may all be horizontal, vertical, or diagonal. Now make slices to the core again, but at right angles to the first slices so as to make a grid of 1-inch squares. A toothpick must be placed in each square to keep it fastened to the core. Replace the top of the pineapple. Serve with **Herbed Yogurt**, mace-sprinkled **Sour Cream**, or other appropriate dip.

PEARS AND ORANGE CHEESE DIP

Peel pears and cut into bite-size cubes or chunks. Dip pear bites quickly into lemon juice, then place in serving bowl with tooth-picks handy. As a dip, use 1 cup **Cream Cheese** blended with ¼ cup orange juice.

CANAPÉS

Remove crust from slices of stale bread, and cut bread into small shapes: rounds, squares, oblongs. Toast on one side and put an acceptable spread and topping on toasted side. Some spread and topping ideas are given below. If desired, garnish serving platter with a decorative border of fresh, uncooked vegetables: radish rosettes, cauliflower pieces, parsley sprigs, etc.

Spreads:
- **Cream Cheese** mixed with parsley and basil flakes
- **Cream Cheese** mixed with garlic flakes
- **Cream Cheese** mixed with caraway seeds

Toppings:
- Slice fresh mushrooms (stem to cap). Sauté mushrooms in water and garlic juice—about 2 tablespoons water and 1 tablespoon garlic juice for each cup of sliced mushrooms. Place one slice on top of each canapé.
- Cook and slice egg whites. Place a slice on each canapé and sprinkle with paprika.

STUFFED CELERY

6 stalks celery	¾ teaspoon caraway seeds
1 cup **Cream Cheese**	Paprika

Cut celery stalks into 6-inch segments. Mix cream cheese and caraway seeds and fill celery with mixture. Sprinkle on paprika.

QUICK DIP

1 cup **Sour Cream**	½ teaspoon onion juice
½ teaspoon garlic powder	1 teaspoon parsley flakes

Combine all ingredients and chill 1 hour. Makes 1 cup.

FRENCH ONION DIP

1 cup **Sour Cream**   2 tablespoons toasted onions

Mix onions with sour cream, cover, and let stand in refrigerator for 24 hours. Delicious! Makes 1 cup.

L.A. BEAN DIP

1 cup cooked and drained   2 tablespoons **Yogurt**
  pinto beans   ½ teaspoon onion powder
2 canned California green   Pinch of cayenne pepper
  chilies, chopped

Combine ingredients and mash in small saucepan. Cook to desired consistency. Makes 1¼ cups.

GARBANZO DIP

To one recipe **Garbanzo Spread** add ½ cup **Yogurt.** Stir or blend. Makes about 2 cups.

LEFSE ROLL-UPS

Spread **Lefse** evenly with **Garbanzo Dip** (above). Roll up lefse jelly-roll style, cut in ¾-inch-wide slices, and skewer each roll-up with a toothpick.

RAW ZUCCHINI SPEARS

Peel zucchini and cut lengthwise, end to end, making spears ¼ to ½ inch thick and about half the length of the zucchini (or full-length, if preferred).

MINIATURE ITALIAN MEATBALLS

Make 20 **Italian Meatballs** no larger than 1 inch in diameter. Cook and serve in **Spaghetti Sauce #3,** in a heated, shallow serving dish. Have skewers or small forks handy.

SOUR CREAM CUCUMBERS

2 cups pared, sliced cucumbers
2 cups **Sour Cream**
3 tablespoons lemon juice
1 teaspoon garlic powder
¼ teaspoon pepper
2 teaspoons frozen apple juice concentrate

Combine all ingredients except cucumber slices in a bowl and mix well. Add cucumber slices and mix lightly with a fork. Chill before serving. When serving, spoon onto bed of lettuce in parfait glass or dessert dish. Makes 4 cups.

SAVORY TOMATO JUICE COCKTAIL

1 cup **Cottage Cheese**
3 cups chilled tomato juice
⅛ teaspoon garlic powder
¼ teaspoon onion powder
¼ teaspoon celery powder

Blend all ingredients thoroughly and serve immediately. Makes 4 cups.

MUSHROOMS WITH CHEESE 'N CHILI

Blend **Cream Cheese** with canned California green chilies, chopped finely. Use 6 parts cheese to 1 part chilies. Spread mixture on fresh mushroom slices (sliced through stem and cap). Sprinkle with paprika and serve. Wonderful!

SANTA BARBARA FISH SKEWERS

½ pound white-flesh fish
1 cup lime juice
1 clove garlic, chopped

1 melon (cantaloupe, honeydew, etc.)
10 small wooden skewers

Cut fish into ½-inch cubes and chill in lime juice and garlic for 45 minutes. Cut the meat of the melon into ½-inch cubes. Place 2 fish cubes and 2 melon cubes on each skewer and cook over charcoal. Makes approximately 10 appetizers.

TURKEY-YOGURT APPETIZER

1 cup finely chopped roast turkey
½ cup **Yogurt**
½ cup **Sour Cream**
½ cup finely chopped celery

¼ cup chopped green peppers
½ cup chopped tomato
1 small onion, chopped finely
½ cup chopped cucumber

Mix ingredients and serve chilled in parfait glasses. Makes 3 cups.

GLAZED BEET CUBES

Make beet cubes according to the recipe for **Glazed Beets,** but cut the beets into ½-inch cubes rather than slices before cooking. Serve hot or at room temperature in a small serving dish. Keep toothpicks and napkins handy.

MINI-KABOBS

½ pound beef chuck shoulder or other lean steak, ½ inch thick or thicker
¼ cup dry red wine (e.g., Burgundy)

½ teaspoon garlic powder
½ teaspoon pepper

One or more of the following:

Water chestnuts
Fresh mushrooms
Jerusalem artichokes
Thick slices of broccoli stem
¾-inch celery slices

Pieces of cooked artichoke heart
Cauliflower stem cut in ¾-inch cubes

Cut steak across grain into thin strips (no thicker than ⅛ inch). Partially frozen meat makes this easier. Strips should be 3 inches to 6 inches long. Combine with wine and seasonings and marinate a few hours in refrigerator (tougher cuts may require longer marinating). Wrap each strip around a water chestnut, section of Jerusalem artichoke, mushroom cap or slice, or whatever, and run skewer or toothpick through. Broil a few minutes only on each side. Makes about 25 mini-kabobs. Allow 3 per guest. Served on a bed of brown rice, mini-kabobs make an unusual main dish. Serves 3 as a main dish.

SEVICHE

¾ pound tender-fleshed fish filets
½ cup lime juice
1 medium tomato, chopped
⅛ teaspoon oregano

¼ cup finely chopped onion
¼ cup finely chopped canned California green chilies
Parsley

Slice raw fish into very thin, tiny strips and marinate in the lime juice (covered, in refrigerator) for 2 hours. Combine fish with remaining ingredients and chill thoroughly. Serve in parfait glasses. Decorate with parsley sprigs. Serves 4.

NACHOS

Corn tortillas   Tiny slices of canned California
Fresh Cheese   green chilies or hotter peppers

Preheat oven to 500°. Cover cookie sheet with aluminum foil. Cut several tortillas into triangular pieces, tortilla chip size. Toast tortilla triangles *on wire cake-cooking rack* on cookie sheet for 3 minutes. Turn each triangle over and fit with a thin slice of cheese. Top each with a tiny slice of pepper. Bake nachos in oven 4 to 5 minutes, or until cheese is melted. Serve hot as an appetizer or first course in a Mexican dinner.

BRUSSELS SPROUTS HORS D'OEUVRE

½ cup sliced fresh mushrooms ¾ cup **Sour Cream**
½ tablespoon garlic juice   3 cups small cooked Brussels
                                                       sprouts

Sauté mushrooms in garlic juice and 1 tablespoon water. Add Brussels sprouts and sour cream and heat. Serve as a hot hors d'oeuvre with toothpicks or little forks. Makes 4 cups.

ANTIPASTI MISTI

Antipasti Misti, seen on the menu in Italian restaurants, is an offering of mixed appetizers. It can consist of any delectables that suit the fancy of the cook. Our *antipasti misti* includes tidbits that one might expect to find in a restaurant in northern Italy. Arrange in an attractive array of little dishes on a serving tray:

- Rings of squid hood prepared as explained in **Insalata di Mare**
- **Raw Zucchini Spears**
- Cherry tomatoes
- Green pepper strips
- Cubes of **Fresh Cheese**
- Artichoke hearts
- **Antipasto Garbanzos**
- **Antipasto Cauliflower**
- Tiny fresh mushrooms sautéed in 1 tablespoon garlic juice and 2 tablespoons water per cup of mushrooms

ANTIPASTO GARBANZOS

2 tablespoons cider vinegar
¼ cup water
1 clove garlic, minced
¼ cup chopped onion
1 cup cooked garbanzo beans

Combine vinegar, water, garlic, and onion to make a marinade for the garbanzo beans. Marinate beans for 3 hours or more, adding a bit of water to the marinade if necessary to cover the beans. Serve as one of the offerings in **Antipasti Misti.**

ANTIPASTO CAULIFLOWER

Prepare marinade as in **Antipasto Garbanzos.** Marinate for 2 hours. Serve along with little forks or as a part of **Antipasti Misti.**

TORTILLA CHIPS

6 corn tortillas
¼ cup liquid from jar of hot
   chili peppers (see page 263)

1 teaspoon paprika
½ teaspoon garlic powder
¼ teaspoon arrowroot

Preheat oven to 500°. Combine chili pepper liquid, paprika, and garlic powder in a saucepan; stir and bring to a boil. Mix arrowroot with 1 teaspoon cold water to make a paste, stir paste into boiling liquid, reduce to simmer, and cook, stirring until liquid thickens. Spread thickened sauce on tortillas, cut each tortilla into eight triangles (pizza pie–style), and place triangles on a wire cake rack. Line cookie sheets with aluminum foil and place cake racks on cookie sheets in oven. Bake 4 or 5 minutes, turn triangles, and bake 4 or 5 minutes more. Serve hot or at room temperature. Makes 48 tortilla chips (about the amount in a medium-sized bag of commercial tortilla chips).

QUICK TORTILLA CHIPS

6 corn tortillas
Garlic powder

Onion powder

Preheat oven to 400°. Cut each tortilla into eight triangles. Place triangles on cake rack and bake 6 minutes. Turn chips over, sprinkle with garlic, onion, or both. Bake 3 minutes more. Makes 48 chips (a nice bowlful). Use with any dip. Goes especially well with **Chili Salsa.**

MEXICAN VEGETABLE DIP

This delicious chili-flavored dip is excellent for dipping carrot sticks, cauliflower pieces, green pepper strips, or other fresh vegetables of any kind. Use it also as a marvelous salad dressing— either thick and creamy, or slightly thinned by the addition of a bit of skim milk.

1 cup **Cottage Cheese**	½ teaspoon dry mustard
½ cup **Buttermilk**	1 tablespoon diced onion
1 tablespoon lemon juice	1 Hard-cooked egg white
2 teaspoons **Chili Salsa** (or to taste)	¼ cup skim milk

Combine all ingredients but the milk in the blender. Adding the milk a bit at a time, chop and blend at high speed until very smooth. Stop the addition of the milk when desired thickness is achieved. Sprinkle paprika over the top and serve. Makes 1½ cups.

PINEAPPLE-CHEESE DIP

This fabulous dip goes well with crackers or **Nachos**. The taste of the spices arrives first, followed by the lingering sweet taste of the pineapple juice and cottage cheese.

½ cup **Cottage Cheese**	2 tablespoons pineapple juice
¼ cup skim milk	Dash of pepper
1 tablespoon lemon juice	Pinch of celery seeds

Combine all ingredients in blender. Blend at high speed until very smooth. Serve chilled. Makes ¾ cup.

PICKLED BEETS

4 medium beets, sliced and cooked
⅔ cup cooking liquid from beets
½ medium onion, sliced

2 tablespoons vinegar
10 peppercorns
6 whole dried cloves
2 dozen mustard seeds

Combine all ingredients and marinate in refrigerator 24 hours. Makes 3 cups.

GINGER-MARINATED PARSNIPS

1 large parsnip
2 teaspoons fresh ginger root slices

¼ cup vermouth
½ cup orange juice

Cut parsnip into thin, small rectangles (should make about 1 cup). Tie ginger root in small cheesecloth bag and bring to boil in vermouth and orange juice. Cover and simmer 5 minutes. Pour mixture, including bag, over parsnip and marinate 1 hour or more. Drain before serving. Makes 1 cup. Serve with toothpicks or little forks. Use also as a relish for **Lamb Curry.**

CHAPTER 4

Soups and Stews

There is no better way to magnify the appetite than to use a light soup as a first course. But we mustn't forget that a hearty soup can be used as a main dish as well. And of course a soup can be perfect for lunch and snacks. Really, soups do it all. They are versatile as a menu component, easy to freeze and store, and easy to make.

The tastiest soups are homemade, using stocks and bases that are also homemade. Commercial soups and stocks are not only less tasty, but also usually contain undesirable ingredients—sugar, salt, and/or fat.

This chapter gives recipes for soups for all occasions (including some fast and easy ones) and tells how to make the critically important stocks upon which the soups are based.

THICKENING SOUPS

Soups may be thickened by the addition of a flour or a grain. In order to thicken a soup with rice, barley, or oatmeal, bring the soup to a boil, add 1 teaspoon of grain per cup of soup, reduce to a simmer, and cook 1 hour. For a soup recipe calling for extended cooking, add the grain 1 hour before cooking is over.

For wheat flour, use 1½ teaspoons of flour per cup of soup, make a paste of the flour in twice its volume of skim milk, and stir the paste into the boiling soup. Simmer for 10 minutes. With arrowroot flour or cornstarch use 1 teaspoon per cup of soup and follow the same procedure.

Legume soups and other starchy soups will separate into a watery layer over a denser layer. To prevent separation, one must "bind" the soup by thickening the soup with arrowroot as discussed above.

STORAGE

Due to their high salt content, most commercial soups and stocks keep fairly well in the refrigerator. Salt acts as a preservative. The saltless soups and stocks in this book do not last quite so long in the refrigerator unless they are boiled from time to time. Thus, unless the soup is used right away, it should either be kept in the freezer or boiled every couple of days to prevent spoilage. For convenience, freeze stock in ice cube trays and store cubes in bags or other containers until needed. Stock cubes make a handy base for almost-instant soups, and are always available when needed to enhance the flavor of rice or other dishes.

STOCKS

It will be quite useful to save and store the cooking liquids that are left over in the preparation of meats, fish, or vegetables. They may be used in the preparation of stocks or in the place of water in many recipes. In this connection, observe these constraints:

- Because of their distinctive fishy taste, use fish residues only in fish recipes.
- Use meat residues in long-cooking recipes, because they do not deteriorate with extended cooking as vegetable and fish residues do.
- Use sparingly the cooking liquids from strong-tasting vegetables like cabbage and turnips.

The purpose of any stock is to concentrate and capture in liquid form the best flavors of food. In stock making, free use is made of items such as celery tops, chicken feet, and bones, which are normally considered castoffs. Old animals and mature vegetables are used rather than young animals and tender vegetables. Stock ingredients are soaked in cold water and cooking is begun in cold water in order to draw the juices of the ingredients into the stock. All these things are done to capture as much flavor as possible.

In preparing the stock ingredients: disjoint or break up bones; trim and discard all visible fat from meat; chop meat; chop or blend vegetables. If a clear stock is desired, avoid mixing raw and cooked bones and avoid starchy vegetables.

A very big factor affecting the flavor of a stock is the manner in which it is cooked. A stock must be cooked with a long and stable simmer. To insure proper cooking, place an asbestos pad on the burner, and the pot on top of the pad. Simmer with the pot lid ajar for 2 hours or more. If bones are included in the stock, simmer for as long as 12 hours.

Just before cooking, season stocks sparingly with whole spices such as bay leaf, cilantro, and peppercorns. Make an **Herb Bundle** by tying sprigs of fresh parsely, chervil, and thyme with white string. A bundle of fresh herbs may be dropped in the stock at the beginning of cooking. Dried herbs should be crumbled, tied in cheese cloth, and dropped in during the last 20 minutes of cooking. When the stock has finished cooking, remove the herb bundle and correct the seasoning to taste.

Remove any fat from a stock or a soup by placing it, tightly covered, in the refrigerator. The fat will rise to the top and form a solid layer that can easily be removed. The fat layer may be left in place as a protective cover until the soup or stew is to be used. Soups and stocks store well in the freezer.

To clarify the stock—to remove any cloudiness from it—skim off the heavy foam generated during the first half hour of cooking as it arises, and wipe the pot at the water line after the last skimming. This makes for a relatively clear stock.

For even greater clarity, add the white and the crumbled shell of an egg to each quart of the completed and cooled stock. Avoiding any boiling, very slowly bring the stock just to a simmer. Gently move the new and thick foam that will result to one side of the pot, exposing a portion of the liquid. The simmering action of the liquid can then be observed and monitored. Simmer for 15 minutes, then set aside and cool for 15 minutes. Make up a filter pot by covering a pot with a cloth wrung out in hot water. (Liquid poured into the filter pot through the cloth will be cleaned of visible particles.) Once again move the foam on the surface of the stock to one side and gently ladle the liquid out of the pot and into the filter pot. Cool further and store covered in the refrigerator.

PORK STOCK

¾ pound cheapest pork cuts (feet and bones)

2 cups assorted vegetable trimmings (aging mushrooms, yesterday's salad, bell pepper, onion and tomato ends, limp carrots, or whatever)

2 quarts water

⅛ teaspoon caraway seeds

⅛ teaspoon dill seeds

About a dozen whole black peppercorns

1 clove garlic, cut in half

Combine all ingredients in a large pot. Bring to a boil, cover, and simmer over low heat for several hours. Strain, refrigerate to congeal fat on surface, and skim. Makes about 1¼ quarts.

SWEET LAMB STOCK

1½ pounds lamb breast,
    cut up
  2 quarts water

4 carrots
1 beet

Slice carrots and beet. In large pot, simmer all ingredients until lamb is very tender. Cool slightly and strain. Refrigerate stock to congeal fat on surface, and skim fat. Makes about 1¼ quarts.

LAMB STOCK

2 pounds lamb bones   6 cups water

Bring to a boil, then simmer, covered, for 6 to 10 hours. Discard bones (lean meat may be cut off and returned to stock) and allow to cool. Chill, and discard surface fat. Use as a base for barley soup or other hearty, flavorful soups. Makes about 1 quart.

EASY BEEF STOCK

6 pounds beef bones
1 gallon water
1 onion, cut up
2 carrots, cut up

6 mushrooms, cut up
Other vegetable tops and
    greens, as available
¼ teaspoon pepper

In large pot, bring all ingredients to a boil. Cover and simmer 6 to 10 hours. Strain, chill, and skim fat. Makes about 3 quarts.

CHICKEN STOCK

1 whole chicken, disjointed
  (excluding giblets)

1 small onion, quartered
1 **Herb Bundle**

½ bay leaf
¼ teaspoon peppercorns
2 stalks celery, whole

1 green pepper, seeded and
quartered

Cut meat from bones and put all ingredients (bones included) into a stew pot with 6 cups of cold water. Gradually bring to a boil, and simmer until meat is tender (2 to 3 hours). Strain, and put aside the chicken meat for use in other recipes. Season with pepper to taste, cool, skim fat, and store in refrigerator or freezer until needed. Makes 1 quart.

FISH STOCK

4 cups of fish leavings: head,
   tail, skin, bones, meat
1 small carrot, chopped finely
1 celery stalk, chopped finely
½ small onion, chopped finely

1 tablespoon garlic juice
6 peppercorns
2 cloves
½ bay leaf
2 tablespoons vinegar

In a saucepan, sauté the vegetables for 3 minutes with garlic juice and a tablespoon or so of water. Add all other ingredients, plus 2 quarts of cold water, and slowly bring to a boil. Simmer 30 minutes and strain. Makes 1½ quarts.

MUSHROOM WINE STOCK

½ cup vermouth

1 cup fresh mushroom stems
   and ends, washed

In a small saucepan, bring wine and mushrooms to a boil, then simmer, covered, for 15 minutes. Strain through cheesecloth. Store broth for future use. Make maximum use of the mushrooms by repeating the process with ½ cup of dry red wine. Store stock. Discard mushrooms. Makes less than ½ cup of strong special-purpose stock.

VEGETABLE STOCK

¼ cup dried navy beans
¼ cup dried split peas
1 medium onion, sliced
1 carrot, quartered

½ stalk celery, chopped
1 **Herb Bundle**
3 whole cloves
⅛ teaspoon mace

Combine all ingredients in pot with 2 quarts of water. Bring to a boil, and simmer, slowly, for 3 to 4 hours. Skim debris from surface, remove herb bundle, and strain. Makes about 6 cups.

ABOUT CONSOMMÉS

Any highly seasoned soup that has been strained and cleared so as to make it translucent is considered a consommé. One can make a consommé using any of the meat stock recipes above, and clearing the stock by the clearing method discussed on page 73. By adding vegetables to an already made consommé, cooking for 20 to 30 minutes, straining, and reclearing, you can create an entirely new consommé, with the flavor of those items added. We give, for example, a consommé recipe below and three others after it that can be made simply by adding vegetables, cooking, straining, and reclearing.

CONSOMMÉ

Here is an old-fashioned consommé that is delicious by itself and can be used as a base for many, many other dishes.

3 pounds cheapest cut, lean
  beef with or without bone
3 pounds beef knuckles

1 small turnip, chopped
½ small onion, chopped
1 stalk celery, chopped

3 quarts cold water
1 quart **Chicken Stock** (or a double handful of chicken bones)
1 small carrot, chopped
2 sprigs each of parsley, thyme, and marjoram
1 bay leaf
1 teaspoon peppercorns
4 cloves

Cut the beef from the bone, chop it up, and brown about half of it in a Teflon pan. Place both the browned and the raw beef into a large stewing pot, along with the beef bone, the beef knuckles (disjointed), and the 3 quarts of cold water. Let stand ½ hour, then slowly bring to a boil. Turn heat down and simmer 3 hours, removing foam as it forms on top of the liquid. Add chicken stock (or chicken bones plus 1 quart water) and simmer 2 hours more. Cook vegetables in small amount of water for 5 minutes. Add vegetables, herbs, and spices to the stewing pot and simmer 1½ more hours. Strain the liquid, refrigerate it, skim the fat from it when cold, and clear further if desired (see page 73). Reheat to serve. Makes about 3 quarts of consommé.

FILIPINI CONSOMMÉ

1 quart **Consommé**
¼ cup canned pimientos

Puree the pimientos in the blender or by forcing through a puree strainer, and add to the consommé. Clear the consommé as explained on page 73. Makes 4 cups. Serve hot or chilled.

TOMATO CONSOMMÉ

1½ quarts **Consommé**
2 cups chopped canned tomatoes
1 tablespoon onion flakes
½ teaspoon celery seed
6 peppercorns

Puree tomatoes in blender, combine with other ingredients and simmer 20 minutes. Strain, cool, and clear (see page 73). Makes about 6 cups.

CARROT CONSOMMÉ

1 quart **Consommé**
1 cup cooked carrot slices
1 teaspoon onion flakes

½ teaspoon celery seed
3 cloves
½ bay leaf

Combine all ingredients and boil 20 minutes. Strain, cool, and clear (see page 73). Makes 1 quart.

VEGETABLE SOUPS

There are an infinite number of ways to combine vegetables in a pot and come out with a delicious soup. In the recipes below we present not only familiar favorites like vegetable soup, tomato soup, julienne soup, and cream of vegetable soup, but also versions of vegetable soup from other countries: borscht from Russia, gazpacho from Spain, and minestrone from Italy. By the time one has sampled a few of the vegetable soup recipes here, canned commercial vegetable soups will seem very plain indeed.

ALPHABET SOUP

2 tablespoons alphabet
  noodles
¼ cup diced potatoes
¼ cup diced tomatoes

¼ cup chopped fresh parsley
¼ cup thinly sliced carrot
½ cup tomato sauce
1 cup water

¼ cup chopped celery

¼ cup chopped onion

¼ cup chopped green pepper

4 cups **Beef Stock** or water

¼ teaspoon celery seed

¼ teaspoon pepper

Combine all ingredients except noodles, bring to a boil, cover, and simmer 20 minutes. Add noodles and simmer, stirring occasionally, until noodles are tender (about 20 minutes). Makes 1½ quarts.

LOUISIANA SOUP

¼ cup chopped green pepper

¼ cup chopped onion

1 tablespoon water

½ tablespoon garlic juice

2 tablespoons arrowroot

1 quart **Beef Stock**

One 15-ounce can of tomatoes

½ teaspoon black pepper

½ teaspoon red pepper

1 teaspoon vinegar

½ cup cooked macaroni

Sauté the peppers and onions until tender in 1 tablespoon water and ½ tablespoon garlic juice. Make a paste of the arrowroot with a bit of cold water and stir into the peppers and onions. Add stock, tomatoes, spices, and vinegar. Bring to a boil, then simmer for 15 minutes. Strain, add macaroni, and serve. Makes 6 cups.

VEGETABLE SOUP

2 pounds beef neck bones

1 onion, chopped

2 medium carrots, diced

2 zucchini squash, sliced

1 large rutabaga, diced

2 medium turnips, diced

One 10-ounce package of frozen
mixed vegetables

2 stalks celery, cut into
½-inch pieces

¼ head cabbage, chopped

2 small potatoes, diced

½ cup pearl barley

½ teaspoon rosemary

Combine beef neck bones with 2½ quarts cold water in large kettle. Bring to rolling boil over high heat, reduce heat to medium, and cook until meat is tender. Remove meat and any visible fat from bone, and put meat back in kettle along with the vegetables, barley, and rosemary. Cover, reduce heat, and simmer several hours. Pepper to taste before serving. Makes 6 to 8 cups.

JULIENNE SOUP

½ cup julienne-sliced onions
¼ cup julienne-sliced carrots
¼ cup julienne-sliced turnips
4 cups **Beef Stock**

½ cup cooked julienne green beans
¼ teaspoon pepper

Combine onions, carrots, and turnips in stock and simmer until tender. Add beans. Add pepper to taste. Heat through and serve. Makes 4 cups.

ONCE-A-WEEK SOUP

To keep little bits of this and that from having to be thrown out, try cleaning out the refrigerator once a week with this flexible soup. Start with the basic recipe, use a little imagination and whatever's on hand, and just have fun.

One 8-ounce can of tomatoes or 3 peeled overripe tomatoes
1 cup **Tomato Sauce** or ¼ cup tomato paste and ¾ cup water, *or* any combination that needs to be used up

(Leftover cooked meat or fish)
3 cups water
2 tablespoons red wine
2 tablespoons alphabet noodles
¼ teaspoon garlic powder
⅛ teaspoon oregano

2½ cups cooked vegetables
    (corn, beans, green beans,
    garbanzos, potatoes,
    cauliflower, peas, or
    whatever sounds good)

⅛ teaspoon cumin
½ teaspoon **Vegetable Powder**
1 tablespoon vinegar

Combine all ingredients except vinegar, bring to a boil, cover, and simmer 20 minutes. Add vinegar and simmer 5 minutes more. Makes 1½ to 2 quarts, more or less, depending on circumstances and imagination.

LOVE SOUP

This soup is as easy as one, two, three. Each vegetable ingredient goes in a few minutes after the preceding ingredient, along with a little more water. This allows time to ready the next ingredient while the earlier ones are cooking. Timing is not critical. Vegetables may be substituted or left out.

1 large onion, chopped
2 cloves garlic, minced
1 cup whole canned tomatoes
½ teaspoon oregano
1 tablespoon parsley flakes
1 leaf basil
½ cup cauliflower flowerets
3 carrots, sliced
½ cup cut fresh green beans

1 cup fresh peas
¼ head cabbage, cut in chunks
2 stalks celery, chopped
2 potatoes, peeled and diced finely
½ cup cooked lima beans
1 cup cooked garbanzos

Make sure the lima beans and garbanzos are cooked and available so they can be added as the last step. Brown onions and garlic in a large pot with two tablespoons of water; add tomatoes and a cup of water, mash, and simmer over low heat. Add spices and stir. Then, keeping the soup always at a simmer, prepare and add each vegetable in the sequence above, along with enough water to keep the mixture soupy. As a last step add the limas and garbanzos, and more water. Continue cooking at a simmer until all vegetables are tender. Makes about 2 quarts.

QUICK VEGETABLE SOUP

1 cup leftover cooked
vegetables

1 cup **Chicken Stock**
½ cup evaporated skim milk

Combine ingredients in blender. Spice as desired and blend. Makes 2½ cups of fabulous cream soup.

INSTANT VEGETABLE BROTH

⅓ cup tomato juice *or* ¼ cup
Tomato Sauce *or* 2
tablespoons tomato paste

1 teaspoon **Vegetable Powder**

Combine tomato juice and vegetable powder in an 8-ounce coffee mug. Add hot water to fill, stir, and drink from the mug. Makes one individual serving.

MINESTRONE

There are many ways to make this old Italian favorite. Rice or pasta may be used in place of the beans, and all kinds of vegetables may be used. Here is our favorite recipe:

1½ cups dried beans (navy,
kidney, red, garbanzo, or
a mixture)

½ cup chopped green onions
1 medium onion, chopped
1 cup chopped celery

1 cup fresh green beans

1 small zucchini squash, diced

1 cup shredded spinach or cabbage

1 cup diced tomatoes

2 tablespoons parsley flakes

¼ teaspoon savory

½ teaspoon pepper

½ teaspoon thyme

½ cup finely grated **Fresh Cheese**

To prepare the dried beans, first clean them, and then either soak them all night in 2 quarts of water or bring them to a boil in 2 quarts of water, simmer 2 minutes, and let stand 1½ hours. Combine the prepared beans, their soaking water, and the fresh green beans in a large soup pot. Bring to a boil, reduce heat, and simmer 45 minutes. Sauté all the remaining vegetables in ¼ cup of water and 1 tablespoon of garlic juice. Add them to the soup pot and continue simmering for another 30 minutes. Add spices and simmer 5 minutes more. Mix cheese in hot soup and serve. Makes about 2½ quarts.

MINESTRONE WITH RICE

½ cup uncooked brown rice

1 medium onion, chopped

1 clove garlic, minced

1 leek, diced

3 stalks celery, chopped

2 medium carrots, diced

2 cups shredded cabbage

2 zucchini, chopped

1½ quarts **Chicken Stock** or water

One 28-ounce can of tomatoes

3 tablespoons tomato paste

2 tablespoons parsley flakes

½ teaspoon thyme

½ teaspoon oregano

3 cups cooked beans (red, navy, lentils, etc.)

Without disturbing the boiling action, slowly add rice to a boiling pot containing all the other ingredients except the beans. Reduce heat and simmer 1 hour. Add beans. Puree ⅓ of the soup in blender, return to pot, stir, heat, and serve. Makes 2 quarts.

BORSCHT

This excellent soup is the Russian version of vegetable soup. Borscht traditionally includes beets and very often cabbage. This borscht includes both.

4 cups shredded cabbage
One 16-ounce can of beets,
    coarsely chopped
1 medium onion, chopped
One 28-ounce can of tomatoes,
    finely chopped

¼ cup apple juice
2 cups water
⅛ teaspoon nutmeg

Combine ingredients in soup pot, bring to boil, and simmer, covered, for about 45 minutes. Thin with water if desired, and serve hot. Makes 6 cups.

LEEK SOUP

1 cup sliced leeks
1 cup diced carrots
1 cup diced parsnips

1 cup sliced zucchini
1 cup diced fresh tomatoes
1 cup diced potatoes

Place leeks in 2 quarts of water and bring to a boil. Cover tightly and let sit for 1½ hours at room temperature. Add carrots, parsnips and potatoes. Cook just below a boil for 45 minutes. Add zucchini and tomatoes and cook for 15 minutes more. Makes 2 quarts.

CREAM OF ANY VEGETABLE SOUP

2 cups **White Sauce**
2 cups well-cooked vegetable
    or vegetables

2 cups of the liquid in which
    vegetables were cooked

Combine ingredients and boil 2 minutes. Strain vegetables from liquid, puree them in blender (or by rubbing through a sieve), return to liquid, season to taste with pepper, and serve. Makes 6 cups.

CREAM OF CELERY SOUP

2 cups finely chopped celery
2 cups water
2 cups **White Sauce**

2 teaspoons onion powder
1 tablespoon parsley flakes
Dash of nutmeg

Put celery and water into a saucepan, cover, bring to a boil, and simmer until celery is tender (about 10 minutes). Add white sauce and spices, heat through, and serve. Makes 6 cups.

ASPARAGUS SOUP

1 pound tender, fresh
asparagus
2 cups water
1 teaspoon lemon juice

Pepper to taste
½ teaspoon **Vegetable
Powder**
½ cup skim milk

Rinse asparagus and snap off and discard the fibrous ends of the stems. (Asparagus will snap where tender part begins.) Cut off top 3 inches of tips and set aside. Cut the rest of the stems into 1-inch sections. Place in 1 cup water, bring to a boil, cover, simmer 15 minutes or until tender, and set aside to cool. Cook tips in the other cup of water until just tender, or about 10 minutes. After the stems have cooled, placed them and their cooking liquid in blender and chop and puree until smooth. In saucepan, combine pureed stems with lemon juice, pepper, vegetable powder, and skim milk, stirring after each addition. Add tips and their liquid and heat through, stirring to prevent sticking. Makes 4 cups.

CREAM OF POTATO SOUP

2 cups **White Sauce**
2 cups cooked potatoes
2 cups of the liquid in which
    potatoes were cooked

1 tablespoon pimiento,
    chopped

Combine all ingredients and boil 2 minutes. Strain vegetables from liquid, puree them in blender (or by rubbing through a sieve), return to liquid, season to taste with pepper, and serve. Makes 6 cups.

SUMMER ASPARAGUS SOUP

Prepare as above, omitting skim milk, and adding pepper, **Vegetable Powder,** and lemon juice while pureed stems are in blender, blending again after these additions. Reserved tips should be soaked in a mixture of 1 teaspoon lemon juice, ½ teaspoon **Vegetable Powder,** and 1 tablespoon water. Strain and chill pureed stems, pour into bowls, and top with a float of **Buttermilk.** Arrange well-drained tips on top of buttermilk and serve cold. Makes 4 cups.

FASTER ASPARAGUS SOUP

One 10-ounce package of
    frozen cut asparagus
1 quart **Chicken Stock**

1 tablespoon arrowroot
2 tablespoons skim milk
Pepper

Place frozen asparagus in a saucepan, add stock, and bring to a boil, breaking up the asparagus as the liquid heats. Make a paste of arrowroot and milk and stir the paste into the boiling liquid. Simmer 10 minutes. Pepper to taste. Makes 4 cups.

ASPARAGUS AND CREAM CHEESE SOUP

4 cups **Asparagus Soup**
½ cup **Cream Cheese**

Place a spoonful of the cheese into each individual serving bowl,
pour hot asparagus soup over the cheese, and serve. Makes 4 cups.

TOMATO RICE SOUP

2 cups **Tomato Sauce**   2 cups skim milk
1 cup cooked rice   Thick slices of **Cream Cheese**

In saucepan, combine tomato sauce and rice. Heat to boiling, then
simmer until rice is very soft. Add milk and heat to serve (do not
boil). Top each bowl with a cheese slice. Pass **Sourdough Bread**.
Makes 4 cups.

TOMATO AND ONION SOUP

1½ quarts tomato juice   1 teaspoon vegetable flakes
1 medium onion, sliced   3 cloves

Combine all ingredients in a saucepan, bring to a boil, and simmer
5 minutes. Makes 6 cups.

TOMATO BOUILLON

One 28-ounce can of tomatoes   1 **Herb Bundle**
½ cup chopped green pepper   6 peppercorns
2 stalks celery, chopped   ½ bay leaf
1 small carrot, sliced

Combine all ingredients with 1 cup of water in a saucepan. Bring to a boil, and simmer 15 minutes. Strain, and pepper to taste. Cool and clear (see page 73). Serve hot or cold. Makes about 4 cups.

FRESH TOMATO RICE SOUP

3 tablespoons uncooked rice
8 medium tomatoes, chopped
1 bunch chives, chopped

4 cups boiling water
2 tablespoons fresh chopped dill weed

Put rice into 3 cups of the boiling water and boil for 15 minutes. Put the tomatoes and chives into the remaining cup of boiling water, boil 5 minutes, cool sufficiently to put into blender, and blend. Pour contents of blender into cooked rice and its water and mix well. Sprinkle with dill and serve hot. Makes 6 cups.

FROZEN PEA SOUP

4 cups frozen peas
1 cup skim milk (or water)

1 tablespoon onion flakes
Pepper

Put peas, milk, and onion into soup pot. Bring almost to boil, then reduce heat and simmer, covered, until the peas are tender. Let cool, blend in blender, return to pot, and heat. Pepper to taste and serve. Thin with water if desired. Makes 4 cups.

BROWN RICE AND CARROT SOUP

¼ cup long-grain brown rice
2 cups boiling water

¼ teaspoon marjoram
¼ teaspoon dill seed

3 cups **stock** (beef, chicken, lamb, or vegetable)
1½ cups diced carrots
¼ cup chopped parsley

⅛ teaspoon pepper, freshly ground
1 tablespoon lemon juice

Add rice to boiling water, cover, and simmer 30 minutes. Add stock, carrots, parsley, and spices. Bring to a boil, cover, and simmer until carrots are very tender (45 minutes to an hour). Add lemon juice and stir. Makes 4 cups.

BARLEY SOUP

¼ cup barley
2 cups water
2 cups **Beef Stock** or water
3 stalks celery, sliced
1 parsnip, sliced
1 potato, diced

¼ cup fresh sliced mushrooms
1 sprig fresh parsley, chopped
¼ teaspoon pepper
1 small bay leaf

Rinse barley and place in saucepan. Add water, bring to boil, remove from heat, and let stand 1 hour. Add stock and simmer 45 minutes. Add remaining ingredients (and, if necessary, more water) and simmer 1½ hours more, removing bay leaf after 30 minutes. Makes 1½ quarts.

PINK SOUP

2 medium cucumbers, sliced
3 cups tomato juice, unsalted
(½ cup parsley chopped)
2 teaspoons fresh lemon juice

2 cups **Buttermilk**
Freshly ground pepper
Dried dill weed
Parsley sprigs

In blender, liquify half of cucumber slices with tomato juice, the chopped parsley, and lemon juice. Add buttermilk and blend again. Immediately pour soup into shallow bowls, float cucumber slices, sprinkle with freshly ground black pepper and dill weed, and decorate with a parsley sprig. Serve chilled. If serving must be delayed, reblend soup a few seconds before serving. Makes 6 cups.

BROTH ARMENIAN STYLE

2 quarts **Beef Stock** or
  Consommé
4 teaspoons flour

4 teaspoons cornstarch
1 cup **Buttermilk**

Cook down broth to half its original volume, or 1 quart. Cool ½ cup of this broth and add flour and cornstarch, stirring until smooth. Stir in remaining stock and heat until thick and bubbly. Turn off heat and allow broth to cool 5 or 10 minutes. Stir·in buttermilk and serve. Makes 5 cups.

POTATO CHOWDER

1 cup water
4 medium potatoes, peeled
  and diced
¼ medium onion, chopped
  fine

2 cups skim milk
1 teaspoon parsley flakes
Pinch of celery seeds
Pepper

Bring water to boil, add potatoes and onion, cover, and cook just below boiling for 15 minutes or until potatoes are soft. Scald the milk. Crush potatotes and onion in their liquid and stir the hot milk into them. Add seasonings and serve. Makes 4 cups.

RICE AND YOGURT SOUP

½ cup partially cooked, drained brown rice (boil rice 15 minutes to partially cook)
1 tablespoon white flour

2 teaspoons mint flakes
3½ cups **Vegetable Stock** or water
1 cup **Yogurt** or **Sour Cream**

Mix rice, flour, and mint flakes in a saucepan. Add stock and yogurt, and bring to a boil, stirring constantly. Reduce heat and simmer until rice is cooked (25 to 30 minutes). Serve hot or cold. Makes about 4 cups.

SPINACH AND SOUR CREAM SOUP

2 cups cooked, chopped spinach
1 cup **Sour Cream**

1 cup hot, freshly made **White Sauce**
1½ cups **stock**

Combine ingredients, heat slowly, and serve. Makes 5 cups.

GAZPACHO

This marvelous cold soup from Spain is simply chopped vegetables in tomato and lime juice. Other liquids may be used in place of tomato juice, and imagination may be used in selecting vegetables. Gazpacho may be used as a soup to go with a salad or as a salad to go with a soup.

2 medium tomatoes
1 green pepper
1 medium zucchini
1 stalk celery
1 clove garlic

1 small red onion
4 cups tomato juice
3 limes
Pepper
½ cup stale bread crumbs

Chop all vegetables fine and place in pot. Add tomato juice, the juice of the limes, and pepper to taste. Chill well and top each individual serving with a bit of the bread crumbs. Makes about 6 cups.

GAZPACHO IN CHICKEN BROTH

3 cups **Chicken Stock**
2 cups tomato juice
2 tablespoons vinegar
2 stalks celery, chopped
1 cucumber, peeled and chopped
6 large, ripe tomatoes, peeled and chopped
8 small green onions, chopped

1 small green pepper, chopped
2 cloves garlic, minced
½ cup chopped fresh parsley
½ teaspoon dill weed
¼ teaspoon thyme
¼ teaspoon mint flakes

Combine all ingredients and stir well. Puree half the soup in blender, combine with balance, stir, cover, and let chill overnight or longer. Stir well (and add water if desired to thin) before serving. Garnish bowls with lemon slices. Makes 2½ quarts.

ONION SOUP

2 medium onions, chopped
½ cup vermouth
½ teaspoon celery seeds

2 cups **Beef Stock**
1 teaspoon onion powder
¼ teaspoon garlic powder

Simmer onions in 2 cups of water in stew pot until tender. With a slotted spoon remove most of the onions from the water (save the onion water) and place in a Teflon frying pan. Add vermouth and celery seed to onions and cook over moderate heat, stirring constantly, until liquid has evaporated and Teflon feels gummy. Cook very carefully until the residue on the pan begins to turn brown. Add small amount of the stock and stir to release this residue. Return onions and liquid to pot; add stock, onion powder, and garlic powder, and simmer 15 minutes before serving. Makes 4 cups.

ICED ONION SOUP

2 cups **Onion Soup**   Green onion, sliced
2 cups **Buttermilk**

Chill soup and combine with chilled buttermilk. Sprinkle with thin slices of green onion. Makes 4 cups.

FRENCH ONION SOUP

4 onions, chopped   4 cups **Beef Stock**

Place ½ cup of onions and 2 tablespoons of stock in saucepan. Heat slowly until onions start to burn, stirring only occasionally. Stir and continue to brown or even burn onions. Add remaining onions and ¼ cup of stock, stir, cover, and simmer 5 minutes. Uncover and stir until liquid has evaporated and onions are dry and brown. Add remaining stock and simmer 20 minutes. Makes 5 cups.

INSTANT FRENCH ONION SOUP

½ cup toasted onions   Cayenne and black pepper to
 4 cups **Beef Stock**   taste

Combine ingredients in saucepan, bring to boil, cover, and simmer 20 minutes. Makes 4 cups.

BEAN AND PEA SOUPS

Soups made from beans and peas are delicious and often more filling than other soups. They are easily stored and reused, and usually are even better with reheating. Because bean and pea soups will separate into a watery layer over a thick layer if they are allowed to stand, it is often useful to "bind" them (see page 71). It will be helpful to read page 155 on methods of preparing dried beans before cooking. Any of the three methods may be used, although we include a specific method in each recipe below.

SPLIT PEA SOUP

1 pound split peas (2 to 2½ cups)	1 cup chopped onions
1 quart **Beef Stock**	1 cup chopped celery
1 quart water	¼ teaspoon marjoram
½ cup tomato juice	¼ teaspoon pepper
	¼ teaspoon thyme

Soak split peas overnight in stock, water, and tomato juice. Drain peas, reserving liquid. Add enough water to liquid to make 2 quarts and return peas to liquid. Bring to boil, reduce heat, and simmer 2 hours. Add vegetables and spices and simmer 30 minutes longer. Bind with arrowroot (see p. 71) and serve. Makes 6 cups.

BLENDER SPLIT PEA SOUP

1 pound split peas (2 to 2½ cups)	½ cup chopped green peppers
1 cup diced, cooked carrots	¼ teaspoon pepper
1 cup diced, cooked potatoes	¼ teaspoon turmeric
2 cups chopped onions	¼ teaspoon cumin

Soak peas overnight in 2 quarts of water. Drain and reserve the liquid. Add enough water to the liquid to make 2 quarts, return the peas to the liquid, bring to a boil, and simmer until tender (2 to 3 hours). Sauté onions and peppers in 3 tablespoons water. Combine all ingredients in the blender and blend. Reheat, binding with arrowroot (see page 71) if necessary, and serve. Makes 6 cups.

SANTA BARBARA SPLIT PEA SOUP

1¼ cups split peas, washed and drained	1 stalk celery, chopped
2 quarts **Chicken Stock**	2 medium carrots, diced
1 medium onion, chopped	½ teaspoon marjoram
	⅛ teaspoon ground cloves

Place all ingredients in soup pot, bring to boil, and simmer covered, stirring occasionally, until peas are mushy (about 1½ hours). Puree half of soup in blender, return to pot, stir and heat. Thicken if necessary (see page 71) and serve. Makes 2 quarts.

LENTIL SOUP

2 cups dried lentils	¼ teaspoon pepper
1 onion, chopped	2 tablespoons fresh parsley, chopped
1 carrot, diced	
3 stalks celery, chopped	½ cup barley

Cover lentils with cold water and soak overnight. Drain. Sauté onion until tender in a few tablespoons of water. Combine all ingredients with 2 quarts hot water in a soup pot and simmer until lentils are tender (45 minutes or so). Puree half the soup in a blender, return the pureed portion to the pot, stir, heat, and serve. Makes 2½ to 3 quarts.

GREEK LENTIL SOUP

1 cup lentils, washed and
  drained
2 quarts **Chicken Stock,** or
  water
1 medium onion, chopped

1 stalk celery, chopped
1 bay leaf
¼ teaspoon oregano
3 tablespoons tomato paste
2 tablespoons wine vinegar

Without disturbing the boil, slowly pour lentils into vigorously boiling stock. Add all other ingredients except vinegar, reduce heat, and simmer, stirring occasionally, until lentils are very soft (about 1½ hours). Add vinegar. Puree half of the soup in the blender, return pureed portion to pot, mix, heat, and serve. Makes 2 quarts.

RED LENTIL SOUP

4 cups red lentils
3 cups boiling water

1 bunch scallions
2 tablespoons **Miso**

Pour lentils slowly into boiling water, without disturbing boil, and boil 5 minutes. Sauté scallions in a small amount of water for 2 minutes, and add to the boiling lentils. Boil 20 minutes. Add miso and serve. Makes 6 cups.

LIMA BEAN SOUP

2 cups fresh shelled lima
  beans
2 potatoes, chopped
1 green pepper, chopped
1 large onion, chopped
2 teaspoons garlic juice *or*
  one clove garlic, minced

2 tablespoons parsley flakes
½ teaspoon thyme (ground or
  leaves) *or* several sprigs
  fresh thyme
2 cups **Cottage Cheese**
½ cup skim milk

Combine all ingredients except the cottage cheese and milk in a saucepan. Add 2 cups water and bring to a boil. Reduce heat and simmer 30 minutes. Blend the cheese and milk until very smooth. Combine with the other ingredients and heat through. Serve with a garnish of parsley sprigs. Makes about 6 cups.

BLACK BEAN SOUP

2 cups dried black beans
1 tomato, chopped
1 green pepper, seeded and chopped
1 celery stalk, chopped
1 large onion, chopped

1 tablespoon parsley
¼ teaspoon ground cloves
¼ teaspoon savory
2 tablespoons arrowroot
¼ cup skim milk

Without disturbing the boil, slowly add the beans to 2½ quarts of boiling water. Reduce heat and simmer for 2 hours. Add vegetables and spices and continue simmering 10 more minutes. Make a paste of the arrowroot and milk. Bring the soup to a boil. Add paste and simmer 10 minutes more. Makes about 2½ quarts.

BEAN WITH BARLEY SOUP

½ cup chopped onions
1 clove garlic, minced
1 cup cooked beans (navy, kidney, or red)
1 cup diced carrots

2 cups diced, peeled potatoes
¼ cup barley
½ teaspoon freshly ground pepper

In a large pot, sauté onions and garlic in 2 tablespoons of water. Add beans, carrots, potatoes, and 6 cups of water. Bring to a boil, reduce heat, and simmer 1 hour. Add barley and pepper, and simmer 2 hours more. Makes about 2 quarts.

BLACK BEAN AND WINE SOUP

1 cup dried black beans
2 cups water
½ cup chopped celery
1 medium onion, chopped
⅛ teaspoon allspice

⅛ teaspoon pepper
4 cups **stock** or water, or a
  combination
¼ cup dry white wine
2 teaspoons lemon juice

Rinse beans, then soak overnight in 2 cups of water (beans should be covered with water). Drain, and combine with celery, onion, allspice, pepper, and stock. Bring to a boil, cover, and simmer 3 hours. Let cool 15 minutes, then puree in blender and return to pot. Add wine and lemon juice, and reheat to boiling, stirring constantly until alcohol odor has gone. Makes 1½ quarts. Serving ideas: drizzle a pinwheel of **Buttermilk** on surface of each bowl; or garnish with hard-cooked egg white; or chill, and blend with **Buttermilk.**

SOUR CREAM AND BEAN SOUP

1 cup dried beans (red,
  kidney, or navy)
1 medium onion, chopped

¼ teaspoon pepper
1 cup **Sour Cream**

Soak beans overnight, drain, and discard water. Add onion, pepper, and 2 quarts hot water. Simmer until beans are very soft (about 2 hours). Stir in sour cream, and serve. Makes 2 quarts.

SENATE BEAN SOUP

1 pound dried white beans
3 medium potatoes, peeled,
  cooked, and mashed

1 teaspoon garlic powder
½ teaspoon thyme
1 teaspoon basil

2 medium onions, chopped   ¼ teaspoon cayenne pepper
1 cup diced celery

Soak beans overnight in cold water. Drain and add water enough to make 5 quarts. Bring to a boil, cover, and simmer until beans begin to mush (about 2 hours). Add remaining ingredients and simmer, covered, 1 hour longer. Makes 5 quarts.

BEAN-PEA SOUP

1 cup dried pinto beans   2 small onions, chopped
1 cup dried navy beans   3 carrots, diced
1 pound package of dried   8 whole peppercorns
   split peas   ¼ teaspoon dry mustard
3 stalks celery, diced

Bring 3½ quarts water to boil in large kettle, add beans and peas, and boil 2 minutes. Turn heat off, cover kettle, and let sit 1 hour. Then add the rest of the ingredients and simmer covered until the beans are soft and the soup is thick (about 2 hours). Puree half the contents of the soup in a blender, return puree to kettle, stir well, and serve. Makes 3 quarts.

SOUPS CONTAINING MEAT

Below are delicious soups in which meat plays a central role. In serving meat soups as an appetizer, it is important to account for the additional meat (and therefore additional fat and cholesterol) that will be added to each person's total intake by eating the soup. Keeping total meat intake to less than ¼ pound per day per person necessitates watching for meat here as well as in the main course.

ALBONDIGAS SOUP

The word *albondigas* means "meatball" in Mexico. Meatball soup is a favorite first course in Mexican restaurants everywhere.

1 recipe of **Italian Meatballs,**   6 cups **Consommé**
   uncooked   (¼ cup dry sherry wine)

Combine consommé and wine in a saucepan and bring to a boil. Add meatballs slowly enough so that boil is not lost. Simmer for 45 minutes. If necessary, cool and skim surface fat; reheat to serve. Makes 8 cups.

AUTUMN SOUP

½ pound leanest ground beef   ¼ teaspoon pepper
1 cup chopped onions   ¼ teaspoon basil
1 cup diced carrots   1 bay leaf
1 cup diced celery   One 28-ounce can of tomatoes,
1 cup diced, peeled potatoes   chopped

In a large saucepan brown meat, drain and discard rendered fat, stir in onions, and cook until tender. Add 1 quart of water and all other ingredients except tomatoes. Heat to boiling, cover, and simmer 30 minutes. Add tomatoes, cover, and simmer 20 minutes more, or until vegetables are tender. Makes 6 cups.

MENUDO

This delicious Mexican soup is reputed to soften the effects of overindulgence in alcohol. It is frequently served on New Year's Eve, in anticipation of the morning after.

1½ pounds tripe   ½ teaspoon garlic powder
One 4-ounce can of chopped   ½ teaspoon crushed
   California green chilies   coriander seeds
1 cup chopped onions   4 ears corn
1 cup chopped tomatoes   1 cup chopped green onions
1 tablespoon parsley flakes

Clean and cut tripe into bite-size pieces. Cover tripe with cold water, bring to a boil, drain, and add 2 quarts boiling water. Add chilies, onions, tomatoes, and spices, and simmer until tripe is tender (about 2 hours). Clean the corn, boil until tender, and slice the kernels from the cob. When the tripe has finished cooking, add the corn kernels and heat through. Pepper to taste. Sprinkle a tablespoon of green onion in each bowl of soup and serve. Makes 8 cups.

OX-TAIL SOUP

1 ox-tail, approximately 1½ pounds, separated into joints
¼ cup white flour
1 onion, chopped
1 carrot, chopped
2 stalks celery, chopped
1 tablespoon barley, rinsed
1 bay leaf
½ cup dry red wine
⅛ teaspoon pepper
1 sprig fresh parsley, chopped

Roll ox-tail in flour. Place 1½ quarts of water in stew pot, add onion, carrot, celery, barley, and bay leaf, and bring to a boil. Drop floured ox-tail into boiling mixture. Allow boil to return, cover, and simmer 3 hours. Strain, separate meat and bone from vegetables, tie the vegetables in cheesecloth bag, and return bag to broth. Allow broth to cool, making sure bag of vegetables stays well submerged. Remove and discard surface fat. Unwrap vegetables and add to soup along with wine, pepper, and parsley. Simmer 15 minutes. Makes 1½ quarts.

SOUPS OF FISH AND FOWL

What delicious soups can be created with the help of a little fish or a little chicken! The recipes below absolutely depend on their fish or fowl content to deliver their marvelous flavors.

EASY FISH SOUP

4 -inch-square piece of dried kelp

½ pound fish, cut in ½ inch cubes

1 stalk celery, chopped in ½ inch pieces

4 green onion tops, chopped

4 small leaves of Swiss chard or similar green, cut in ½-inch strips

Parsley

To rid kelp of salt: rinse kelp, place it in 2 cups water, bring rapidly to a boil, and discard water. To cook kelp: add 4 cups fresh water and bring to a boil; simmer for ½ hour. Add fish and celery, and simmer 10 minutes. Add onions and Swiss chard; simmer 1 minute. Serve, topping each bowl with a sprig of parsley. Makes 4 cups.

CHANNEL STREET CHOWDER

¼ green pepper, chopped

½ medium onion, chopped (2 green onions, bottoms and tops, sliced)

1 cup fresh or frozen broccoli

2 cups canned or cooked tomato, with liquid

⅛ teaspoon oregano

⅛ teaspoon cumin

Dash of cayenne pepper

1 teaspoon dried parsley

Dash of garlic powder

Black pepper to taste

¾ pound rock cod or other firm-fleshed fish filets

2 tablespoons dry red wine

2 tablespoons wine vinegar

Combine all ingredients except fish, wine, and vinegar in a 2-quart saucepan. Add 1 cup of water and bring to a boil. Cover and simmer 20 minutes. Cut fish into 1-inch pieces, removing all small bones missed in fileting. Add fish, wine, and vinegar to the soup, return to a boil, and simmer 15 to 20 minutes more. Serve with hot **Sourdough Bread.** Delicious! Makes 1 quart.

CREAM OF SALMON SOUP

½ cup **Broiled Salmon Steak** scraps (skin, bones, tiny flakes)
½ cup dry vermouth
¼ teaspoon white pepper
2 tablespoons white flour

2 tablespoons cornstarch
¼ cup regular nonfat dry milk
2 cups skim milk
1 cup **Broiled Salmon Steak,** crumbled

Combine salmon scraps, vermouth, and pepper with 1½ cups of water. Bring to a boil. Simmer uncovered for 10 minutes. Strain, discarding the salmon scraps. Combine flour, cornstarch, and dry milk with ½ cup of the liquid milk to make a paste. Stir the remaining liquid milk into the paste and add to the simmering salmon liquid. Bring to a boil, simmer 1 minute, add salmon, and simmer 1 more minute. Makes 6 cups.

TUNA MUSHROOM SOUP

2 cups **Tuna Mushroom Sauce**

3 cups skim milk

Heat and serve. Makes 6 cups.

FISH IN CHICKEN STOCK

3-inch-by-2-inch piece of kelp
1½ quarts **Chicken Stock**
1 medium onion, sliced
¼ pound firm-fleshed fish filet, cut in 1-inch cubes

2 cups coarsely chopped fresh parsley leaves
Alfalfa sprouts

Pour 1 cup hot water over kelp in bowl. Let soak several minutes, drain, and rinse. Add kelp to stock and bring to a boil. Add onion, cover, and simmer. When onion is tender, remove kelp and add fish and parsley. Simmer until fish is tender (about 3 minutes). Serve with alfalfa sprouts floating in each bowl. Makes 1½ quarts.

NEW ENGLAND STYLE FISH STEW

¾ pound black cod or other tender-fleshed fish, cut into 1-inch pieces
3 tablespoons chopped onion
¾ cup vermouth
1½ quarts **Cream of Celery Soup**
¾ teaspoon cayenne pepper

Cook fish and onion in vermouth in Teflon frying pan or saucepan until the odor of the fish is stronger than that of the vermouth. Add cream of celery soup and pepper, and heat to boiling. Simmer a minute or two for thicker soup. Makes 1½ quarts.

FISH AND SQUID CHOWDER

4 squid (fairly small: hood 4 to 6 inches long)
1 small potato, peeled and diced
½ cup water
1 quart **Channel Street Chowder**

Clean squid. Cut hood into rings. Separate tentacles (eight tentacles plus two arms per squid). Combine squid, potato, and water in saucepan, bring to a boil, cover, and simmer 45 minutes. Combine with chowder, bring to a boil, and simmer 10 minutes. Makes 1½ quarts.

DAY-AFTER-THANKSGIVING TURKEY SOUP

1 turkey carcass
2 stalks celery
Pepper

Remove all stuffing. Break up carcass and place into stewing pot with as much of the unused meat as desired. Add celery, cover with cold water, gradually bring to a boil, then simmer 2 hours. Strain, cool, and remove fat. To serve, reheat and season to taste with pepper. Makes 1 to 4 quarts, depending on turkey size and amount of water used.

CHICKEN 'N RICE SOUP

1 quart **Chicken Stock**   1 cup well-cooked rice

Add rice to stock and reheat. Makes about 1½ quarts.

WHIPPED CHICKEN BROTH

4 cups **Chicken Stock**   2 tablespoons lemon juice
2 teaspoons **Vegetable**   1 tablespoon chopped, fresh
   Powder   parsley
2 egg whites

Bring stock and vegetable powder to a boil and reduce to low heat. Beat egg whites until frothy, add lemon juice, and beat again. Add 1 cup of stock to egg whites, a tablespoonful at a time, beating after each spoonful. Remove stock from heat and pour egg mixture into stock, stirring constantly. Serve immediately in large coffee mugs, topped with chopped parsley. Makes 4 cups.

STEWS

A stew is a simple way to please many different tastes and several delicious recipes for these handy one-meal dishes follow. They are particularly appreciated when the weather turns cold and there is a snap in the air.

BEEF AND GREEN BEAN STEW

1½ pounds top round, cut into
    ½-inch cubes
1 cup chopped onions
¼ teaspoon pepper
1 cup chopped fresh tomato
2 cups cooked green beans

Brown the meat and onions in a large Teflon frying pan. Add pepper while the mixture is browning. Add ½ cup of water and tomatoes. Cover, and cook over low heat until the meat is tender (about 1 hour). Add the cooked green beans and continue cooking until the beans are heated through. Serves 8.

BEEF STEW

¾ pound lean stewing beef, cut up
3 cloves of fresh garlic, sliced
1 onion, coarsely chopped
⅛ teaspoon pepper
3 carrots, coarsely chopped
3 parsnips, coarsely chopped
1 turnip, coarsely chopped
1 potato, coarsely chopped
½ cup fresh mushrooms, sliced
1 green pepper, cut in chunks
1 onion, sliced
1 medium tomato, peeled, in chunks
4 sprigs of parsley, chopped
½ cup dry red wine
2 tablespoons whole wheat flour

Trim visible fat from meat and discard. Brown meat over high heat in Teflon frying pan. Bring 1 quart of water to boil and add meat, garlic, onion, and pepper. Return to boil, cover, and simmer 2 hours, stirring occasionally to prevent sticking. Strain to separate meat from broth. Chill broth, skim fat, then recombine meat and broth. Add carrots, parsnips, turnip, and potato, and simmer 15 minutes. Add mushrooms, green pepper, sliced onion, tomato, parsley, and red wine. Simmer 20 more minutes, or until all vegetables are tender. To make brown gravy, place the 2 tablespoons of whole wheat flour in Teflon frying pan. Heat and stir dry flour with wooden spoon, lifting and shaking pan as needed to prevent flour from burning. When flour is medium brown, add ½ cup of broth from stew and stir to thicken. Return thickened gravy to stew, deglazing pan with additional stew broth. Cook and stir stew to thicken. Stew liquid should be light brown and slightly thickened. Serve over rice, noodles, bread, or in bowl by itself. Serves 6 to 8.

CHILI STEW

1½ cups diced potatoes
1 cup pinto beans, cooked
½ medium onion chopped
2 small fresh tomatoes, cut up

2 teaspoons chili powder
1 tablespoon **Vegetable Powder**
¼ cup **Bean-Thickened Gravy**

Combine all ingredients with 1½ cups water, bring to a boil, and simmer 45 minutes. Flavor improves with reheating. Makes 1 quart.

YANKEE CHICKEN GUMBO

One 8-ounce can of tomatoes
1½ cups **Chicken Stock**
1 small zucchini, sliced
1 medium onion, chopped
1 green pepper, chopped
1 clove garlic, finely chopped
1 teaspoon paprika
Pinch of saffron

½ teaspoon thyme
¼ teaspoon pepper
⅛ teaspoon cayenne pepper
1 chicken breast (½ pound)
5 fresh okra
1 potato
¼ cup freshly chopped parsley
2 teaspoons cornstarch

Combine tomatoes, stock, zucchini, onion, green pepper, garlic, and spices in a large pot. Bring to a boil, cover, and simmer for 10 minutes. Remove fat and bones from chicken breast, cut meat into ½-inch cubes, and Teflon-fry until white and separate. Cut okra into ½-inch slices. Cut peeled potato into ½-inch cubes. Add chicken, okra, potato, and parsley to simmering pot, and cook until all vegetables are tender. Mix cornstarch with small amount of water, add to pot, and cook, stirring constantly, until thickened, boiling down to reduce liquid if necessary. Serve over brown rice. Serves 4.

EASY RATATOUILLE

½ eggplant, peeled and cut into slabs ("vanilla wafer" size)

3 zucchini squash, peeled, ends trimmed off, and also cut in wafers

1 green pepper, thinly sliced

1 onion, thinly sliced

1 clove garlic, chopped very fine

2 large tomatoes, halved, dejuiced, and cut into ½-inch strips

2 tablespoons parsley flakes

¼ teaspoon pepper

Combine all ingredients in a large, heavy pot. Cover and cook over low heat for 20 minutes. Uncover and cook 15 minutes more over moderate heat, stirring with a wooden spoon to prevent scorching. Serves 4.

Alternate cooking method: Place all ingredients in a covered casserole and bake in the oven at 350° until vegetables are tender (about 1 hour). (See also **Ratatouille Sans Oil.**)

CHILI CON CARNE #1

1 cup dried kidney or pinto beans

One 15-ounce can of tomatoes

2 tablespoons chili powder

½ pound leanest ground beef
1 large onion, sliced
1 green pepper, coarsely
  chopped

1 bay leaf
¼ teaspoon cumin
½ teaspoon oregano

Rinse beans. Bring beans to a boil in 3 cups of water, simmer 3 minutes, and let stand 1 hour. Cook until tender (2 to 3 hours). Drain beans, reserving liquid. Brown meat in large Teflon pan. Discard all fat. Add remaining ingredients to meat, stirring and cooking over high heat until mixture boils. Add drained beans to mixture, cover, and simmer at very low temperature for 1 to 1½ hours, stirring occasionally to prevent sticking. Add bean liquid if mixture becomes too thick. Remove bay leaf. Serves 4 to 6.

CHILI CON CARNE #2

1 pound leanest ground beef
¼ cup pimiento, cut up small
2 cloves garlic, minced
2 teaspoons chili powder
1 teaspoon cumin

½ teaspoon oregano
(½ teaspoon cayenne pepper)
3 cups cooked red or kidney
  beans
1 tablespoon flour

Brown beef in Teflon pan, then add 2 cups water and all other ingredients except beans and flour. Cover and simmer very slowly 2 hours. Stir in beans and flour and simmer 30 minutes more. Serve with hot corn tortillas and lettuce and tomato salad. Serves 6.

CHILI CON CARNE #3

1 pound kidney beans
½ pound leanest ground beef
1 medium onion, chopped

One 15-ounce can of tomatoes
2 tablespoons chili powder
½ teaspoon pepper

Soak beans overnight in 2 quarts cold water. Drain. Brown beef in large kettle. Drain rendered fat. Add beans and enough water to cover. Bring to rolling boil, add remaining ingredients, reduce heat, and simmer until beans are tender (2 or 3 hours). Stir occasionally, adding water if necessary. If desired, serve over or with rice or macaroni. Serves 6.

JIFFY CHILI CON CARNE

This is a faster version that uses canned pinto beans. Most of the salt and sugar in the canned product is eliminated by rinsing.

½ pound leanest ground beef
One 15-ounce can of pinto beans
½ medium onion, chopped
½ green pepper, chopped
2 cups cooked or canned tomatoes
2 bay leaves

1 teaspoon chili powder
⅛ teaspoon garlic powder
½ teaspoon onion powder
¼ teaspoon oregano
⅛ teaspoon pepper
¼ teaspoon cumin
Four 1-inch cubes of
Buttermilk Fresh Cheese

Brown beef and drain off and discard all fat. Drain beans, discarding liquid from can. Rinse beans under running water. Cook onion and pepper slowly in small amount of water (3 tablespoons) until tender. In large pot, combine all ingredients and simmer uncovered for 15 minutes, stirring occasionally. Remove bay leaves. (If time permits, cover and increase simmering time.) Add cheese and simmer 5 minutes more, stirring constantly. Serves 4.

LEFTOVER-TURKEY STEW

3 cups leftover turkey, coarsely chopped
½ medium onion, coarsely chopped

1 stalk celery, coarsely chopped
1 medium carrot, coarsely chopped

Cook onion, celery, and carrot in 1 cup water until tender. Put turkey in saucepan with 2 additional cups of water and liquid from cooked vegetables and cook about 2 hours over low heat. Add vegetables, bring to boil, and cook covered over medium heat for 10 minutes. Makes 6 cups.

DAD'S OLD GOULASH

1 pound leanest ground beef
1 medium onion, chopped
2 cups of **Tomato Sauce**
One 10-ounce package of frozen cut green beans (or peas, or limas, or mixed vegetables), cooked and drained

⅓ pound spaghetti, cooked and drained
1 small can of mushroom pieces, packed in water

Cook beef, chopped onion, and tomato sauce in covered frying pan, separating beef into small pieces as it cooks. Add other ingredients, mix, serve, and enjoy. Serves 6.

HAMBURGER STEW

¾ pound extra-lean ground beef
1 medium onion, sliced
One 16-ounce can of tomatoes, coarsely chopped
3 medium carrots, peeled and sliced

3 medium potatoes, peeled and sliced
2 stalks celery, chopped
½ teaspoon pepper
½ teaspoon garlic powder

Brown meat and onion in large frying pan, breaking up meat, then add remaining ingredients. Bring to a boil, reduce heat, and simmer 30 minutes or until vegetables are tender, adding water if necessary. Serves 4.

MIXED VEGETABLE STEW

6 pearl onions, peeled, whole

2½ cups **Chicken Stock**

6 new potatoes, whole, with skins

6 small carrots, cut in half

4 small leeks, chopped

4 small zucchini, chopped

4 stalks celery, chopped

2 medium tomatoes, quartered

1 head cauliflower, broken into flowerets

2 teaspoons arrowroot

2 tablespoons parsley flakes

Boil onions gently in 1 cup water for 20 minutes. Add remaining ingredients except arrowroot and parsley flakes, and simmer until tender (about 1 hour). Add parsley flakes, thicken with arrowroot, and serve. Makes 2½ quarts.

CHAPTER 5

Salads and Salad Dressings

Because of the fresh greens and vegetables in most salads, these dishes are of key importance to a healthy diet. They are our primary source of certain vitamins and minerals. They satisfy a need to chew, and they provide our greatest source of needed bulk.

Salads can be especially important for the person just beginning to eat low-gremlin foods, because salads provide an excellent way to educate one's taste buds. The delicate, natural flavors of greens, fruits, and vegetables are often more readily enjoyed in a salad than in other dishes. When foods are uncooked and lightly dressed, as is normally the case with salads, the individual flavor of each ingredient is easily distinguished from the others and can be appreciated in its own right. The impact of spices and herbs on overall flavor is also easier to recognize and appreciate in a salad than in other dishes.

CHRYSANTHEMUM SALAD

1 small head Boston lettuce
½ cup chrysanthemum petals

2 cups sliced mushrooms
½ cup **French Dressing**

Line salad bowl with leaves of lettuce. Toss flower petals and mushrooms and add to bowl. Before serving, moisten with dressing. Serves 6.

ZESTY GREEN SALAD

1 cup shredded cabbage
1 cup watercress tops
½ cup raw broccoli flowerets
¼ cup chopped green onion
    tops

½ bunch red lettuce, broken
    into small pieces

Wash, dry, and chill cabbage and watercress. Toss with other ingredients, and moisten with favorite dressing. Serves 6.

INTERNATIONAL SALAD

½ pound fresh spinach
1 bunch watercress
1 sweet red onion, thinly
    sliced

½ small jicama, peeled and
    thinly sliced (see Glossary)
½ cup **French Dressing**

Wash spinach and tear into bite-size pieces. Remove and discard watercress stems, and toss tops with spinach. Make rings from onion slices, and add rings and jicama to salad. Moisten salad with dressing and serve. Serves 4.

DANISH CUCUMBERS

3 young, medium cucumbers
½ cup cider vinegar
1 teaspoon celery seed

½ teaspoon freshly ground
    pepper

Wash cucumbers thoroughly. Slice paper-thin, unpeeled. Mix together vinegar and ½ cup water, and to this add celery seed and pepper. Pour over cucumbers and chill 1½ to 2 hours. Drain. Serves 4.

GARDEN GREEN SALAD

8 to 12 large leaves of lettuce, torn into small pieces

4 onion slices, quartered and separated

4 sprigs of parsley, torn up, stems removed

¼ cup diced celery

4 Swiss chard leaves, torn into small pieces

Toss all ingredients, moisten with favorite dressing, and serve. Serves 4.

RUSSIAN SALAD

4 medium potatoes, boiled, cooled, peeled, and diced

1 medium cucumber, peeled and diced

1 small zucchini, peeled and diced

1 medium tomato, chopped

1 medium onion, finely chopped

1 stalk celery, chopped

2 tablespoons parsley flakes

2 tablespoons chopped pimiento

⅛ teaspoon celery seed

⅛ teaspoon dill weed

⅛ teaspoon pepper

½ cup **Sour Cream**

2 large green onions, chopped

Combine all ingredients except spices, sour cream, and green onions. Toss with spices mixed well with the sour cream. Top with green onions, and chill. Serves 6.

RAINY DAY SALAD

1 large beet, cooked, cooled, and diced
1 large potato, cooked, cooled, and diced
1 medium apple, diced
1 medium green pepper, diced
1 stalk celery, diced

Toss all ingredients lightly. Moisten with **Buttermilk Spring Dressing** and tint with some of remaining beet juice. Serves 6.

SATURDAY TOSSED SALAD

2 artichoke hearts, cooked and chopped
1 medium cucumber, diced
1 medium tomato, chopped
1 cup shredded cabbage
8 large lettuce leaves, torn into small pieces
6 parsley sprigs, chopped
6 water chestnuts, sliced thin
1 cup alfalfa sprouts

Combine all ingredients except sprouts and toss. Add sprouts and toss lightly. Excellent plain, but favorite dressing may be added. Serves 6.

HOLIDAY SALAD

¾ cup fresh asparagus tips, steamed
¾ cup fresh green beans, steamed
¾ cup diced cucumbers
½ cup raw young peas
½ cup sliced radishes
2 artichoke hearts, cooked and sliced
2 egg whites, hard-cooked and sliced

Toss all ingredients lightly. Moisten with **Buttermilk Spring Dressing**. Serves 6.

STUFFED TOMATO SALAD

6 medium tomatoes   1 cup **Sour Cream**
¼ cup lemon juice   Lettuce
1 teaspoon pepper
2 medium cucumbers,
   peeled and diced finely

Peel tomatoes (see page 55), remove and discard a thin slice from the top of each, and remove seeds and some of the pulp. Mix lemon juice and pepper, and pour mixture into one of the tomatoes. Let sit a minute or so, and pour the same mixture into the next tomato. Repeat process for all six tomatoes, then discard lemon and pepper mixture. Invert tomatoes on cake rack, and let drain a few minutes. Fill tomatoes with the diced cucumber mixed with about half the sour cream. Use the remainder of the sour cream to top the tomatoes. Arrange on lettuce leaves, and serve cold. Serves 4.

STUFFED TOMATO SALAD—RUSSIAN-STYLE

6 medium tomatoes, peeled   1 tablespoon vinegar
¼ cup lemon juice   ½ cup cold cooked chicken,
½ cup pulp from tomatoes   diced finely
¼ cup finely diced cucumbers   ½ cup **Sour Cream**
¼ cup cold cooked peas   Parsley
½ teaspoon pepper   Lettuce

Cut and discard a thin slice from top of each tomato. Remove and reserve pulp. Pour lemon juice into one tomato and let sit a minute or so. Pour same juice into next tomato; repeat process for all 6 tomatoes. Invert tomatoes on cake rack and let drain a few minutes. Mix ½ cup of reserved pulp with cucumbers, peas, pepper, and vinegar; put in a piece of cheesecloth and squeeze. Add chicken and sour cream to tomato mixture mix, and use to stuff tomatoes. Garnish with finely chopped parsley, and serve each to-mato on a lettuce leaf. Serves 6.

MACÉDOINE SALAD

½ cup vinegar
½ cup water
2 tablespoons lemon juice
1 tablespoon garlic juice
1 cup cooked, diced carrots

2 cups cooked peas
2 cups cooked cauliflower
  pieces
3 stalks celery, cut into sticks
1 large tomato, sliced

Combine vinegar, water, lemon juice, and garlic juice to make a marinade for the vegetables. Marinate the vegetables separately, 10 minutes in the refrigerator. Drain the vegetables, and spoon the carrots and peas into a single pile in the center of a serving platter, alternating a spoonful of carrots with a spoonful of peas. Top the pile with the cauliflower bits. Decorate the serving dish with the celery sticks and tomato slices. Serve cold. Serves 6.

GARBANZO AND BEET SALAD

1 cup cooked and drained
  garbanzo beans
2 cups cooked and diced beets
1 cup cooked, cut green beans

1 cup grated carrot
1 cup **Boiled Dressing** *or* **Sour Cream Dressing**

Toss vegetables, moisten with dressing, serve chilled. Serves 8.

GREEN BEAN SALAD

2 cups French-cut green
  beans

1 teaspoon mustard seeds
3 tablespoons vinegar

Add beans and mustard seeds to 1 cup boiling water and cook until tender. Add vinegar and 3 tablespoons water. Chill. Serves 4.

PEA SALAD

1 cup peas, cooked
1 cup garbanzo beans, cooked
¼ cup **Buttermilk Mock Sour Cream**

1 teaspoon moldiest areas of very ripe blue cheese
1 cup alfalfa or bean sprouts

Moisten peas and beans thoroughly with a mixture of the sour cream and blue cheese. Chill. Toss with sprouts, serve. Serves 4.

LENTIL SALAD

3 cups cooked lentils, drained and cooled
4 medium carrots, grated
1 medium green pepper, chopped

4 stalks celery, chopped
4 medium tomatoes, cut in wedges
2 cups **Thousand Island Dressing**

Mix all ingredients except dressing. Pour dressing over top, and let sit a few minutes before serving. Serves 8.

ASPARAGUS TIP SALAD

Two 15-ounce cans of asparagus tips, drained and chilled

2 cups **Sour Cream**
2 tablespoon parsley flakes

Place asparagus tips in individual serving dishes and cover with a mixture of the sour cream and parsley. Serves 4.

MUSHROOM SALAD

4 cups (about ¾ pound) large, fresh mushrooms
1 small onion
1 small green pepper
¼ cup garlic juice
¾ cup watercress, finely chopped

½ cup **White Sauce**
1 tablespoon parsley flakes
1 tablespoon lemon juice
Lettuce

Slice mushroom caps from stems, and place caps in a large frying pan or saucepan that has a tight-fitting lid. Chop mushroom stems, onion, and green pepper finely and combine with the mushroom caps. Add garlic juice and ½ cup water, and sauté, covered, a few minutes. Drain and chill. Combine, mix, and chill all remaining ingredients, except lettuce, to make a sauce for the mushroom mixture. Serve the mixture on lettuce, topped with the sauce. Makes 6 servings.

ZUCCHINI SALAD

2 medium zucchini, sliced
2 medium tomatoes, peeled and chopped

½ green pepper, chopped
1 cup **Creamy Salad Dressing**

Sauté zucchini in 2 tablespoons of water for 1 or 2 minutes and let cool. Place dressing in bowl, add all vegetables, stir, and serve. Serves 4.

ZUCCHINI-APPLE SALAD

1 pound zucchini, thinly sliced
3 medium Delicious apples, diced
1 medium green pepper, chopped
½ medium mild red onion, chopped

2 tablespoons wine vinegar
1 tablespoon lemon juice
1 teaspoon frozen apple juice concentrate
1 teaspoon basil
¼ teaspoon pepper

Combine all ingredients, chill, and serve. Serves 4.

CUCUMBER SALAD

2 cups sliced, peeled cucumbers
1 cup **Yogurt** or **Sour Cream**

1 green onion top, chopped fine

Divide cucumbers among four individual serving bowls, pour ¼ cup yogurt or sour cream over each bowl, top with a sprinkle of green onion, and serve. Serves 4.

MACARONI SALAD

2 cups macaroni
1 cup **Sour Cream** or other mock sour cream
2 radishes, finely chopped
1 tablespoon pimiento, finely chopped

1 tablespoon onion flakes
1 tablespoon parsley flakes
¼ teaspoon garlic powder
⅛ teaspoon celery seeds

Cook and drain macaroni. Combine all other ingredients and stir. Fold into macaroni, toss, chill, and serve. Serves 6.

BULGUR SALAD

1 cup bulgur wheat
¼ cup sliced scallions
½ cup sliced mushrooms
2 stalks celery, chopped
1 cup chopped fresh parsley
½ cup **stock**

2 tablespoons vinegar
¼ teaspoon marjoram
¼ teaspoon thyme
6 leaves of lettuce
1 medium tomato, sliced

Bring 2½ cups water to a boil, add bulgur wheat, cover, and simmer 30 minutes. Drain and cool. Add scallions, mushrooms, celery, and parsley. Mix. Stir in the stock, vinegar, and spices, and chill. Serve individually on lettuce leaves. Top each serving with a tomato slice. Makes 6 servings.

GARDEN SQUASH SALAD

1 medium yellow squash
1 medium zucchini squash
½ cup favorite salad dressing
1 cup alfalfa sprouts

1 medium tomato, chopped
¼ cup very thin mushroom
   slices
¼ cup chopped fresh parsley

Cut both kinds of squash into matchsticks. Toss with a spoonful of the dressing to coat. Layer squash, sprouts, tomatoes, and mushrooms in salad bowl. Pour dressing over top, and sprinkle with parsley. Serves 4.

POTATO SALAD

4 cups peeled, diced, and
   cooked potatoes
5 egg whites, hardcooked,
   diced

1 tablespoon parsley flakes
¼ to ½ teaspoon garlic
   powder
½ teaspoon pepper

1 cup chopped celery
¼ medium onion, chopped
3 tablespoons chopped
  green onion
3 tablespoons chopped
  green pepper

1½ teaspoon Italian Seasoning
½ cup **Sour Cream**
½ cup **Yogurt**
4 teaspoons prepared
  mustard (or to taste)
(2 teaspoons cider vinegar)

Combine all ingredients except sour cream, yogurt, and mustard. Combine sour cream, yogurt, and mustard, and stir into other ingredients. Refrigerate 2 or 3 hours before serving. Makes 6 cups.

CREAMY COLESLAW

1½ cups **Creamy Salad Dressing**
2 teaspoons celery seed
½ teaspoon dill weed

3 cups finely shredded cabbage
1 cup diced apple

Combine salad dressing with celery seed and dill weed and mix well. Add cabbage and apple and serve. Makes 1 quart.

BUTTERMILK COLESLAW

¾ cup **Buttermilk**
1 tablespoon lemon juice
2 tablespoons regular dry
  nonfat milk

¾ teaspoon pepper
¾ teaspoon celery seed
3 cups shredded cabbage
½ cup shredded carrots

Combine all ingredients except cabbage and carrots, and mix well to make creamy coleslaw dressing. Toss cabbage and carrots with dressing and let sit 2 hours before serving. Makes 1 quart.

GARDEN SQUASH SLAW

1 medium yellow squash
1 medium zucchini squash
1 cup shredded cabbage
½ cup tender mung bean
   sprouts

¼ cup carrot shavings
¾ cup **Herbed Yogurt**
¼ teaspoon pepper.

Cut squash into matchsticks and combine with other vegetables. Add enough yogurt to coat all vegetables, then add pepper and mix. Makes ¾ quart.

CABBAGE SALAD

1 cup chopped cabbage
1 teaspoon green onion tops,
   chopped
¼ cup alfalfa sprouts, firmly
   packed

¼ medium tomato, chopped
¼ cup **Sour Cream**
¼ teaspoon celery seed
⅛ teaspoon paprika
Pepper

Layer cabbage, onion tops, sprouts, and tomato in an individual salad bowl. Combine remaining ingredients and pour over the vegetables. Serves 1.

FOUR-BEAN SALAD

1 cup cooked kidney beans
1 cup cooked green beans
1 cup cooked wax beans
½ cup cooked garbanzo beans
½ cup apple juice
2 teaspoons vinegar

½ cup chopped onion
1 tablespoon chopped
   pimiento
1 teaspoon **Vegetable
   Powder** or onion powder
½ teaspoon pepper

Combine all ingredients and marinate in refrigerator several hours. Makes 1 quart.

STRING BEAN SALAD

1 cup cooked, chopped string beans
1 cup cooked kidney beans
1 medium onion, chopped

2 cloves garlic, chopped
¼ cup vinegar
¼ cup water
1 tablespoon lemon juice

Combine beans, onion, and garlic. Cover with vinegar, water, and lemon juice. Chill thoroughly. Serves 4.

CURRIED RICE SALAD

2 large dried tamarind pods
¼ cup orange juice
One 10½-ounce can of mandarin orange sections, water-packed

One 8-ounce can of pineapple tidbits, juice-packed
½ teaspoon curry powder
3 cups cooked rice
½ cup **Sour Cream**

Remove and discard shells of tamarind pods, leaving flesh and seeds. In a small saucepan combine tamarind flesh, orange juice, juice from the canned fruits, and curry powder. Bring to a boil, cover, and simmer until tamarind flesh is very soft. Simmer uncovered, force seeds from flesh by mashing with spoon, and discard seeds. Continue simmering, stirring, and mashing until reduced to about ¼ to ⅓ cup of viscous, pulpy liquid. Toss liquid with rice. Stir in sour cream, breaking up any rice lumps. Fold in fruit, and chill. Serves 6.

RICE SALAD

2 cups cooked rice
½ cup finely chopped celery
¼ cup finely chopped onions
¼ cup chopped radishes

½ teaspoon mint flakes
¼ teaspoon pepper
Tangy Salad Dressing

Combine all ingredients except dressing, and chill. Before serving, break up any lumps, and moisten slightly with dressing. Serves 4.

BANANA-STUFFED SALAD

This delightful old favorite is always fun to serve and only takes a minute to fix.

4 bananas
½ cup **French Dressing** or
   Sour Cream and Curry
   Dressing

Wash bananas (skins may have been sprayed for insects; do not eat skins). Remove one section of skin from each banana and take out the fruit portion, leaving the skin intact to form a boat for stuffing. Slice three of the fruit portions into cubes, marinate the cubes in the dressing, and refill all four skins. Slice the remaining fruit into thin slices. Serve the stuffed bananas on individual plates, using the banana slices as decoration. Serves 4.

FRUIT AND COTTAGE CHEESE SALAD

On individual salad plates, make a bed with a lettuce leaf, place a mound of cottage cheese in the center, arrange bite-size pieces of fruit around the mound, and top it with a strawberry. Delicious, attractive, and so easy to do. The following portions are sufficient to make 6 individual fruit salads.

6 leaves of lettuce
2 cups **Cottage Cheese**
6 strawberries
2 medium apples, quartered, cored, and sliced thin
1 cup pineapple chunks
2 oranges, sectioned and seeded
3 bananas, sliced
1 bunch seedless grapes
3 cups melon balls

CLOVED PEACH SALAD

6 freestone peaches
Whole cloves
1 cup **Cottage Cheese**

¼ teaspoon frozen apple juice
  concentrate
¼ teaspoon lemon juice

Halve, peel, and pit peaches. Insert 2 to 4 cloves in each peach half, and chill 1 hour. Mix cottage cheese, apple juice concentrate, and lemon juice. Fill chilled peach halves with this mixture, put peach halves back together, forming whole stuffed peaches, remove cloves, and serve on a lettuce leaf or individual salad plates. Serves 6.

SAVORY COTTAGE CHEESE SALAD

½ cup **Sour Cream**
1 teaspoon skim milk
2 cups **Cottage Cheese**
½ stalk celery, chopped fine
1 medium cucumber, peeled
  and diced

2 tablespoons chopped
  pimiento
½ teaspoon garlic powder

Blend sour cream and milk until very smooth, and combine with cottage cheese to produce a "creamed cottage cheese" effect. Combine with remaining ingredients and mix well. Serves 6.

COTTAGE CHEESE AND TOMATO SALAD

6 medium tomatoes, peeled
2 cups shredded lettuce
2 medium cucumbers, peeled
  and sliced

2 cups **Cottage Cheese**
1 tablespoon parsley flakes

Slice each tomato into six wedges, leaving the wedges connected at the bottom. On each of six individual salad plates, place a bed of lettuce, a ring of cucumber slices, and one of the tomatoes. Gently open the tomato wedges to form a rosette, and spoon 4 or 5 spoonfuls of the cottage cheese mixed with the parsley flakes into the center. Serves 6.

PINEAPPLE COTTAGE CHEESE SALAD

One 8-ounce can of pineapple tidbits, juice-packed
2 tablespoons juice from pineapple

4 cups **Cottage Cheese**
¼ cup evaporated skim milk
½ head shredded lettuce

Combine half of the pineapple tidbits, 1 cup of the cottage cheese, the pineapple juice, and the skim milk in the blender, and chop and blend until very smooth. Add remainder of pineapple tidbits and cottage cheese, and blend for a few seconds only. Serve over shredded lettuce. Serves 4.

PINEAPPLE AND GRAPEFRUIT SALAD

2 cups crushed pineapple
½ cup grapefruit sections
½ teaspoon mint flakes

2 tablespoons chopped green pepper

Mix all ingredients, chill 1 hour, and serve. Serves 4.

PINEAPPLE SOUR CREAM SALAD

1½ cups drained crushed pineapple
1 cup **Sour Cream**

¼ cup tiny cubes or bits of **Fresh Cheese**
4 lettuce leaves

Combine pineapple, sour cream, and cheese, and serve cold on individual salad plates with a lettuce leaf as a bed. Serves 4.

GREEN BEAN ASPIC

One 12-ounce can of unsalted vegetable juice
1 tablespoon unflavored gelatin
1 teaspoon lemon juice
1 cup cooked and thoroughly drained French-cut green beans
½ cup cooking liquid from green beans (or water)

Pour ¼ cup vegetable juice into a flat bowl. Sprinkle gelatin evenly over surface, and let soften 5 minutes. Combine lemon juice and beans, toss thoroughly, and set aside. Bring liquid from green beans to a boil, add to gelatin, and stir to completely dissolve all gelatin. Add remaining vegetable juice and stir well. Fold in beans and pour into aspic mold. Chill until set, unmold, and serve. Serves 4.

TUNA MOLD

One 7-ounce can of tuna
1 tablespoon unflavored gelatin
½ cup tomato paste
1 cup **Cottage Cheese**
1 cup skim milk
1 fresh egg white
½ medium green pepper, chopped fine
½ medium onion, chopped fine
1 stalk celery, sliced very thin

Drain tuna thoroughly. Pour ½ cup of cold water into 2-quart saucepan, sprinkle gelatin on top, and let stand 5 minutes to soften. Add tomato paste, heat and stir to dissolve gelatin. Cool to room temperature. In blender, combine cottage cheese and half of milk. Chop and blend until very smooth. Add remaining milk and egg white, and blend. Combine with gelatin, water, and tomato paste mixture, and chill until partly set. Add vegetables and tuna, pour into mold, and chill until firm. Serves 4 to 6.

CARROT AND PEA ASPIC

1 tablespoon unflavored gelatin
1 cup pure carrot juice
2 tablespoons vinegar
1 tablespoon lemon juice
½ cup clean carrot peelings

1 cup cooked and drained peas
1 tablespoon chopped pimiento
¼ teaspoon pepper

Sprinkle gelatin over ½ cup water in saucepan, allow 5 minutes to soften, then heat and stir to dissolve gelatin. Stir in all liquid ingredients, followed by remaining ingredients. Pour into serving dish, and chill until set. Serves 4.

GREEN BEAN MOLD

1 tablespoon unflavored gelatin
1½ cups **stock**
¼ cup chopped celery
2 teaspoons white vinegar

2 teaspoons lemon juice
½ teaspoon garlic powder
¼ teaspoon pepper
1¾ cups cooked chopped green beans

Sprinkle gelatin over surface of ¼ cup cold water, and let sit 5 minutes to soften. Place stock, celery, vinegar, lemon juice, and spices in saucepan, bring to a boil, then remove from heat. Add softened gelatin and stir until dissolved. Add beans, pour into 4 small ring molds, and chill until set (about 1 hour). Serves 4.

TACO SALAD FOR 12

1 pound extra-lean ground beef, crumbled, cooked, drained, and cooled
3 cups grated **Fresh Cheese**
One 15-ounce can of kidney beans, drained and rinsed under cold running water
1 large head lettuce, chopped
2 tomatoes, chopped
1 bunch green onions, chopped
1 cup **Creamy Salad Dressing**
¼ cup **Red Molé Sauce**
1 Recipe of **Tortilla Chips**

Combine all ingredients except tortilla chips. Before serving, crush and add tortilla chips. Serves 12.

TUNA SALAD #1

One 7-ounce can of tuna, drained
1 small head lettuce, chopped fine
1 cup chopped celery
1 cup diced cucumber
¼ cup vinegar
¼ cup lemon juice
2 teaspoons onion powder
½ teaspoon pepper
4 small tomatoes cut in eighths
4 green pepper rings

Mix tuna, lettuce, celery, and cucumber. Mix vinegar, lemon juice, onion powder, and pepper. Combine with tuna mixture. Place mixture on top of tomato wedges. Top with green pepper rings. Serves 4.

TUNA SALAD #2

One 7-ounce can of tuna
1 teaspoon lemon juice
½ cup **Sour Cream**
2 tablespoons chopped
   green pepper

2 tablespoons chopped onion
Sprinkling of pepper
Sprinkling of **Vegetable**
   Powder *or* onion powder
Lettuce

Drain tuna, mix with lemon juice, combine with other ingredients, and serve on lettuce as a luncheon salad. Serves 4.

TUNA MACARONI SALAD

1 cup **Tuna Salad**
1 quart cooked macaroni
   (small elbow or seashell)

Toss macaroni with tuna salad, chill, and serve. Makes 1 quart.

INSALATA DI MARE

This delicious salad is typical of the seafood salads served in restaurants in northern Italy.

4 squid (fairly small; hood 4
   to 6 inches long)
¼ cup coarsely chopped
   green pepper
1 clove garlic, chopped

¼ cup sliced celery
¼ teaspoon freshly ground
   pepper
Juice of 1 lemon

Clean squid. Separate tentacles and cut each in half. Cut hood into rings. Add tentacles and hood rings to small amount of boiling water. Boil 3 to 4 minutes *only* (tentacles will turn a lovely pink purple). Drain, combine with all other ingredients, and let sit in refrigerator 3 to 4 hours. Serve as is on a bed of ¼ head lettuce, torn into small pieces, or toss with:

¼ head lettuce, torn into
  small pieces
1 small tomato, chopped

3 sprigs fresh parsley,
  chopped.

Serves 4.

SALAD DRESSINGS

Salads are usually marvelously low in fat and other gremlins wherever they are found, in this book or elsewhere. But salad *dressings* are a different matter entirely. Outside this book, a salad dressing is almost always high in fat or sugar or salt or all three. This includes the old favorites (French, Thousand Island, and oil and vinegar) as well as the many rare and exotic dressings found in the cooking literature.

On the following pages we offer a variety of dressings: French, Thousand Island, blue cheese, and many others. All of them are unique in the fact that, like the salads themselves, they are free of gremlins—no fat, no sugar, no salt. Frankly, the French dressing we offer does not taste like the usual French dressings at the market. It's different. It's unique. But it's delicious. The same is true of some of the other old favorites. They're not always identical to the dressing from which they derive their name. They can't be. There really is no way to achieve complete fidelity in taste without using all the same ingredients. And that would mean putting the gremlins right back in again. Fidelity to old tastes, we feel, is not really the answer in longevity cookery.

BLUE CHEESE DRESSING

Overripe blue cheese

1 cup **Sour Cream**

Scrape moldiest areas off blue cheese to get 1 tablespoon of very concentrated blue cheese. Stir into sour cream and thin to desired consistency with **Buttermilk.** Makes 1 cup of delicious blue cheese dressing.

FRENCH DRESSING

½ cup water
2 tablespoons powdered
   pectin
3 tablespoons lemon juice
¼ teaspoon frozen apple juice
   concentrate

⅛ teaspoon pepper
¼ teaspoon dry mustard
¼ teaspoon paprika

Combine ingredients in a jar large enough to leave an air space. Shake well to mix ingredients and to fill the dressing with tiny air bubbles. Chill. Shake before serving. Makes ¾ cup.

THOUSAND ISLAND DRESSING

1 cup **Yogurt**   ¼ cup **Hamburger Sauce**

Combine yogurt and sauce, and stir to blend. Use on tossed green salads or vegetable salads. Makes 1 cup.

SPICED VINEGAR DRESSING

¼ cup wine or cider vinegar
2 tablespoons water
1 tablespoon lemon juice
1 tablespoon onion flakes
1 tablespoon parsley flakes

¼ teaspoon pepper
¼ teaspoon tarragon
¼ teaspoon oregano
¼ teaspoon paprika

Mix ingredients, chill, and stir before serving. Goes great as a light dressing on tossed green salads. Makes ½ cup.

GARLIC AND VINEGAR DRESSING

2 cloves garlic, sliced
½ cup vinegar
¼ cup water
2 teaspoons frozen apple
   juice concentrate

¼ teaspoon paprika
½ teaspoon ground thyme

Combine all ingredients and shake well before serving. Makes ¾ cup.

BUTTERMILK SPRING DRESSING

1 cup **Buttermilk**
1 teaspoon frozen apple juice
   concentrate
1 teaspoon lemon juice

1 teaspoon onion flakes
1 teaspoon dill weed
Pepper
Ground allspice

Mix all ingredients except pepper and allspice. Add pepper and ground allspice to taste. (Begin with about ⅛ teaspoon each, and add more if necessary.) Chill. Makes 1 cup.

AUTUMN BEAN DRESSING

One 16-ounce can of cooked
   red or pinto beans
1 tablespoon vinegar
¼ cup apple or pineapple
   juice

½ teaspoon onion flakes
½ teaspoon dill weed
⅛ teaspoon pepper

Combine all ingredients, including liquid from beans, and chill. Makes 2 cups.

BOILED DRESSING

This simple, old-fashioned dressing may be served cold over vegetable salads, tomato slices, aspics, etc.

3 tablespoons flour	¾ teaspoon dry mustard
¾ cup skim milk	2 tablespoons lemon juice
½ teaspoon paprika	½ teaspoon garlic powder.

Make a paste of the flour and ¼ cup of the milk. Stir paste into remaining milk, add remaining ingredients, and mix. Cook and stir in the top of a double boiler over boiling water until thickened. (Curdling is normal prior to thickening; have faith.) Chill. If desired, thin before serving by adding 1 tablespoon of skim milk and mixing in the blender on the chop or puree cycle. Makes 1 cup.

TANGY SALAD DRESSING

¾ cup tomato juice	2 tablespoons finely chopped
3 tablespoons lemon juice	onion
	¼ teaspoon pepper

Combine all ingredients, chill, and stir before using. Makes 1 cup.

HERBED YOGURT

1 cup **Yogurt**	2 teaspoons parsley flakes
½ teaspoon dill weed	¼ teaspoon chervil

Combine all ingredients, and let sit 24 hours in refrigerator. Makes 1 cup.

GREEN DRESSING, YOGURT-STYLE

½ cup **Corn Pudding**   ⅛ teaspoon pepper
½ cup **Yogurt**

Combine ingredients and mix. Makes 1 cup.

GREEN DRESSING

4 green onions, finely   2 tablespoons grated green
  chopped   cheese
½ cup **Buttermilk**   ½ cup **Cottage Cheese**

In blender, chop and blend all ingredients until smooth. Heat in
small saucepan to make even smoother. Cool and use on tossed
salads or vegetable salads. Use hot as an artichoke dip. Makes 1
cup.

PIMIENTO DRESSING

1 cup **Mexican Mock Sour**   2 tablespoons sliced pimientos
  Cream

Place ingredients in blender, chop, then liquify at high speed. A
mild, sweet dressing. For tang, add 2 teaspoons **Tomato Sauce** and
½ teaspoon vinegar before blending. Makes 1 cup.

CREAMY SALAD DRESSING

1 cup **Cottage Cheese**
½ cup **Sour Cream**
1 tablespoon lemon juice
½ teaspoon garlic powder

Combine ingredients in blender and blend until smooth. Thin with a bit of skim milk during blending, if desired. Excellent on vegetable or tossed green salads. Makes 1½ cups.

LEMON MOCK SOUR CREAM

This mock sour cream is excellent as a dip, and may be used as a salad dressing or a topping for baked potatoes. Best of all, it can be thrown together in a matter of minutes.

¼ cup skim milk
1 cup **Cottage Cheese**
2 tablespoons lemon juice

(2 tablespoons parsley flakes *or* onion flakes)

Combine all ingredients in blender, mix at chopping speed, then switch to high speed and liquify. Makes 1 cup.

BUTTERMILK MOCK SOUR CREAM

1 cup **Cream Cheese**   ⅓ cup **Buttermilk**

In blender, combine buttermilk and cheese. Blend until very smooth. Chill. Makes 1 cup.

MEXICAN MOCK SOUR CREAM

1 cup **Cream Cheese**   ½ cup skim milk

Mix cheese and milk in the blender at a chopping speed, then liquify at high speed. Makes 1 cup.

SOUR CREAM AND GARLIC DRESSING

1 cup **Sour Cream**   1 teaspoon minced fresh
¼ teaspoon garlic juice   onion

Mix ingredients well, and serve over vegetable or tossed green salads. Makes 1 cup.

SOUR CREAM AND ONION DRESSING

1 cup **Sour Cream**   1 tablespoon lemon juice
1 tablespoon onion flakes   ¼ teaspoon paprika
1 tablespoon parsley flakes   ¼ teaspoon curry powder

Combine ingredients, mix well, and serve chilled over **Asparagus Tip Salad, Saturday Tossed Salad,** or any tossed green salad. Makes 1 cup.

SOUR CREAM AND CURRY DRESSING

1 cup **Sour Cream**   ½ teaspoon curry powder
1 tablespoon lemon juice

Combine ingredients and mix well. Makes 1 cup.

CHAPTER 6

Main Dishes

What may be a main dish to one person may not be one to another. In fact, one meal's main dish may be only an appetizer to another. Indeed, this dish is simply the one occupying the spotlight; the one around which the meal is designed. Since the choice of which dish to feature is a matter of personal taste, there is no universal way to make a distinction between main dishes and side dishes. But as a general rule the recipes in this chapter are the sort one might wish to use as a featured main dish. The final decision, however, is up to the meal planner.

The chapter is divided into five sections:
1. Vegetable Main Dishes and Vegetable Accompaniments
2. Combination Casseroles and Pastas
3. Fish Dishes
4. Chicken and Turkey Dishes
5. Meat Dishes

This way of categorizing the main dishes intentionally de-emphasizes meat, fowl, and fish dishes, by placing them last. And, indeed, one of the best ways to keep meat (this includes fowl and fish as well as beef, lamb, and pork) intake down is to use a non-meat main dish as frequently as possible. The more sparingly one uses meat as a main dish, the more freedom one has to use meat in appetizers, soups, salads, and as a flavoring in other dishes, without exceeding the limit of one-quarter pound of meat per person per day. So our advice is to take meat out of the mealtime spotlight. Use it instead, in small quantities, to add flavor and meaty fragrances to the many other courses one can prepare.

Even when meat is served as a main course, don't hesitate to serve it in small portions so long as other more filling dishes accompany it. "Main" course does not have to mean "big" course. Many of the meat dishes in this chapter are purposely designed to provide small portions.

VEGETABLE MAIN DISHES AND VEGETABLE ACCOMPANIMENTS

Until recently it has been customary in Western cultures to use vegetable dishes almost exclusively as side dishes, and rarely as main dishes. Today, however, a vegetable dish is a welcome main dish. In this chapter we've mixed vegetable main dishes and side dishes, and we leave to the reader the decision as to which of these delicious recipes to spotlight where during the course of the meal.

A final comment: the estimate given in each recipe of the number of people the recipe serves is based on using the recipe as a main dish. A recipe will usually serve more than indicated if used as a side dish.

CREAMY MUSHROOM CASSEROLE

⅔ cup canned mushrooms (stems and pieces), drained
1 teaspoon garlic juice
1 tablespoon arrowroot
¼ cup **Mock Cream Cheese**
½ cup skim milk

One 10-ounce package of frozen peas
One 8½-ounce can of small white onions
1 tablespoon minced fresh parsley

Sauté mushrooms in garlic juice and 2 tablespoons water for 5 minutes. Blend arrowroot and cream cheese. Add sautéed mushrooms, then gradually stir in milk. Combine with peas and onions in a 1-quart casserole dish, cover, and bake 30 minutes at 425°. Sprinkle with parsley and serve. Serves 4.

SWEET AND SOUR VEGETABLES

1 tablespoon cornstarch
2 tablespoons vermouth
¾ cup **Chicken Stock** or water
One 8-ounce can of crushed
  pineapple, juice-packed
½ cup bean sprouts
¼ cup alfalfa sprouts
2 tablespoons sliced green
  onions, tops and bottoms
2 small carrots, cut in thin,
  2-inch-long strips
½ cup thinly sliced Chinese
  celery-cabbage
½ teaspoon grated fresh
  ginger root (or ¼ teaspoon
  ground ginger)
½ cup sliced fresh
  mushrooms

¼ cup jicama, cut in strips
  ½″ × 2″ × ⅛″ (see
  Glossary) or substitute
  canned water chestnuts
10 snow pea pods
¼ cup green pepper, in
  ¾-inch pieces
¼ cup fresh broccoli stems,
  cut across grain in thin
  slices
1 Jerusalem artichoke, sliced
  thin
2 tablespoons chopped
  pimiento
1 tablespoon vinegar
(½ pound cooked chicken, in
  small cubes)

Mix cornstarch and vermouth. Combine with chicken stock and juice from pineapple, in 2-quart saucepan, and cook over medium heat, stirring constantly, until thickened. Add remaining ingredients, and simmer, stirring frequently, until vegetables are just slightly tender but still crisp and colorful (6 to 7 minutes). Serve over cooked brown rice. Serves 4.

GARDEN CASSEROLE

1 medium onion, chopped
1 teaspoon chili powder
1 teaspoon oregano
⅛ teaspoon ground cumin
Dash of cayenne pepper
1 medium green pepper, cut
   in strips

2 large zucchini, sliced
1 cup corn kernels,
   preferably fresh off the cob
2 medium tomatoes, sliced
½ cup tiny sourdough bread
   cubes
Paprika

Place onion, spices, and ¾ cup water in small saucepan, and heat to boiling. Pour into casserole dish; add peppers, zucchini, and corn; cover; and bake 1 hour at 350°. Then stir in tomatoes, top with bread cubes, sprinkle with a bit of paprika, and bake uncovered an additional 25 minutes. Serves 4.

MILLET AND VEGETABLES

½ cup millet
1½ cups boiling water
2½ cups mixed raw vegetables
   (for example, 2 leaves of
   spinach torn in pieces, 3
   chopped sprigs of parsley,
   ½ cup coarsely chopped
   onion, ¼ cup sliced
   mushrooms, ¼ cup thinly
   sliced cauliflower, ¼ cup
   diced zucchini, ¼ cup
   sliced or diced carrot, 1
   tomato cut in eighths, ¼
   cup sliced celery)

1 teaspoon **Vegetable**
   Powder
1 teaspoon grated lemon
   peel
1 teaspoon lemon juice
Generous pinch of saffron

In heavy pan, toast millet until lightly browned, stirring constantly. Steam vegetables. In large casserole dish, combine millet and boiling water. Add all other ingredients and stir. Bake covered at 350° for 40 minutes. Serves 6.

EASY ARTICHOKES

For casual occasions, skip the time-consuming preparation of the artichokes before cooking. Simply wash the artichokes, drop into boiling water, bring to boil again, reduce heat, and simmer 40 minutes. Artichokes are served and eaten (one per person) as described above, with a little care in handling the pointy ends of the leaves. **Green Dressing** is required (½ cup per person), as well as a bowl to catch the discarded leaves.

ARTICHOKES

Hot, freshly prepared, whole artichokes are a welcome dish at any meal. The task of working through the leaves to the artichoke heart adds liveliness and fun that heightens the eating pleasure of young or old. Allow one artichoke per person, and be sure to provide bowls to hold the discarded artichoke leaves after the edible meat on them is eaten.

Artichokes (1 per person)
Green Dressing (½ cup per
    person), hot

Rinse artichokes, cut off stems, and square off bottoms with knife. Remove the sharp point at the tip of each leaf: with sharp knife cut off cluster of points at top of each artichoke; with kitchen scissors cut off rest of points. Dip artichokes in vinegar water (1 tablespoon vinegar per quart water) to prevent discoloration. Drop artichokes in large pot of boiling water. Bring to boil again, reduce heat, cover, and simmer 40 minutes. Gently lift artichokes from pot, shaking off excess water. Serve hot. To eat, pull off each leaf, dip in dressing, and eat the fleshy part of the leaf by scraping leaf against front teeth. When leaves are gone, carefully remove the inedible "choke" fibers to expose the superbly delicious heart and edible part of stem. Cut up, dip, and enjoy.

VEGETABLE CASSEROLE

Use those aging vegetables in the vegetable bin and the leftover vegetables from Tuesday night's dinner in this delicious, quick casserole. This recipe is a "for instance." Use it as a guide, but use whatever's on hand. (The onions and the tomatoes are always used.) Hard fresh vegetables, like carrots, will need to be partially cooked first.

4 cups cooked and drained shell or elbow macaroni
2 large tomatoes, sliced
1 large onion, sliced
1 medium zucchini, sliced

1 cup sliced fresh mushrooms
1 cup fresh broccoli pieces
1 cup grated **Fresh Cheese**
2 cups **Versatility Sauce**

In a glass baking dish 13″ × 9″ × 2″, layer the ingredients in the following sequence:
    half the onions and tomatoes;
    a third of the macaroni;
    half the zucchini, mushrooms, broccoli, and fresh cheese;
    another third of the macaroni;
    remainder of zucchini, mushrooms, broccoli, and fresh cheese;
    remainder of the macaroni.
    Pour sauce over casserole. Add remainder of onions and tomatoes as a topping layer. Cover and bake 30 minutes at 350°. Serves 6.

BAKED CHERRY TOMATOES

30 cherry tomatoes
 1 cup dry bread crumbs
 2 teaspoons **Vegetable Powder**
 ¼ teaspoon garlic powder
 1 teaspoon chili powder
 ¼ cup water

Cut tomatoes in half, and place in shallow pan, cut side up. Combine bread crumbs with seasonings, add water, toss lightly, and sprinkle onto tomato halves. Bake at 375° for 15 minutes. Serves 4 to 6.

BRASSICA OLERACEA BAKE
(Brussels sprouts and cauliflower)

2 cups cooked Brussels sprouts
2 cups cooked cauliflower clusters
2 cups **Cheese Sauce**
½ cup cracker crumbs
½ cup grated **Fresh Cheese**

In a casserole dish, arrange Brussels sprouts and cauliflower clusters in an attractive pattern. Smother with hot cheese sauce, top with cracker crumbs and grated cheese, and bake at 375° for 30 minutes. Serves 4.

CAULIFLOWER IN BLOOM

1 head cauliflower
2 bunches broccoli
2 lemons, cut in lengthwise wedges
Thyme
Savory

Cut out green stem and pulpy center of cauliflower (a shallow, cone-shaped plug), taking care not to separate head. Rinse. Cut off the inedible bottom parts of the broccoli stems, and wash broccoli. Place a vegetable steaming rack at bottom of a large pot, and add water just to the level of the rack bottom. Place cauliflower and broccoli in rack, add spices to taste, cover pot tightly, and steam until tender (about 20 minutes). Serve on a large platter with cauliflower in center and broccoli groups radiating outwards, interspersed with lemon wedges. Serves 6.

CAULIFLOWER IN SOUR CREAM

1 medium head cauliflower	1 small onion, minced
1 teaspoon lemon juice	⅛ teaspoon pepper
1 cup **Sour Cream**	
1 tablespoon prepared mustard	

Remove thick leaves from cauliflower, leaving small tender leaves. Place whole cauliflower, head up, in a saucepan. Add lemon juice and ¼ cup water. Cover, and cook 25 minutes over low heat. Combine and heat remaining ingredients. Pour over cauliflower and serve. Serves 6.

MARINATED CAULIFLOWER

1 head cauliflower	⅛ teaspoon cayenne pepper
½ cup white wine	⅛ teaspoon mild paprika
½ cup white vinegar	1 teaspoon dill seed
1 teaspoon peppercorns	½ clove garlic, sliced

Remove leaves and woody stem from cauliflower, separate into flowerets, and cook, covered, in ½ cup boiling water for 10 to 15 minutes. Combine the remaining ingredients with cooking liquid to make a marinade. Marinate the cauliflower 24 hours in the refrigerator. Use as an appetizer (excellent with **Mexican Vegetable Dip**), a cold salad, or a vegetable side dish. Makes 2 to 4 cups, depending on size of cauliflower.

BROCCOLI WITH CHEESE

3 cups cooked broccoli
Dash of thyme
Dash of nutmeg
1 cup grated **Fresh Cheese**

Combine broccoli and spices in a casserole dish. Top with cheese, cover, and bake at 350° for 20 minutes. Serves 4.

GRATED BEETS WITH ORANGE

4 large beets, peeled and grated
¾ cup orange juice
15 to 20 drops Angostura Bitters

Place beets in saucepan, stir in juice and bitters, heat, and simmer 5 minutes. Beets will be slightly crisp. Delicious! Serves 4.

GLAZED BEETS

8 medium beets, trimmed, peeled, and sliced
1½ cups water
2 teaspoons cornstarch
4 teaspoons vinegar

Combine beets and water in pot, cover, and cook until tender (about 20 minutes). Remove beets from liquid. Combine cornstarch with ¼ cup cold water and add to liquid. Cook and stir until thickened. Add vinegar and beets and heat through. If desired, increase acidity with more vinegar. Serves 4.

BEETS IN SOUR CREAM

2 cups diced uncooked beets
½ cup chopped onion
⅛ teaspoon caraway seeds
1 cup water

½ cup **Sour Cream**
2 teaspoons white vinegar
½ teaspoon powdered
horseradish

Combine beets, onion, caraway seeds, and water in a saucepan, cover tightly, and simmer until beets are tender (about 15 mintes). Mix sour cream, vinegar, and horseradish thoroughly, add to beets, and serve hot. Serves 4.

ASPARAGUS

2 pounds fresh asparagus
2 teaspoons lemon juice
(½ teaspoon tarragon, or to
taste)

(½ teaspoon marjoram, or to
taste)

Snap off and discard asparagus butts, then rinse asparagus thoroughly. Line up spears and slice stems into ½-inch pieces, leaving top 3 or 4 inches of spear. Bring 1 quart water to boil, add lemon juice and stem pieces, return to boil, cover, and simmer 5 minutes. Add tips and continue simmering until stems and tips are tender (about 15 minutes). Serves 6.

ABOUT RICE

Confucius said: "With coarse rice to eat and my bended arm for a pillow I have joy." Even in Confucius's time, 2500 years ago, both white and brown rice were available. The "coarse rice" Confucius mentions is brown rice. It has its bran coat and germ still intact. White rice is the result of removing the bran and germ. It is milder than brown rice and slightly faster cooking, but it is nutritionally inferior, lacking the important vitamin thiamin. The widespread use of polished white rice in the early part of this century was responsible for much of the world's incidence of the deficiency condition called beriberi. Thus in recipes calling for rice, we recommend the use of brown rice, not white rice or instant rice products.

Recent grain hybridization has produced two varieties of rice—long grain and short grain. Short-grain rice cooks up a bit more tender and moist than long-grain rice and is thus preferred in some dishes. Long-grain rice is good for use in soups and stuffings, where the ability of the grain to hold together is an asset.

When a recipe in this book calls for cooked rice, it means boiled rice. To boil rice, allow 2½ cups stock (or water) for each cup of rice. Combine liquid and rice in a saucepan, bring to a boil, cover, and simmer slowly for 1 hour. Remove from heat, let stand 5 minutes, fluff with fork, and the rice is ready to serve.

For variety, try one of the following just before serving:

- Add 1 teaspoon prepared mustard for each cup cooked rice, and mix with fork.
- Add 1 tablespoon parsley flakes for each cup cooked rice, and mix with fork.

A fact to remember: 1 cup raw rice swells to about 3½ cups after being boiled. If rice is toasted first, expect less swelling.

A WHEY TO COOK RICE

2 cups slightly sour **Whey**   1 cup chopped mushrooms
1 cup brown rice   1 cup water

Bring all ingredients to a boil in a saucepan, cover, and simmer 1 hour. Serves 4.

RICE AND ONIONS WITH CURRY

2 cups cooked rice
6 medium onions, sliced very thin
1 teaspoon curry powder

1 cup evaporated skim milk
1 tablespoon garlic juice
Pinch of mace
Pinch of nutmeg

Add onions to 1 cup boiling water, boil gently 15 minutes, and drain. Combine remaining ingredients, except rice. Add to onions. Add rice, mix, heat through (do not boil), and serve. Serves 4.

RISOTTO CON FUNGHI E PISELLI
(Rice with mushrooms and peas)

1 cup long-grain brown rice
2 cups **Beef Stock** *or* Water
One 4-ounce can of sliced mushrooms
1 cup cooked peas

1 cup **Cream Cheese**
½ cup skim milk
1 fresh mushroom cap
2 tablespoons vermouth
Parsley sprigs

Bring rice and stock to a boil, cover, and simmer until tender (45 minutes to 1 hour). Toss rice with mushrooms and peas. Blend cheese and skim milk in blender until very smooth, and add all at once to rice mixture, stirring quickly to coat all rice. Heap rice mixture lightly into serving bowl. In a very small saucepan, simmer fresh mushroom cap and vermouth until vermouth has evaporated, and use the mushroom cap to top the rice. Decorate with parsley and serve. Serves 4.

SPANISH BROWN RICE

¾ cup brown rice
¾ cup chopped tomato
¼ cup chopped onion
¼ cup **Chili Salsa**
2 tablespoons chopped green
   pepper

¼ teaspoon cayenne pepper
⅛ teaspoon paprika
Pinch saffron

In a saucepan, combine all ingredients except rice. Add 2¼ cups water and bring to a boil. Add rice, return to a boil, cover, and simmer 1 hour. Serves 4.

ACAPULCO GOLDEN RICE

2 cups brown rice
2 cups **Chicken Stock** *or* water
1 cup tomato puree

2 medium onions, chopped
1 clove garlic, minced
1 tablespoon parsley flakes

Heat heavy skillet over medium flame, add dry uncooked rice, and toast lightly, stirring constantly. In a separate pan, bring stock and puree to a boil, and add to the skillet. Add remaining ingredients, cover, and reduce heat to very low. Cook about 40 minutes or until all liquid is absorbed. Serves 6.

APPLED RICE

1 cup brown rice
½ cup wild rice
2 medium apples

1 tablespoon lemon juice
⅛ teaspoon cardamom

Bring 1 quart of water to a boil in open pressure cooker. Add rice and cook under 15 pounds of pressure for 10 minutes. (For rocking-cap type cooker, cook for 10 minutes after pressure cap begins rocking.) Remove from heat and allow pressure to drop by itself. Peel, core, and finely chop apples into lemon juice, stirring to coat. Stir apples and cardamom into rice, cover, let sit 5 minutes, and serve. Serves 4.

RICE AND BEANS

3 cups cooked rice, still hot
2 cups cooked beans (pinto, red, or kidney)
2 cups **Tomato Sauce**

1 large onion, chopped
1 medium green pepper, chopped
1 cup frozen corn

Combine all ingredients except rice and heat until piping hot. Pour over bed of rice on individual serving plates. Serves 4.

GARBANZO-RICE MEDLEY

½ cup uncooked brown rice
One 15-ounce can of garbanzo beans
Three 15-ounce cans of tomatoes
1 medium green pepper, coarsely chopped
2 medium onions, sliced

1 small eggplant, coarsely chopped
2 stalks celery, coarsely chopped
2 medium carrots, diced
4 tablespoons Italian Seasoning

Combine all ingredients in pot, bring to boil, cover, and simmer until rice is tender (about 1 hour). Delicious hot or cold. Makes 6 cups.

ABOUT KASHA

Kasha is the name used in Russia for the delicious seed of the buckwheat plant. It is sold under the name buckwheat, buckwheat groats, groats (an Old English word meaning "little chunk"), or kasha. It may be used as a side dish in place of rice or as a delicious hot breakfast cereal with milk and fruit. To prepare kasha use:

1 part kasha
2 parts water
(Diced green pepper, minced onions, spices, etc.)

Pour kasha on a preheated heavy skillet, and toast it lightly over a medium flame, stirring frequently. Pour water (and pepper, onions, spices, etc., if desired) over toasted kasha and turn flame to low. Cover and let steam 30 minutes.

ABOUT BEANS

Beans develop in pods. While still young, the pods themselves can be eaten, and are delicious. The pods are what we find in the market under the names green beans or snap beans. Green beans have also been called string beans. However, since today's improved varieties are practically stringless, the name is somewhat of a misnomer.

As beans mature, the pods become fibrous and inedible, but within the pods the seeds increase in size and become kidney beans, white beans, navy beans, etc. These beans can be cooked and eaten fresh from the pod, or they can be dried first and cooked and eaten later. Mature beans fresh from the pod take longer to cook than green beans, but not so long as the mature beans after they have been dried.

TO COOK GREEN BEANS USE:
1½ pounds fresh green beans   (Spices: marjoram, oregano,
½ cup water   rosemary, dill)

Bring water to a boil, add green beans and spices, cover, and simmer 15 minutes or until tender. Add a little water, if necessary, to prevent water from evaporating completely. Serves 4.

TO COOK FRESH BEANS:

FOR FRESH LIMAS USE:
3 cups shelled limas   (Spices: curry powder, dill,
½ cup water   rosemary, sage)

Bring water to a boil, add limas and spices, cover, and simmer 20 minutes or until tender. Serves 4.

FOR OTHER FRESH BEANS USE:
3 cups shelled beans   (Spices: **Herb Bundle,** rosemary,
1 cup water   sage)

Bring water to a boil, add beans and spices, cover, and simmer 45 minutes to an hour or until tender. Serves 4.

TO COOK DRIED BEANS:

Wash 1 pound of dried beans in cold water and pick out and discard beans that float. Discard pebbles masquerading as beans. Prepare the beans first, by using any of the three precooking preparation techniques below. Add an **Herb Bundle** to the pot of prepared beans, cover, and simmer until beans are tender (½ to 2 hours, depending on variety of bean). Season to taste, using spices such as pepper, rosemary, thyme, and oregano. One pound (about 2½ cups) dried beans makes about 1½ quarts cooked beans.

PRECOOKING PREPARATION METHOD #1:
Combine beans with 2 quarts cold water in pot, and let soak overnight.

PRECOOKING PREPARATION METHOD #2:
Combine beans with 2 quarts cold water in pot, bring to a boil, boil 2 minutes, remove from heat, and let stand 1 hour.

PRECOOKING PREPARATION METHOD #3:

Add beans to 2 quarts rapidly boiling water so slowly as not to disturb the boil. Reduce heat to simmer. Beans are now prepared for cooking.

PIMIENTO GREEN BEANS

2 pounds fresh green beans, cut up (or two 10-ounce packages of frozen, cut green beans)

2 tablespoons chopped canned pimiento
⅛ teaspoon **Vegetable Powder**
⅛ teaspoon paprika

Cover green beans in small amount of boiling water and add pimiento, vegetable powder, and paprika. Cover, reduce heat, and simmer until tender (about 15 minutes). Serves 4.

GREEN BEAN CASSEROLE

1½ pounds fresh green beans
¼ teaspoon pepper
1 tablespoon **Chili Salsa** (or more, to taste)

1½ cups grated **Fresh Cheese**
2 cups **Versatility Sauce**

TOPPINGS:
(½ cup grated **Fresh Cheese**)
(¼ cup fresh bread crumbs)

(3 hard-cooked egg whites, shredded)

Simmer green beans, covered, in ½ cup water for 20 minutes. Drain. Combine green beans, pepper, chili salsa, and fresh cheese in shallow glass baking dish. Pour sauce over all, top with any or all of toppings, and bake at 350° until surface browns (about 20 minutes). Serves 6.

GREEN BEANS WITH NUTMEG

4 cups fresh, cut, green beans

¼ teaspoon nutmeg

Bring 1 cup water to a boil, add green beans already sprinkled with nutmeg, reduce heat, and simmer until beans are just tender (about 20 minutes). Drain and serve. Serves 4.

FRENCH-CUT GREEN BEANS

Two 10-ounce packages of frozen French-cut green beans

2 teaspoons **Vegetable Powder**

6 Jerusalem artichokes, sliced thin and cut into almond-size pieces

Bring 1 cup water to a boil and add vegetable powder and green beans, breaking apart frozen beans with a fork. Simmer until tender. Teflon-fry artichoke pieces over high heat until slightly dry and beginning to brown. Drain beans, stir in artichoke pieces, and serve. Serves 4 to 6.

GREEN PEAS WITH VEGETABLE FLAKES

While frozen peas cook up into a delicious dish all by themselves, the addition of vegetable flakes and marjoram does wonderful things to them.

One 10-ounce package of frozen peas

2 teaspoons vegetable flakes
¼ teaspoon marjoram

Bring 1 cup water to a boil, add vegetable flakes and marjoram, add frozen peas, and cook over medium heat until just barely tender (5 to 10 minutes). Serves 4 as a side dish.

FRESH BLACK-EYED PEAS

3 cups shelled, fresh,
    black-eyed peas
1 quart **Pork Stock** *or* water

¼ teaspoon cayenne pepper
¼ cup toasted onions

Combine all ingredients, bring to a boil, cover, and simmer until tender (at least 45 minutes). Serves 6.

BAKED BEANS

1 cup dried white beans
1 cup **Beef Stock**
½ medium onion, sliced
¼ cup **Bean-Thickened Gravy**

2 tablespoons **Tomato Sauce**
½ teaspoon mild dry mustard
Juice of 1 orange
2 teaspoons grated orange rind

Soak beans overnight in 2 cups water. Add stock, cover, and cook until beans are tender (about 1 hour). Add remaining ingredients, place in a covered baking dish, and bake at 300° for 6 hours. Stir, and bake uncovered until beans reach desired dryness (about ½ hour). Serves 4.

INSTANT BAKED BEANS

1¾ cups boiling water
1 cup Hallmark Pre-Cooked
    Beans
2 tablespoons **Tomato Sauce**
¼ cup **Bean-Thickened Gravy**

¼ teaspoon mild dry mustard
½ clove of garlic, minced
2 tablespoons finely chopped
    onion
¼ cup orange juice

Combine boiling water and beans in a baking dish. Stir in all other ingredients and bake covered at 450° for 30 minutes. Uncover, stir, and bake 15 minutes more, or to desired dryness. Serves 4.

BARREGO-STYLE BEANS

1 pound dried beans
(kidney beans are especially good)
One 28-ounce can of whole tomatoes

2 cups chopped celery
2 cups chopped onions
2 fresh red jalapeño chilies, diced, some seeds included

Wash and pick over beans. Place beans in large pot, cover generously with water, and simmer 1½ hours. Add remaining ingredients and simmer until beans are tender (1 to 2 hours). One note of caution: jalapeño chilies vary in hotness from mildly hot to painfully hot. After testing hotness by carefully tasting one or two of the seeds, you might wish to reduce the amount of chilies used. This recipe makes approximately 1½ quarts of delicious hot beans.

CHILI BEANS

1 pound dried red beans
2 medium onions, chopped
2 stalks celery, chopped
1 medium green pepper, chopped

1 teaspoon chili powder (more or less, to taste)
½ teaspoon pepper
½ cup **Chili Salsa** (more or less, to taste)

Wash and pick over beans. Bring 3 quarts of water to a boil in a 4- to 6-quart saucepan. Add beans a few at a time, so as not to disturb boiling action. Slowly add onions and celery to boiling water. Cook 30 minutes over medium heat. Add green pepper, spices, and chili salsa. Continue cooking until beans are tender (1 to 1½ hours). Makes 2 quarts. May be frozen for future use.

REFRIED BEANS

1½ cups dried pinto beans,   2 tablespoons onion flakes
   washed and picked over   1 teaspoon pepper
 1 teaspoon onion powder

Add beans slowly to 1½ quarts boiling water, making sure not to lose the boil. Reduce heat to medium, add spices, cover, and cook just below boiling until beans are tender (about 1½ hours). Drain, mash beans, and stir and cook over medium-to-low flame until beans begin to look dry. Use refried beans in making burritos, tostadas, and other Mexican dishes. Makes 1 quart.

LENTIL AND SPINACH LOAF

2 cups cooked lentils   ¾ medium onion, chopped
2 cups chopped, cooked   ½ cup bread crumbs
  spinach   ¾ teaspoon sage
1 cup **Yogurt**   2 egg whites, stiffly beaten
1 cup evaporated skim milk

Partially mash lentils and combine with all the other ingredients except the egg whites. Fold in egg whites. Spread flat in baking dish and bake at 350° for 45 minutes. Cut in squares and serve hot. Serves 6.

BLENDER REFRIED BEANS

1½ cups dried pinto beans,   V-8 juice
   washed and picked over   2 tablespoons **Hot Sauce**
2 cloves garlic   Pepper
1 whole medium onion,
  peeled

Add beans slowly to 1½ quarts boiling water, making sure not to lose the boil. Reduce heat to medium, add garlic and onion, cover, cook just below boiling until beans are tender (about 1½ hours), and drain. When beans are cooled enough to handle easily, put through the blender, a cup at a time, adding enough V-8 juice to blend. Let sit 24 hours. Add hot sauce and pepper to taste, reheat, and serve alone or on Mexican dishes such as tostadas or burritos. Makes 1 quart.

LENTIL LOAF WITH SPINACH TOPPING

2 cups cooked lentils	1 medium tomato, sliced
1 cup evaporated skim milk	2 cups chopped, cooked
¾ medium onion, chopped	spinach
½ cup bread crumbs	1 cup **Yogurt**
¾ teaspoon sage	2 hard-cooked egg whites
2 egg whites, beaten	Lettuce leaves

Partially mash lentils, and combine with milk, onion, bread crumbs, sage, and beaten egg whites. Spread flat in baking dish, and bake at 350° for 30 minutes. Lay tomato slices over top, and bake 15 minutes more. In blender, combine spinach and yogurt and blend until very smooth. Heat yogurt and spinach mixture through and place in a bowl lined with lettuce. Top with hard-cooked egg slices. Serve loaf and topping in separate serving dishes. Serves 6.

QUICKIE LENTIL BURGERS

1 cup dried lentils	1 medium onion, minced
¼ teaspoon basil	⅔ cup flour
1 bay leaf	

Combine lentils, basil, and bay leaf in a saucepan. Add 2 cups of water, cover, and boil very slowly 25 minutes. Add minced onion and flour, and let sit 15 minutes. Form into patties and Teflon-fry. Serve on a bun with lettuce, tomatoes, and **Hamburger Sauce** or serve as a plate patty with **Chili Salsa** or **Hot Sauce.** Makes 6 big burgers.

ABOUT SQUASH

Squash comes in two varieties: summer squash and winter squash. Zucchini is typical of summer squash and is probably the most popular of all the summer squashes. Other varieties of summer squash include: crookneck, straight neck, cocozelle, and cymling (often called simply "summer squash" in the market). They have soft, thin skins, and both the skins and the seeds are edible. Tough-skinned squashes should be avoided, or else pared and seeded before eating. Summer squashes are delicious cooked or raw. Any summer squash may be used in place of any other in most recipes.

Winter squashes are characterized by their hard rinds and seedy, pulpy center interior to the edible flesh. Typical of winter squash is the acorn squash, but the most famous winter squash of all is the pumpkin. Other varieties of winter squash are turban, butternut, Hubbard, and banana. Winter squashes may also be substituted for each other in recipes.

TEFLON-FRIED ZUCCHINI

So fast and so good, this dish is perfect for a fast lunch or a last-minute side dish at dinner.

4 medium zucchini, sliced   Pepper
2 tablespoons garlic juice

Put half (about 1 cup) of the zucchini into a frying pan with 1 tablespoon of the liquid garlic, 2 tablespoons of water, and a dash of pepper. Cover tightly, and cook 2 or 3 minutes over a hot flame, occasionally shaking the pan to stir. Repeat process for the other half of the zucchini. Serve immediately. Fantastic! Serves 4.

ZUCCHINI IN MEDITERRANEAN SAUCE

4 medium zucchini, sliced 1½ cups water
1½ cups **Richer
 Mediterranean Sauce**

Combine ingredients in saucepan, cover, and simmer until zucchini are tender, stirring occasionally. Serve in bowl alone, or over bread cubes. Serves 4.

JANET'S SPICY ZUCCHINI

This marvelous dish is quite spicy. Use it as a "relish" side dish to dress up other dishes. A little goes a long way.

1 large zucchini, diced   1 teaspoon oregano
1 medium onion, chopped   1 teaspoon basil
1 medium green pepper,   1 teaspoon chili powder
  chopped   1 teaspoon garlic powder
1 medium tomato, chopped

Mix ingredients in a pot with ¼ cup water and simmer, covered, 1 hour. Serves 6.

ZUCCHINI ITALIANO

4 small zucchini, sliced
½ cup chopped onion
1 clove garlic, crushed

1 cup **Tomato Sauce**
¼ teaspoon oregano

Combine zucchini, onion, and garlic in saucepan. Add 1½ cups water and cook over medium heat until zucchini is tender (about 15 minutes). Add tomato sauce and oregano, heat through, and serve. Serves 4.

CONTINENTAL ZUCCHINI

4 small zucchini, diced
One 10-ounce package of frozen corn
One 2-ounce jar of chopped pimientos

2 cloves garlic, sliced
¼ teaspoon pepper
½ cup **Cottage Cheese**

Combine all ingredients except cottage cheese in Teflon skillet. Add 3 tablespoons water, and cook over medium flame, stirring occasionally until zucchini is just tender (5 to 10 minutes). Stir in cottage cheese, heat through, and serve. Serves 4.

CHILI BAKED SQUASH

3 medium zucchini (or yellow) squash
1 cup **Corn Pudding**

⅓ cup finely chopped chives *or* green onion tops
½ cup dry bread crumbs
1 teaspoon chili powder

Slice squash in half lengthwise and simmer 10 minutes in water to cover. Gently scrape out seeds. Arrange squash in single layer in shallow pan, cut side up, with enough of the cooking water to barely cover bottom of pan. Stuff hollows with corn pudding, and top with chives. Combine bread crumbs and chili powder with ¼ cup water, and sprinkle mixture over all cut squash surfaces, as well as over corn filling. (By doubling bread mixture, the bread may be substituted for the corn pudding.) Bake at 350° for 20 minutes. Serves 6.

ARMENIAN STUFFED ZUCCHINI

4 large plump zucchini,   ½ cup tomato juice
  8 to 10 inches long   ½ cup chopped fresh parsley
¼ pound leanest ground beef ¼ teaspoon pepper
1 cup cooked brown rice   8 fresh mint leaves, finely
  (cook in **Beef Stock**)   chopped
½ cup finely chopped onion

Cut top off zucchini (about 1½ inches). With potato peeler and small, sharp knife, hollow out inside of zucchini, leaving a thin shell (about ¼ inch). Carve top into a stopper to fit shell. Teflon-fry and drain beef. Combine with other ingredients, stuff into zucchini, and insert plugs. Place stuffed zucchini in shallow pan. Add enough water or stock to cover bottom of pan. Bake at 375° until tender (about 45 minutes). Serves 4.

STEAMED BUTTERNUT SQUASH

2 butternut squashes   (¼ teaspoon allspice)
(½ teaspoon cinnamon)   (¼ teaspoon ginger)
(¼ teaspoon nutmeg)

In a large pot, steam whole squashes on steaming rack for ½ hour. Cut in half, scrape out seeds, and mash pulp. The squash may be enjoyed plain, or it may be spiced. Use only the cinnamon and nutmeg for a lightly spiced taste, or all the spices for a heavier spice taste reminiscent of pumpkin pie spice. Serves 4.

MASHED SQUASH

4 cups cubed fresh banana   1 cup orange juice
  squash (½-inch cubes)

Place squash and orange juice in saucepan, cover, and cook over medium heat until tender. Mash and serve. Serves 4.

SQUASH EMPANADA

1 butternut squash (about   ¼ teaspoon ground cinnamon
  medium in size: enough to   Dash of nutmeg
  make approximately 1 cup   4 pita breads
  when cooked)   2 egg whites
2 tablespoons orange juice
1 teaspoon grated orange
  rind

Steam squash, remove seeds, and mash flesh. Add orange juice, grated orange rind, and spices. Slitting around their perimeters, separate the 4 pita breads into 8 pita rounds. Place a spoonful of squash mixture on each round, brush edges with egg white, and fold round turnover style, pressing moistened edges together but being careful not to tear round. Teflon-fry to heat through and seal edges. Makes 8 delicious empanadas, which are excellent for accompaniments, snacks, or unusual desserts.

BAKED ACORN SQUASH

2 acorn squashes   Cinnamon
(2 cups unsweetened
  applesauce *or* drained
  crushed pineapple)

Bake squash whole at 350° for 1 hour. Slice in half, remove seeds, and fill the four squash halves with applesauce, pineapple or **Acorn Squash Stuffing** (below). Put filled squash back in oven and bake until squash is tender (about ½ hour more). Sprinkle with cinnamon. Serves 4 generously.

ACORN SQUASH STUFFING

This recipe uses mashed banana squash as a stuffing for acorn squash.

2 cups **Mashed Squash**   8 drops Angostura Bitters
  (p. 166)   1 cup crushed pineapple
¼ cup orange juice   Nutmeg

Combine mashed squash with orange juice and bitters. Stuff cavity of acorn squash with this mixture. Top with crushed pineapple, then sprinkle with nutmeg. Makes stuffing enough for 2 acorn squashes cut in half.

SQUASH GOURMET

2 pounds Hubbard squash   ½ cup finely chopped onion
1 cup **Lemon Mock Sour**   ¼ teaspoon pepper
  Cream

Quarter squash; remove and discard seeds, rind, and fiber; cut flesh into cubes. Fill the bottom of a large saucepan with an inch of water. Heat to boiling, add squash, cover, and boil gently until tender (15 or 20 minutes). Drain, mash, add remaining ingredients, and stir. Turn into a 1-quart casserole dish, and bake uncovered 25 minutes. Serves 4.

ABOUT POTATOES, SWEET POTATOES, AND YAMS

Potatoes, sweet potatoes, and yams are not closely related biologically. The three come from entirely different families in the plant kingdom. Even though the sweet potato gets its name because it resembles a potato somewhat, the two are quite different in taste, and no one will confuse the two in the kitchen or substitute one for the other in a recipe. The yam, however, is so similar to the sweet potato in taste and texture that the two are often confused. They can, in fact, be used interchangeably in most recipes, including the recipes in this book.

As far as ordinary potatoes are concerned, a potato is a potato. Whether it is called an Irish potato, a russet, or an Idaho potato is not critical. The important distinction among potatoes is their size, and whether they are young or mature. When young, the potato is small, round, and thin-skinned. Mature potatoes are larger, more irregular, and thicker-skinned. Be sure to use young (or new) potatoes in recipes calling for them. In other recipes, simply use mature potatoes of the size called for.

MASHED POTATOES

6 large potatoes, cleaned and peeled
2 cloves garlic, cut in half

Skim milk
2 tablespoons parsley flakes
½ teaspoon pepper

Drop potatoes and garlic into 1½ quarts boiling water, and boil until potatoes are soft enough to mash (30 or 40 minutes). Drain potatoes, remove and discard garlic, and mash potatoes with potato masher, adding skim milk as necessary. Add parsley flakes and pepper, mix, and serve. Serve with a sauce or gravy if desired. Serves 6.

COMPANY POTATOES

4 large potatoes	2 cups **Sour Cream**
½ cup parsley flakes	2 egg whites
¾ cup chopped onions	¼ teaspoon caraway seed
4 cloves garlic, finely chopped	¼ teaspoon dill seed
	1 teaspoon pepper

Peel, slice, and boil the potatoes with half of the parsley flakes. Drain, combine with all remaining ingredients, and mix with electric mixer to the consistency of thick mashed potatoes. Spread mixture over bottom of shallow casserole dish, sprinkle bread or cracker crumbs over top if desired, and bake ½ hour at 375°. Serves 6.

MASHED POTATO CAKES

1 cup cooked, sliced potatoes	¼ cup flour
2 tablespoons evaporated skim milk	1 tablespoon finely chopped fresh onion
¾ teaspoon onion powder	1 tablespoon finely chopped fresh parsley
1 egg white	

Mash potatoes. Add remaining ingredients and mix well. Spread (in pancake shapes) onto preheated Teflon frying pan and cook over low-to-medium heat. Do not attempt to turn until spatula can lift cake without sticking. Turn, flatten, and fry second side. Serve topped with **Sour Cream.** Makes 4 cakes.

STUFFED POTATOES

4 large potatoes, suitable for baking
1 cup **Sour Cream**
½ cup **Buttermilk**
½ teaspoon onion powder
¼ teaspoon pepper

¼ teaspoon dill weed
2 tablespoons finely chopped chives
2 tablespoons toasted onions *or* **Browned Onions**
Paprika

Bake potatoes at 450° until tender (about 1 hour; longer if foil-wrapped). Making an end-to-end slice, slice away one third of the potato. Scrape the pulp out of both parts of the potato, saving the larger shell for restuffing. Combine pulp with sour cream and buttermilk, beat until smooth with mixer, add remaining ingredients except paprika, and mix well. Use a decorator tip, and pipe mixture through a pastry sleeve back into potato shells, making attractive design on top. Or spoon mixture back and swirl a design on top. Sprinkle with paprika. Bake 30 minutes at 400°. Serves 4.

SCALLOPED POTATOES

6 large potatoes, pared and very thinly sliced
¼ cup flour
¼ cup very finely chopped onion

1 tablespoon parsley flakes
¼ teaspoon pepper
2 cups skim milk
Paprika

Combine potatoes and flour in plastic bag and shake to coat potatoes. Layer potatoes into baking dish in three layers, with a layer of onions between the layers of potatoes. Add parsley flakes and pepper, pour on milk, and sprinkle paprika over top. Bake 1½ hours at 350°. Serves 4.

YOGURT SCALLOPED POTATOES

6 new potatoes, washed (not peeled) and sliced
3 cups **Yogurt**
1½ cups **Cottage Cheese**
½ pound leanest ground beef
½ cup **Beef Stock**
¾ cup chopped fresh parsley
¾ cup sliced green onions

Cover potatoes with boiling water, boil gently until just tender, and drain. Blend yogurt and cottage cheese in blender until very smooth. Brown beef and drain fat. Add stock, parsley, and green onions, and cook until onions soften a little. Add yogurt and cheese blend to make a sauce. Arrange potato slices in shallow casserole dish, pour sauce over top, and bake 30 minutes at 350°. Place under broiler close to flame for 2 minutes before serving. Serves 4.

SCALLOPED POTATOES WITH VEGETABLES

6 tablespoons skim milk
4 medium potatoes, cooked, cooled, and peeled
½ cup cooked peas
½ cup cooked cauliflower pieces
½ cup cooked chopped celery
¼ cup cooked diced carrots
½ cup **White Sauce**
¼ teaspoon turmeric
1 tablespoon parsley flakes
Matzo meal
Paprika

Pour half of the skim milk into bottom of rectangular baking dish. Slice 2 potatoes and layer into dish. Mix peas, cauliflower, celery, carrots, white sauce, and spices, and place this mixture as a layer over the potatoes. Slice remaining two potatoes as a top layer, pour rest of milk over top, sprinkle with matzo meal and paprika, and bake at 400° until top is browned and casserole is hot. Serves 6.

TOMATOED POTATOES

6 medium potatoes, peeled and sliced
One 16-ounce can of tomatoes
1 cup tomato juice
¼ teaspoon basil
¼ teaspoon pepper
Parsley

Place potatoes in 1½-quart casserole dish. Combine remaining ingredients, except parsley, with 2 cups of water. Bring to a boil and stir into potatoes. Cover, and bake 1 hour at 375°. Garnish with snipped parsley. Serves 6.

MUSHROOM AND POTATO GARDEN

4 large potatoes, suitable for baking
1½ cups **Sour Cream**
½ pound fresh mushrooms, sliced
1 tablespoon garlic juice
1 teaspoon onion juice
1½ cups alfalfa sprouts
3 medium tomatoes, cut into wedges
½ green pepper, sliced

Wash potatoes and bake until done at 350° (about 1 hour). Sauté mushrooms in garlic juice, onion juice, and 2 tablespoons water, until liquid is gone. Place each potato in center of individual serving plate, slit open, fill with sour cream, and top with mushrooms. Surround each potato with heaps of sprouts. Symmetrically arrange tomato wedges and pepper slices around the potato, on top of the sprouts. Beautiful and delicious! Serves 4.

STOVE POTATOES

5 medium potatoes, peeled
and diced
1 large onion, diced

1 tablespoon parsley flakes
½ teaspoon pepper

Combine all ingredients in saucepan, add enough water to cover, and cook over medium flame until tender (about 20 minutes). Drain and serve. So good and so easy to fix! Serves 4.

GLAZED YAMS

3 large yams, pared and
sliced
2 cups orange juice

⅛ teaspoon Angostura Bitters
4 tablespoons raisins
2 tablespoons cornstarch

Combine all ingredients except cornstarch in a saucepan. Add 3 cups of water and cook over medium heat until yams are tender (about 30 minutes). In a separate pan mix cornstarch with ¼ cup cold water; add to this mixture the cooking liquid from the yams, and cook until thickened. Pour thickened liquid over yams, stir to coat, and serve. Serves 4.

MASHED YAMS

4 large yams, peeled and
sliced
1 tablespoon lemon juice
2 tablespoons skim milk

¼ teaspoon fresh ground
nutmeg
1 banana, sliced

Cover yams with boiling water, add lemon juice, and boil until yams are tender (about 30 minutes). Drain, add milk, and mash. Top with nutmeg and banana slices, and serve. Serves 4.

STUFFED YAMS

2 medium-to-large yams,
washed well

½ cup **Lemon Mock Sour
Cream**

⅛ teaspoon fenugreek *or*
curry powder

½ cup finely grated **Fresh
Cheese**

Bake yams in foil at 450° until fork tender (about 1 hour). Remove yams and cool enough to handle. Cut yams in half lengthwise, scrape out most of tender flesh, being careful to keep shell intact, and put flesh into blender. Add sour cream and spice, and blend until smooth. Spoon creamy mixture back into yam shells and top with cheese. Bake on cookie sheet for 20 minutes at 350°. Serves 4.

EGGPLANT

Eggplant is a strange and wonderful food. It adds a flavor and texture reminiscent of meat, yet has none of the fat and cholesterol drawbacks associated with meat. It can be stuffed, sliced, chopped, boiled, baked, fried, or casseroled, and may be eaten with or without the skin. To prevent the fleshy part from discoloring when cut, rub with lemon juice and cook in glass or stainless steel.

EGGPLANT AND CHICK-PEAS

1 medium eggplant, peeled
and cubed

4 medium onions, chopped

2 cups cooked chick-peas
(also called garbanzo beans)

One 28-ounce can of tomatoes

1 teaspoon mint flakes

½ teaspoon pepper

Simmer eggplant and onions 30 minutes in 1 cup water. Add remaining ingredients and simmer 30 minutes more. Serve cold. Serves 4.

STEWED EGGPLANT

1 medium eggplant, pared and cut in ½-inch cubes
1 medium onion, chopped
1 clove garlic, finely diced
½ cup vinegar water (half vinegar and half water)

One 28-ounce can of whole tomatoes
1 tablespoon parsley flakes
1 teaspoon basil
½ teaspoon mild paprika

Add onions and garlic to boiling vinegar water, return to boil, then reduce heat and simmer until onions are tender. Add two cups of water and remaining ingredients, cover, and cook over moderate heat 15 minutes. At this point a delicious stew is ready to serve. To serve as a casserole, place in casserole dish, cover with bread cubes, and bake ½ hour at 350°. Serves 4.

MOM'S SPICY EGGPLANT

1 medium eggplant sliced, unpeeled, into ¼-inch slices
One 15-ounce can of green beans, drained
1 large onion, sliced thin
2 tablespoons diced canned California green chilies
One 15-ounce can of whole tomatoes, cut up
(2 ounces raw hamburger, broken into small pieces)
¼ teaspoon thyme

Combine ingredients in a medium baking dish, cover securely, and bake 1 hour at 350°. Serves 4.

ABOUT CORN

A friend has advised us that the proper way to boil corn is to bring the pot to a boil before picking the live ear from the stalk. It is true that the most delicious results occur when the delay between picking and cooking is minimized. We all know how delicious fresh corn on the cob can be—incomparably more flavorsome than frozen corn on the cob or canned corn. Try using fresh corn kernels cut from the cob instead of canned corn in recipes calling for canned corn. Use specially designed corn-scraping tools for this purpose, or slice the kernels off with a knife. In using the knife, don't cut too deeply. After slicing, use the back of the knife to scrape the tasty juices and the heart of the kernels into the pot with the kernels.

CORN PUDDING

2 cups corn (fresh sliced from cob, or frozen corn, defrosted)
1 medium zucchini squash, finely chopped
1 medium green pepper, finely chopped

Combine squash and pepper in blender. Add corn and blend until smooth (about like applesauce). To accomplish blending, every blender trick will be needed: removing blender container and shaking from time to time, alternating short bursts with steady blending, scraping sides with rubber spatula, etc. Scrape blended mixture into saucepan, bring to a boil, and simmer uncovered until thick, stirring occasionally. Serve hot, as a side dish or as a main dish. Goes great with **Yeast Corn Muffins, Corn Pancakes,** or **Polenta.** Is used in the making of **Chili Baked Squash.** Makes about 2 cups.

CREOLE CORN

One 10-ounce package of frozen corn

1 cup **Tomato Sauce**
One 2-ounce jar of pimientos

¼ cup chopped green pepper   ¼ teaspoon pepper
¼ cup chopped onion

Sauté green pepper and onion in ¼ cup water. Add remaining ingredients, cover, and simmer until corn is tender. Serves 4.

SKILLET CORN AND PEPPERS

2 canned California green chilies, chopped

2 cups fresh corn kernels (slice kernels from about 4 ears)

2 green peppers, chopped

2 medium onions, chopped

4 medium tomatoes, cut in large cubes

(1 fresh tomatillo, chopped)

½ teaspoon whole cumin seeds

⅛ teaspoon cayenne pepper

Combine all ingredients in large Teflon frying pan, add ¼ cup water, and fry, stirring frequently, until vegetables are tender (about 30 minutes). Serve in bowls over cooked brown rice. Mix leftovers with rice and reheat in casserole dish. Serves 6.

CORN AND PEPPER NOODLE BAKE

2 cups leftover **Skillet Corn and Peppers** (above)
4 cups **noodles,** cooked and drained
1 cup **Yogurt**
Pepper

Combine all ingredients in a casserole dish, season with pepper, cover, and bake 30 minutes at 375°. Serves 4.

CHILI STEAMED CORN

There is no better way to prepare fresh corn on the cob than to steam the ears of corn while still in the husk. Served in the husk, this dish is uniquely attractive.

Fresh ears of corn, unshucked   Onion powder
Chili powder

Carefully pull down (but not off) the husks of the corn, exposing the kernels. Remove corn silk. Sprinkle the kernels with chili powder and onion powder, replace the husks, and tie with a string. Place corn on a vegetable steaming rack in a large pot. Add water to the level of the bottom of the rack, cover pot, and steam 15 minutes. Serve corn in husks, snipping string and shucking corn at the table. (Because the corn is not washed, it is wise to use corn that has not been sprayed with pesticides: homegrown or organically grown.)

STUFFING A VEGETABLE

Probably every known vegetable has been prepared stuffed and cooked by someone at some time or place. Stuffed tomatoes, stuffed peppers, and stuffed zucchini are popular, as are stuffed grape leaves and stuffed cabbage leaves. Below are a few tips for stuffing tomatoes, peppers, and zucchini, and a stuffing that will work for nearly any vegetable:

Tomato: Cut plug in top of tomato and scoop out pulp and seeds. Stuff, then replace plug. Place tomatoes on a rack in a baking pan containing a small amount of water. Bake 10 to 15 minutes at 350°.
Green peppers: Cut top off pepper, keeping lid. Scoop out pulp and seeds. Stuff, replace lid, and place on a rack in a baking pan with water. Bake until fork tender (about 45 minutes) at 350°.
Zucchini: Slicing lengthwise, cut off about one fifth of the zucchini. The small slice will be the lid. The rest of the zucchini will

be stuffed. Use a paring knife to slice a perimeter around the area to be stuffed, then scoop out the inside of the perimeter with a spoon. Stuff, replace lid, and place on a rack-and-pan arrangement like that for the tomatoes and peppers. Bake until tender (about 25 minutes) at 350°.

STUFFING FOR ANY VEGETABLE

¼ pound leanest ground beef
1 cup cooked rice
½ cup cooked corn
½ cup **Beef Stock**
¼ cup chopped pimiento

1 canned California green chili, chopped
2 cloves garlic, minced
1 teaspoon chili powder
Dash of cayenne pepper

Lightly brown ground beef. Combine all ingredients and use for stuffing. Makes 2½ cups.

STUFFED TOMATOES

4 large firm tomatoes
1½ cups cooked small elbow macaroni
1 cup **White Sauce**

½ cup grated **Fresh Cheese**
¼ cup fresh bread crumbs
⅛ teaspoon oregano
⅛ teaspoon marjoram

Slice top off tomatoes and scoop out pulp and juice. Discard juice. Drain pulp of juice, chop pulp, and mix together with remaining ingredients. Fill tomatoes with mixture. Place filled tomatoes on a trivet in a saucepan containing ¼ cup water. Cover and cook over low heat until filling is hot and tomatoes are tender (about 20 minutes). Serves 4.

ITALIAN STUFFED PEPPERS

4 large green peppers, seeds and pith removed, tops saved

SAUCE:

One 15-ounce can of
    tomatoes
1 stalk celery, chopped

1 teaspoon parsley flakes
½ teaspoon garlic flakes
½ teaspoon onion flakes

STUFFING:

2 cups cooked garbanzo
    beans with cooking liquid
2 cups cooked brown rice
½ medium onion, chopped
1 stalk celery, chopped
2 egg whites
1 tablespoon parsley flakes

1 teaspoon vegetable flakes
1 teaspoon garlic flakes
½ teaspoon pepper
¼ teaspoon oregano
⅛ teaspoon thyme
⅛ teaspoon cumin

To make sauce, blend tomatoes in blender 15 seconds, add remaining sauce ingredients, and mix. To make stuffing mixture, blend garbanzos in blender until very smooth, add remaining stuffing ingredients and ½ cup of the sauce, and mix. Stuff peppers with this stuffing mixture and replace lids. Place peppers in deep baking dish, cover with remaining sauce, and bake 40 minutes at 350°. Serves 4.

VEGETARIAN STUFFED PEPPERS

4 large green peppers
1 cup long-grain brown
    rice (uncooked)
1 cup thin mushroom slices
One 8-ounce can of
    tomatoes

¼ teaspoon **Vegetable**
    Powder
⅛ teaspoon pepper
Tiny pinch of ground saffron
    (or 5 or 6 crumbled whole
    saffron strands)

Bring 2½ cups water to a boil, add rice, return to boil, reduce heat, and simmer very slowly 45 minutes. Cut tops off peppers to make lids, remove seeds from peppers, and boil peppers and lids 5 minutes. Drain. In separate pan combine mushrooms, tomatoes, and spices. Adding a little water if necessary, bring to a boil, cover, and simmer until mushrooms are tender (about 10 minutes). Stir in rice and simmer 5 minutes more. Stuff peppers with this mixture, replace lids, and bake 25 minutes at 350°. Serves 4.

NADA'S VEGETARIAN CABBAGE ROLLS

1 large head cabbage

STUFFING:
2 cups cooked and drained red, kidney, or garbanzo beans
1 cup chopped onion
1 cup diced celery
½ cup partially cooked brown rice (to partially cook, boil vigorously 10 minutes in 1½ cups water; drain)
One 16-ounce can of whole tomatoes, drained and chopped finely
1 cup **Tomato Sauce**
1 egg white
1 tablespoon parsley flakes
½ teaspoon garlic flakes
¼ teaspoon oregano flakes
⅛ teaspoon pepper

SAUCE:
One 28-ounce can of tomatoes packed in puree (blended 5 seconds in blender)
1 stalk celery, diced
1 tablespoon parsley flakes
⅛ teaspoon garlic flakes

Place whole cabbage in a large pot, add 1 cup water, cover tightly, and steam until cabbage leaves can be separated (about 20 minutes). Mix all stuffing ingredients together. On each cabbage leaf, place a small amount of stuffing (about 3 tablespoons), tuck in ends, roll up, and place in shallow baking dish. Largest leaves may be cut in half to keep rolls more or less uniform in size. Combine sauce ingredients. Chop unused center of cabbage, and add ½ cup of this chopped cabbage to sauce. Pour sauce over cabbage rolls, cover, and bake 25 minutes at 350°. Remove cover and bake 20 minutes more. Makes about 16 rolls. Serves 8.

VEGETABLE POT PIES

2 medium zucchini, diced
1 small onion, diced
½ cup cooked diced carrots
½ cup cooked diced celery
One 10-ounce package of
    frozen peas
One 2-ounce jar of chopped
    pimientos

½ cup **White Sauce**
1 teaspoon curry powder
¼ teaspoon turmeric
4 pita breads
2 egg whites

Place zucchini and onions in frying pan that has a tightly fitting lid. Add 2 tablespoons water, hold lid on tightly, and cook over high flame 2 or 3 minutes, until the zucchini and onions are nearly cooked. Add carrots, celery, frozen peas, pimientos, and white sauce, and mix well. Blend in spices. Cut around the outside of each pita bread to separate each bread into two rounds. Put one round, rough side up, into an individual-size aluminum pie pan. Fill with a portion of vegetable mixture. Place the other round, rough side down, as a top for the pot pie. Moisten the edges of the two rounds, where they touch, with a generous amount of egg whites, so that the rounds will close during baking to seal the pie. Bake 15 minutes in preheated oven at 400°. Serves 4.

FARMER'S ONION-CHEESE PIE

1 cup **Cottage Cheese**
1 cup skim milk
½ cup diced onions
⅜ cup parsley flakes
4 egg whites
1 teaspoon prepared hot mustard

⅛ teaspoon garlic powder
2 tablespoons chopped pimiento
1½ teaspoons onion flakes

Put all ingredients except pimiento and onion flakes into blender and blend at high speed until mixture becomes creamy. Pour into an 8-inch Teflon pie pan, and bake 30 minutes at 325°. Garnish with pimiento and onion flakes, and continue baking until crust is nicely browned (about another 30 minutes). Serves 4.

SPINACH AND ONIONS

½ cup chopped onions
1 tablespoon garlic juice
One 10-ounce package of frozen chopped spinach
¾ cup **Chicken Stock**

⅛ teaspoon nutmeg
⅛ teaspoon thyme
⅛ teaspoon cayenne pepper
1 tablespoon arrowroot

Sauté the onions in garlic juice and 2 tablespoons water. Add frozen spinach and all but a few tablespoons of the chicken stock. Bring to a boil, separating spinach pieces, and cook 5 minutes. Add spices and stir in a paste made by mixing the arrowroot in the remaining cold chicken stock. Reduce heat to medium, and cook and stir until thickened. Serves 4.

CARROTS WITH PINEAPPLE

Neither carrots nor pineapple ever tasted so good. This sweet and delicious recipe comes from a Hindu ashram in Boston. Use it as a side dish when serving pastas, bean dishes, or meat dishes.

    4 medium carrots, peeled and diagonally sliced (¼-inch slices)
    One 28-ounce can of juice-packed crushed pineapple (room temperature)
    ⅛ teaspoon ginger

Place carrots in saucepan and add juice from canned pineapple. (Add additional pineapple juice or water, if necessary, to cover carrots.) Cover, boil gently until carrots are tender (about 20 minutes), and drain. Stir in crushed pineapple and ginger. Serves 4.

MIXED GREENS

    ½ pound spinach, washed and chopped
    ½ pound swiss chard, washed and chopped
    3 sprigs parsley, chopped
    2 large green onion bottoms, chopped
    ¼ teaspoon Italian Seasoning

Combine still wet vegetables and seasoning in pot. Adding no water, cover tightly, and cook 5 to 10 minutes over low heat. Serve hot. Serves 4.

SUMMER GARDEN PLATE

4 ears fresh corn, shucked and cleaned	2 medium crookneck squash, sliced
4 small summer squash (cymling), sliced	⅓ medium red onion, sliced thin
2 medium zucchini, sliced	½ cup **Sour Cream**

Bring 2 quarts of water to a boil, drop in ears of corn, and boil until tender (about 10 minutes). Steam squash in a covered frying pan, using 2 or 3 tablespoons water and a hot flame. The squash will require only 2 or 3 minutes of steaming. It should not be over-cooked so as to brown, nor oversteamed so as to become soggy. Avoid crowding the squash in the frying pan. Cook about a cup of the squash slices at a time, keeping the already-cooked squash warm while subsequent batches are being cooked. Serve squash and corn piping hot on individual serving plates. Garnish each plate with the onion slices. Use the sour cream in place of butter on the corn. (Delicious!) A sourdough bread and a cool beverage go well with this dish. Serves 4.

CABBAGE AND PEPPERS

1 medium head cabbage, cut in large chunks	2 cups **Beef Stock**
4 canned California green chilies, chopped	½ teaspoon celery seed
2 medium potatoes, peeled and sliced thin	¼ teaspoon freshly ground pepper
2 medium onions, sliced	¼ teaspoon dill seed
	2 tablespoons lemon juice

Combine all ingredients in saucepan except for lemon juice. Cook over medium heat until cabbage and potatoes are tender (about 30 minutes). Toss with lemon juice and serve. Serves 6.

COMBINATION CASSEROLES AND PASTAS

Combination casseroles are oven main dishes that join meat with other ingredients such as vegetables, cheese, or noodles to produce a special magic. Easy to make, delicious, and convenient to store and reuse, combination casseroles occupy a traditionally important place in the diet of nearly everyone. They play the same sort of role in the menu that is played by the all-time favorite pasta dishes: spaghetti, lasagna, manicotti, noodles, etc. Both combination casseroles and pasta dishes are contained in this section.

ABOUT PASTAS

Any food made from a flour paste or a flour dough may rightfully be called a pasta. The Italians take credit for the widespread promulgation of these wonderful foodstuffs; in fact the word *pasta* in Italian means paste or dough. Over 500 kinds of pastas are in use, from the familiar spaghettis, macaronis, and noodles to the not-so-familiar fusilli, gnocchi, and grandini. Pasta naming has followed no convention or format, and for this reason confusion in names abounds. A single product is often called different names by different commercial manufacturers. Technically, any dried pasta, regardless of shape, is called a macaroni. But whoever heard anyone call spaghetti or alphabet noodles macaroni?

The trick to cooking dried pasta is to use plenty of water. Use a gallon or a gallon and a half of water for each pound of pasta. Bring the water to a rolling boil, and without disturbing the boil, gradually add the pasta. (A long pasta, such as spaghetti, may not fit into the pot all at once. For a long pasta one has two choices. One may either break it up and add it to the boiling water in smaller pieces, or one may add it as is, allowing the long sticks to hang out of the pot. In the latter case, as the submerged ends soften, gradually feed the rest into the boiling water until all the pasta is completely submerged.) Boil the pasta vigorously until done, stirring once or twice in the beginning if necessary to prevent the pasta from clumping. Leave pot uncovered to prevent foaming over. Test doneness by biting a piece of the pasta in two and examining it in cross section. If the pasta feels tender, and the cross section is uniform in coloration, the pasta is done. If a whitish center is observed in the cross section, more cooking is needed. Cooking time will vary from 2 minutes for tiny pastas like grandini, to 15 minutes for larger pastas like manicotti. Do not overcook. In fact, a slightly undercooked pasta is preferred by many because it offers a nice amount of resistance to chewing. Slightly undercooked pasta is referred to as pasta cooked *al dente*. Why? Because *al dente* is Italian for "to the tooth," and thus pasta cooked *al dente* is pasta cooked just till it's firm to the tooth.

After cooking, drain the pasta well and use immediately. Pastas that have been cooked or partially cooked prior to stuffing and further baking need to be stuffed immediately and put in the oven. Pastas that will be sauced and served need to be covered with sauce immediately and served. Any spaghetti sauce will work not only as a topping for spaghetti but as a topping for other pastas as well. Several spaghetti sauce recipes are given in the next chapter.

LASAGNA

One 8-ounce package of lasagna noodles	½ teaspoon pepper
3 cups **Cottage Cheese**	(½ teaspoon thyme)
3 egg whites	(½ teaspoon basil)
2 teaspoons parsley flakes	(½ teaspoon garlic powder)
	1 quart **Spaghetti Sauce**

Cook lasagna noodles to *al dente* stage. Drain and place in cool water while casserole is being made. Combine cottage cheese, egg whites, and spices. Place a thin layer of spaghetti sauce on the bottom of a rectangular baking dish. Then layer in a portion of the noodles, followed by a layer of the cottage cheese mixture, followed by a layer of spaghetti sauce. Repeat this sequence several times, using up all of the ingredients, and ending with a topping of spaghetti sauce. Bake at 375° until slightly browned on top (about 45 minutes). Serves 6.

FRESH CHEESE SPAGHETTI

½ pound spaghetti *or* 2 cups mostaccioli

3 cups **Spaghetti Sauce**

½ cup **Fresh Cheese**, in ¼-inch cubes or chunks

Flour

Cook pasta. Heat sauce to boiling and remove from heat. Dredge cheese cubes in flour, and stir into sauce. Cover for 1 minute, and serve on hot spaghetti or mostaccioli. Serves 4.

MEATBALLS AND SPAGHETTI

25 **Italian Meatballs** (about 1 recipe)

1 quart **Spaghetti Sauce**

1 pound spaghetti

Cook browned meatballs in spaghetti sauce. Serve over hot cooked spaghetti. Serves 6.

MANICOTTI

12 manicotti noodles (usually the contents of a single package)

2 cups **Cottage Cheese**

1 cup grated **Fresh Cheese**

3 egg whites

2 teaspoons parsley flakes

½ teaspoon pepper

(½ teaspoon thyme)

(½ teaspoon basil)

(½ teaspoon garlic powder)

1 quart **Spaghetti Sauce**

Cook manicotti noodles to *al dente* stage. Drain and place in cool water while casserole is being made. Combine cottage cheese, fresh cheese, egg whites, and spices, adding a little water if necessary to optimize the mixture for stuffing. Spread a cup of the spaghetti sauce over the bottom of a baking dish. One by one, drain each noodle, stuff it with the cottage cheese mixture, using a long-handled spoon, and lay it in the baking dish. Pour remaining sauce over top and bake at 375° until slightly browned on top (about 30 minutes). Serves 6.

VENICE COMBINATION PIZZA
(Recipe for two pizzas)

DOUGH:

1. Soften ½ package (1 teaspoon) active dry yeast in 2 tablespoons warm water (110°–115°). Let stand 5–10 minutes.

2. Meanwhile, pour 1 cup warm water into large bowl. Blend in 2 cups sifted flour. Stir softened yeast. Add to flour-water mixture and mix well.

3. Measure 2 cups sifted flour. Add about half of the flour to the yeast mixture and beat until very smooth. Mix in enough remaining flour to make a soft dough. Turn mixture onto a lightly floured surface. Allow to rest 5–10 minutes. Knead.

4. Lightly grease a deep bowl that is large enough to allow dough to double. Shape dough into smooth ball and place in bowl. Turn dough to bring greased surface to top. Cover with waxed paper (or plastic wrap) and towel and place in warm place (about 80°) until dough is doubled (about 1½ to 2 hours).

5. Punch down with fist. Fold edge toward center and turn dough over. Divide dough into two equal balls. Lightly grease a second bowl. Place each ball of dough into a lightly greased bowl. Turn dough to bring greased side up. Cover as before. Let rise again until almost double (about 45 minutes).

6. Roll each ball of dough into a round to fit a 14″ Teflon (or lightly greased) pizza pan or into a 10″ × 14″ rectangle to fit a rectangular pan. Shape edge of pizzas by pressing dough between thumb and forefinger to make ridge.

TOPPING:

One 6-ounce can of tomato paste

1 medium onion, chopped

⅔ medium green pepper, chopped

(½ pound leanest ground beef, crumbled)

2 cups **Cottage Cheese**

One 4-ounce can of drained sliced mushrooms

4 teaspoons oregano

2 cloves garlic, finely minced

COOKING:

1. Divide the topping ingredients and sprinkle in order of listing over each pizza.

2. Bake at 400° approximately 25 minutes, or until slightly browned on top.

Serves 6.

BUTTON PASTA WITH SAUCE

Button pasta is made in a jiffy, and is delicious with this sauce. This dish makes an excellent accompaniment for any main dish.

PASTA:

¼ cup milk

1 cup sifted, unbleached, white flour

3 egg whites, slightly beaten

SAUCE:

1 tablespoon chopped onion

3 tablespoons chopped green pepper

1 cup chopped canned tomatoes

2 teaspoons cornstarch

⅛ teaspoon cayenne pepper

TOPPING:

(½ cup finely diced **Fresh Cheese**)

Make the pasta: add milk and flour to eggs and mix well; place one third of the mixture into a colander over a pot of boiling water, and force the mixture through the holes; skim the buttons of pasta into a hot serving bowl as they float to the surface; rinse colander in cool water and repeat process. (A steamer works even better than a colander because of its flat bottom. Use a hole-less potato masher to force the pasta through the holes in the steamer. Rinsing the steamer or colander in cold water before the pasta is turned into it prevents some of the stickiness that occurs when the pasta is being forced through the holes.) Make the sauce: sauté onions and peppers in 2 tablespoons water; add tomatoes, cornstarch, and cayenne pepper; cook over medium heat until thickened (about 5 minutes). Pour sauce over pasta, top with cheese, and serve. Serves 4.

FRESH CHEESE LASAGNA

1 cup **Cottage Cheese**

2 cups grated **Fresh Cheese**

2 teaspoons grated green
  cheese

½ cup skim milk

4 egg whites

½ teaspoon pepper

2 tablespoons parsley flakes

1 quart **Spaghetti Sauce,**
  warmed

12 to 15 lasagna noodles,
  cooked to *al dente* stage

Make a cheese mixture by combining in the blender cottage cheese, fresh cheese, grated green cheese, skim milk, egg whites, pepper, and parsley flakes. In shallow, square or rectangular casserole dish, alternate thin layers of sauce, noodles, and cheese mixture, ending with sauce. Top with a few very thin slices of fresh cheese. Bake at 300° for 45 minutes. Let stand 10 minutes to firm up, then cut into squares. Serves 4.

SPINACH LASAGNA

Wow! Who would think spinach would go so well in a lasagna dish! Try this recipe for a real taste treat.

2 bunches fresh spinach	1 teaspoon oregano flakes
1 pound lasagna noodles	1 teaspoon basil flakes
2 small onions, chopped	2½ cups **Cottage Cheese**
½ cup sliced mushrooms	2 egg whites
½ large green pepper, chopped	1 cup grated **Fresh Cheese**
½ teaspoon minced garlic	1 tablespoon parsley flakes
One 28-ounce can of tomatoes, with half the liquid in the can	½ teaspoon pepper
	Bread crumbs

Prepare spinach: wash leaves thoroughly and remove stems; wilt spinach by placing in colander and then plunging in hot water 10 seconds; chop wilted spinach fine. *Prepare noodles:* cook and drain. *Prepare sauce:* sauté onions, mushrooms, green pepper, and garlic in 3 tablespoons water; add the canned tomatoes and juice after chopping 2 or 3 seconds in blender; add spices; simmer 30 minutes; then add spinach. *Prepare cheese mixture:* mix cottage cheese with egg whites, then add fresh cheese, parsley flakes, and pepper. *Prepare lasagna for baking:* place one third of the noodles in the bottom of a baking dish 13″ × 9″ × 2″; layer in one third of cheese mixture followed by one third of sauce; repeat process twice more, using up all of the noodles, cheese mixture, and sauce. Top with bread crumbs and bake at 350° for about 30 minutes. Serves 10.

ZUCCHINI LASAGNA

4 small zucchini squash,
  peeled and sliced
  lengthwise
2 cups grated **Fresh Cheese**
2 cups **Cottage Cheese**
1 cup egg whites (about 8
  eggs)
¼ cup parsley flakes
½ teaspoon pepper
1 pound lasagna noodles,
  cooked *al dente* and
  drained
1 quart **Spaghetti Sauce**

Cook zucchini 10 minutes in vegetable steamer. Make a cheese mixture by combining cheese with egg whites, parsley, and pepper. Layer ingredients as follows: noodles, cheese mixture, spaghetti sauce, zucchini, cheese mixture, spaghetti sauce. Repeat until all ingredients have been used. Bake 1 hour at 350°. Serves 8.

MACARONI AND BEANS

1 cup dried kidney beans
1 pound elbow macaroni
1 medium onion, chopped
3 cloves garlic, chopped
One 28-ounce can of whole
  tomatoes packed in puree
2 bay leaves
½ teaspoon pepper
½ cup cooked chopped
  spinach
½ cup **Sour Cream**

Soak beans 1 hour, then drain. Cook macaroni *al dente* and drain. Sauté onion and garlic in 3 tablespoons water until tender. Chop tomatoes with their liquid 2 or 3 seconds on chop cycle of blender. Combine tomatoes and spices in saucepan with onion and garlic. Add beans, cover, and simmer until beans are tender (3 to 4 hours). Add macaroni and spinach and heat through. Stir in sour cream and serve. Serves 6.

ZUCCHINI WITH PASTA

½ pound mostaccioli *or* large elbow macaroni
3 small zucchini, sliced
1½ cups chopped fresh tomatoes
¼ cup finely chopped onion
¼ cup finely chopped green pepper
¼ teaspoon pepper
3 fresh mushrooms, thinly sliced

Cook and drain pasta. Combine all other ingredients in saucepan. Stir a few minutes over medium heat, cover, and simmer 30 minutes, checking occasionally for adequate liquid. Add water as needed. Serve over cooked pasta. Serves 4.

MACARONI CUSTARD

1 cup shell macaroni, cooked *al dente*
1½ cups scalded skim milk
4 egg whites
1 cup grated **Fresh Cheese**
1 cup bread crumbs
1 green pepper, chopped
2 tablespoons chopped onion
1 teaspoon chopped pimiento
½ teaspoon cumin
¼ teaspoon pepper

Combine all ingredients except half the bread crumbs in a baking dish. Top with the remaining bread crumbs. Place baking dish in a pan of hot water and bake 40 minutes at 350°. Serves 4.

MACARONI AND CHEESE

3 cups cooked and drained small elbow macaroni
2 cups grated **Fresh Cheese**
2 egg whites, slightly beaten

1 cup **Sour Cream**　　　　　Paprika
2 cups **Cottage Cheese**

Combine all ingredients except macaroni and paprika in casserole dish. Stir in macaroni, sprinkle with paprika, and bake 45 minutes at 350°. Serves 8.

BEEFARONI

1 cup elbow macaroni　　　　1½ cups **Sour Cream**
2 cups **Spaghetti Sauce**　　 ½ cup grated **Fresh Cheese**
½ pound leanest ground beef,　½ cup bread crumbs
　broken in pieces

Cook macaroni. Combine macaroni, spaghetti sauce, and ground beef in baking dish. Spread top with sour cream. Sprinkle with fresh cheese and bread crumbs. Bake at 400° for 20 minutes. Serves 4.

RICE CASSEROLE

¼ pound lean beef chuck,　　　3 ounces sliced fresh
　sliced across grain, no　　　　　mushrooms
　thicker than ¹/₁₆ inch　　　　3 tamarind pods, peeled
¾ cup frozen peas　　　　　　3 tablespoons chopped
¾ cup brown rice　　　　　　　pimiento
⅓ cup cooked garbanzo beans　Pinch of saffron

Fry meat in Teflon pan until just barely browned. Bring 2 cups water to a boil, and add all ingredients. Return to boil, cover, and simmer 1 hour (or bake 1½ hours at 350°). Remove tamarinds before serving. Serves 4.

PASTA E FAGIOLI
(Pasta and beans)

2 cups cooked and drained   1 quart **Spaghetti Sauce**
   pinto or red beans   1 pound flat **noodles,** cooked
   (approximately ¾ cup dried)

Combine beans and sauce, and heat through. Toss noodles with
sauce and beans, and serve. Serves 6.

COOKED RICE CASSEROLE

 2 cups cooked brown rice   1 cup sliced fresh mushrooms
½ pound leanest ground beef   Pepper
½ cup **Beef Stock**

Brown and drain beef. Combine all ingredients in casserole dish,
cover, and heat at 350° for 30 minutes. Serves 4.

CHILI CORN PIE

½ pound leanest ground beef   ½ teaspoon paprika
½ cup (1 envelope) Plus-Meat   ½ teaspoon onion powder
½ cup flour   ¼ teaspoon pepper
One 28-ounce can of tomatoes   Dash of cayenne pepper
One 15-ounce can of corn   4 corn tortillas
¼ teaspoon garlic powder   Cornmeal
½ teaspoon chili powder   Skim milk or evaporated skim
                                      milk

Brown ground beef. Drain off all fat. Add ½ cup water to Plus-
Meat, let stand 5 minutes, then stir. Add to ground beef and stir.

Add flour to meat mixture to coat meat, then add all other ingredients except tortillas, cornmeal, and skim milk. Pour mixture into casserole. Cut tortillas into chip-size triangles, moisten with milk, then dip in cornmeal. Arrange tortilla triangles on top of casserole, then sprinkle surface with additional cornmeal. Bake at 400° for 30 minutes. Just before serving, place under broiler for a few minutes to brown topping. Serves 4 to 6.

SPAGHETTI-FLAVORED RICE

1 cup brown rice	2½ cups boiling water
1 cup hot **Spaghetti Sauce**	
(¼ pound leanest ground beef)	

Combine ingredients in casserole dish. Cover and bake 1 hour at 350°. Serves 4.

CORN TORTILLA PIE

2 cups (1 recipe) **Corn Pudding**	½ cup finely chopped onion
1 cup corn	½ cup **Cottage Cheese**
8 corn tortillas	2 cups cold water
1 medium tomato, sliced thin	1 cup cornmeal
	½ teaspoon chili powder

Combine corn and corn pudding. Layer tortillas and corn mixture into casserole dish, ending with corn mixture. Top with tomato, sprinkle with onion and cottage cheese. Combine cold water, cornmeal, and chili powder in saucepan. Cook and stir until thick (3 minutes). Spread over all. Bake at 350° for 45 minutes. Serves 6.

ENCHILADAS

This is a truly excellent vegetarian enchilada dish.

18 corn tortillas

SAUCE:

4 cups **Tomato Sauce**
2 to 4 tablespoons **Chili Salsa**

1 tablespoon parsley flakes
1 teaspoon vinegar

FILLING:

4 cups drained **Chili Beans**
   (reserve liquid)
½ cup liquid from **Chili Beans**
One 4-ounce can of chopped
   mushrooms

1 medium onion, chopped
2 cups grated **Fresh Cheese**

Combine all sauce ingredients and heat through, over low flame. Combine all filling ingredients, except cheese, in saucepan and cook over medium heat 20 minutes. Add 1½ cups of the cheese and cook 5 minutes more. In a Teflon pan heat each tortilla on both sides until soft and pliable. Place 2 or 3 tablespoons of filling in the center of each tortilla, roll up, and place in a glass baking dish 11" × 14" × 2". Continue until all filling is used. Pour sauce over enchiladas and top with remaining cheese. Bake at 350° for 20 minutes. Serves 6.

CHICKEN ENCHILADAS

To make marvelous chicken enchiladas, simply add 1½ cups shredded chicken to the filling ingredients in the recipe above. More tortillas will be needed, perhaps 22 instead of the 18 called for. Serves 8.

ENCHILADAS DE TIJUANA

2 cups diced, cooked turkey *or* chicken *or* chopped beef
1½ cups cooked drained kidney, pinto, or red beans
2 small onions, chopped fine
1 clove garlic, minced
½ medium green pepper
3 cups **Tomato Sauce**
¼ cup canned California green chilies, diced and seeded
1 teaspoon oregano
12 corn tortillas
2 medium green onions, chopped

Prepare filling: Mash down turkey and beans until they adhere to each other. Add half of chopped onions, and mix. *Prepare sauce:* Sauté the rest of the chopped onions with the garlic and green pepper in ½ cup water. Add the tomato sauce, chilies and oregano, and simmer 5 minutes. *Prepare for baking:* Dip tortillas one by one in simmering sauce. Place a large spoonful of filling on each tortilla, roll tortilla up, and place seam-side down in a shallow baking dish. Pour sauce over top. Bake 20 minutes at 350° or until heated through. Garnish with green onions and serve. (For vegetarian enchiladas, double the amount of beans, eliminate the turkey, and add ½ teaspoon of cumin with the oregano.) Serves 6.

STACKED ENCHILADAS

1 cup **Enchilada Sauce** *or* **Red Molé Sauce** *or* **Red Molé Sauce with Tomato**
6 tortillas
½ pound leanest ground beef, browned and drained of fat
1½ cups grated **Fresh Cheese**

In a round casserole dish, layer sauce, tortillas, meat, and cheese until all have been used, ending with a tortilla topped with sauce and cheese. Cover and bake 1 hour at 300°. If desired, remove cover and place under broiler for a few minutes to brown cheese before serving. Serves 4.

EGGPLANT ENCHILADA PIE

½ medium eggplant (cut the eggplant in half crosswise)
1 medium onion, chopped
2 cups tomato juice
2 tablespoons tomato paste
1 tablespoon **Vegetable Powder**

1 teaspoon chili powder
Dash of nutmeg
3 medium tomatoes, thinly sliced
8 corn tortillas
1 cup **Sour Cream**

Peel eggplant and cut into very thin crosswise slices (20 or so slices). Sauté onion in 3 tablespoons water until just barely tender. Make a sauce by combining tomato juice, tomato paste, and spices. Using a round casserole dish a little larger in diameter than the corn tortillas, layer in the ingredients. Make 8 layers, each one made with a bit of sauce, 1 tortilla, 2 or 3 slices of eggplant, 3 or 4 tomato slices, and some of the sour cream. Top with sauce over all. Cover and bake 1 hour at 350°. Uncover and bake 10 more minutes. Remove from oven and allow to sit 10 minutes to firm up before cutting and serving. Makes 6 servings.

CARROT AND NOODLE CASSEROLE

1 cup cooked carrot slices
2 cups cooked **noodles**

¼ cup carrot juice
¼ cup **Sour Cream**

Combine carrots and noodles in shallow casserole dish. Combine carrot juice and sour cream, beat until smooth, and pour over carrots and noodles. Bake at 350° for 25 minutes. Serves 4.

RATATOUILLE SANS OIL

½ medium eggplant, peeled and cut into bars 3″ × 1″ × ½″

3 medium zucchinis, cut into similar bars

1 medium green pepper, sliced thin

1 medium onion, sliced thin

1 clove garlic, chopped very fine

2 large tomatoes, halved, squeezed of seeds and juice, and French-cut into ½-inch slices

2 tablespoons parsley flakes

Pepper

Teflon-fry eggplant and zucchini over low heat, drying them, but browning only slightly if at all. Make a base mixture: sauté green peppers and onions in ½ cup water in covered pan, until tender; add garlic and tomatoes and cook for 5 minutes over very low heat; add parsley and pepper, stir gently, and boil off excess juice. Cover bottom of a casserole dish with one third of this base mixture. Add half the eggplant and zucchini, then a second third of the base mixture. Add remaining eggplant and zucchini, and top with final third of base mixture. Cover casserole and simmer on stove over low heat 10 minutes. With bulb baster, moisten vegetables with any rendered juices. Remove cover, increase heat slightly, and cook 10 minutes, basting frequently and rearranging vegetables as necessary to prevent scorching. Serves 4.

TUNA NOODLE CASSEROLE

3 cups **noodles** (about 6 ounces or half a recipe

One 7-ounce can of tuna

1¼ cups **Cream of Celery Soup**

Bread crumbs

Drop noodles into boiling water, stir, cook until done (about 15 minutes), and drain. Combine noodles, tuna, and cream of celery soup in a 1½-quart casserole dish, top with bread crumbs, and bake at 350° until bread crumbs are lightly browned (about 40 minutes). Serves 4.

TUNA MUSHROOM CASSEROLE

2 cups **Tuna Mushroom Sauce**
2 cups seashell macaroni, cooked *al dente,* and drained
1½ cups cooked peas (or a 10-ounce package of frozen peas)
Bread crumbs

Combine sauce and macaroni in casserole dish. Fold in cooked peas. Top with bread crumbs and bake 30 minutes at 350°. Serves 6.

CREAM OF SALMON CASSEROLE

2 cups **Cream of Salmon Soup**
1 cup whole wheat elbow macaroni, cooked and drained
½ cup bread crumbs
Paprika

Heat soup, and combine in a casserole dish with macaroni. Top with bread crumbs and bake 30 minutes at 350° or until bread is lightly toasted. Garnish with paprika and serve. Serves 4.

POTATO-SALMON BAKE

6 medium potatoes, cooked, cooled, then peeled (keep in cold water until used)
One 7¾-ounce can of salmon

1 tablespoon cornstarch
½ cup cold skim milk
¼ teaspoon tarragon
2 egg whites

2 medium onions, chopped
fine
1 medium green pepper,
chopped fine
1 clove garlic, minced
2 medium zucchini squash,
sliced
One 10-ounce package of
frozen peas

1 cup **Cottage Cheese**
2 tablespoons parsley flakes
1 tablespoon grated green
cheese
½ cup sliced mushrooms
1 tablespoon garlic juice
Paprika
Matzo meal crumbs

Sauté onions, green pepper, and garlic in ½ cup water until nearly tender. Add zucchini and peas and cook briefly over hot flame until zucchini is nearly tender. Make paste of cornstarch, half of the milk, and the tarragon. Blend salmon into paste, add to sautéed vegetables, and cook over medium flame until liquid thickens (add more liquid or more cornstarch if necessary, to produce a creamed-salmon-and-vegetable effect). Slice 3 of the potatoes. Layer the slices onto the bottom of a large baking dish. Spread the creamed salmon and vegetables over the potatoes, then slice and layer on the other 3 potatoes. Spread over all a mixture of the egg whites, cottage cheese, parsley, and 2 tablespoons of water. Sprinkle on grated hard green cheese and top with mushrooms sautéed in the garlic juice and 2 tablespoons water. Bake at 375° for 30 minutes. Sprinkle with paprika and matzo meal crumbs, and bake 5 minutes more. Serves 8.

EASY BROWN RICE AND CHICKEN

2 chicken breasts (about ½
pound each)
2 cups brown rice,
uncooked

1½ cups **Chicken Stock**
1 cup **Onion Soup**

Place chicken into a pot of cold water, bring to a boil, and boil until tender. Remove skin and visible fat and cut into bite-size pieces. Combine chicken pieces with remaining ingredients in a 2-quart casserole dish. Bake 1 hour at 350°, stirring once or twice during baking. Serves 6.

BROWN RICE AND CHICKEN

1 chicken breast (weight ½ pound or less including fat and bones)
1 cup brown rice
½ cup wild rice
½ cup sliced mushrooms
½ cup **Bean-Thickened Gravy**
1 cup fresh or defrosted frozen peas
1 tablespoon **Vegetable Powder**
½ cup chopped fresh parsley
2 tablespoons chopped pimiento

Remove skin and fat from chicken. Cut meat off bones and into ½-inch cubes. Teflon-fry until pieces stay separate and turn white. Rinse rice. In a large pot, combine rice and 3 cups water, bring to a boil, and stir once. Combine rice and water with all other ingredients in large casserole dish, cover, and bake at 350° for 1 hour. Serves 6.

LIMA BEAN PATTIES

1 pound dried lima beans, soaked overnight
2 egg whites
Bread crumbs

Boil beans until soft. Cool (enough to handle) and force through a puree strainer. Form into small patties, roll in crumbs, dip in egg whites, and again in crumbs. Teflon-fry and serve. Makes 6 patties.

BEEF SHEPHERD'S PIE

2 cups (about ¾ pound) chopped leftover roast beef
1 cup leftover gravy (see page 52)
2 medium carrots, cubed
½ cup coarsely chopped onions
4 cups mashed potatoes

Combine roast beef and gravy in a 1½-quart casserole dish. Cook carrots and onions until carrots are soft, and add to the beef and gravy. Cover top with potatoes and bake at 425° until potatoes are lightly browned (about 20 minutes). Serves 6.

MEATBALL SHEPHERD'S PIE

1 pound leanest ground beef
3 cups soft bread crumbs
1 egg white
¼ teaspoon pepper
1 small onion, chopped fine
1 teaspoon arrowroot
One 4-ounce can of sliced mushrooms, with juice
One 16-ounce can of tomatoes
One 10-ounce package of frozen peas and carrots
¼ teaspoon oregano
3 cups leftover mashed potatoes

Mix ground beef, bread crumbs, egg white, and pepper. Form into balls and brown on all sides in Teflon skillet. In saucepan, cook onions until tender in ½ cup water. Blend in a paste made of arrowroot and 1 tablespoon cold water, and cook and stir over medium heat until slightly thickened. Add mushrooms, tomatoes, and meatballs. Cover and simmer 30 minutes. Add peas and carrots and oregano, bring to a boil, and cook until peas and carrots are tender (8 to 10 minutes). Pour into a 1½-quart casserole dish, spread potatoes on top, and put under broiler until lightly browned. Serves 6.

MEATBALLS WITH NOODLES

½ pound leanest ground beef
2 cups **Tomato Sauce**
1 cup **Sour Cream**
½ cup fine dry bread crumbs
1 egg white
1 teaspoon parsley flakes
⅛ teaspoon pepper
1 small onion, chopped

1 clove garlic, minced
1 bay leaf
1 teaspoon lemon juice
1 teaspoon paprika
2 cups uncooked **noodles**
   One 4-ounce can of
   mushrooms

Combine ground beef with 2 tablespoons of the tomato sauce, 1 tablespoon of the sour cream, the bread crumbs, the egg white, the parsley, and the pepper. Shape into small balls and cook in the skillet until well browned, draining off any rendered fat. Sauté onions and garlic in a roomy saucepan, using ¼ cup water as sauté liquid. Add meatballs and all other ingredients except noodles and mushrooms, bring to a boil, cover, and simmer 20 minutes. Uncover and simmer 10 minutes more. Cook and drain noodles. Combine noodles with mushrooms and arrange in border around a hot platter. Remove meatballs from sauce and place in center of platter. Cover meatballs with sufficient amount of sauce and serve. Serves 6.

BEEF AND RICE CASSEROLE

¾ pound leanest ground beef
1 cup uncooked rice
1 small onion, chopped
2½ cups tomato juice

1½ cups boiling water
1 teaspoon paprika
½ teaspoon pepper
½ cup **Cottage Cheese**

Combine broken-up meat, rice, and onion in a saucepan and cook so as to lightly brown meat. Add remaining ingredients except cottage cheese and bring to a boil. Put into a 1½-quart casserole dish, cover, and bake 1 hour at 300°. Cover with cottage cheese and return to oven 5 minutes. Serves 6.

MACARONI AND GROUND BEEF CASSEROLE

1 cup elbow macaroni
¾ pound leanest ground beef
½ small onion, chopped

1 clove garlic, minced
Dash of pepper
Bread crumbs

Cook and drain macaroni. Combine beef, onion, and garlic in skillet and brown beef lightly. Add pepper. Place all ingredients except bread crumbs in a 1-quart casserole dish, add ½ cup water, cover with bread crumbs, and bake 15 minutes at 350°. Serves 4.

BEEF, POTATO, AND BEAN CASSEROLE

¾ pound leanest ground beef
⅛ teaspoon pepper
¼ teaspoon oregano
2 cups thinly sliced, peeled potatoes

2 cups cooked red kidney beans, drained
1 medium onion, sliced thin
½ cup **Chili Salsa**

Lightly brown beef with spices. Layer beef and remaining ingredients into a 1½-quart casserole dish, beginning and ending with beef. Cover and bake 40 minutes at 350°. Uncover and bake 15 minutes more. Serves 6.

FISH DISHES

Those delicate, subtle, marvelous flavors and aromas of fish dishes—what would we do without them? A source of human nourishment for millions of years, fish are used as much today as ever before. Scientists tell us that our nourishment in the future may depend even more than it does today on fish and on other products coming from the fish's environment.

Fish contains cholesterol, just as beef, lamb, pork, and other meats do. For this reason its consumption should be limited to a quarter of a pound per day per person, just as other meats are limited. The advantage that fish holds over other meats (and we *do* classify fish as a meat) is its relatively low fat content. Other things being equal, one who dines on fish will consume less fat than one who eats beef, pork, or lamb. Not all varieties of fish are equally lean, however. Varieties that are particularly high in fat should probably be avoided. Among those in this class are: herring, kipper, sardine, shad, smelt, and eel.

BROILED FISH FILETS

1 pound tender-fleshed fish filets (such as cod, whiting, or flounder)
2 medium lemons
¼ teaspoon basil
⅛ teaspoon thyme
⅛ teaspoon pepper
¼ cup dry white wine
Fresh parsley sprigs

In a shallow pan, arrange filets in a single layer. Brush or sprinkle fish with juice from one of the lemons, then sprinkle with basil, thyme, and pepper. Pour wine into pan around (not on top of) fish. Broil close to heat until fish begins to brown and looks slightly dry, with juices congealing. Do not attempt to turn fish. Serve with parsley trim and wedges cut from remaining lemon. Serves 6.

FISH IN WINE SAUCE

4 tender-fleshed fish filets (3 ounces each)
Dash of white pepper
¼ cup chopped onion

Freshly ground black pepper   4 teaspoons lemon juice
½ cup vermouth
Bones and juice from the filets,
    if any

Sprinkle freshly ground black pepper over filets. Arrange filets in flat casserole or place each in a separate shallow ramekin. Combine remaining ingredients in a saucepan, add 1 cup water, bring to a boil, and simmer, uncovered, to boil off alcohol. Pour through a tea strainer onto filets. Bake at 350° for 25 minutes. Serves 4.

FISH PATTIES

¾ pound tender-fleshed fish   8 egg whites, beaten to soft
    filets   peaks
¼ cup chopped onion   ¼ cup evaporated skim milk
1 cup grated raw potato   Pepper
2 cups bread crumbs

Chop fish into tiny pieces. Combine all other ingredients, then add fish. Mix well. Drop by large spoonsful onto hot Teflon skillet, shape into patties, and fry both sides. Serves 6.

FISH IN CHEESE SAUCE

¾ pounds butterfish filets or   1 cup **Fresh Cheese Sauce**
    other very tender-fleshed   (page 253)
    fish (4 filets)   Dill weed

Arrange filets in shallow casserole or in separate shallow ramekins. Sprinkle each filet lightly with dill weed and smother each with ¼ cup of the cheese sauce. Bake 25 minutes at 350°. Serves 4.

OVEN-FRIED FISH FILETS

4 fish filets (3 ounces each)   ¼ cup evaporated skim milk
4 egg whites, slightly beaten   Cornmeal

Preheat ovenproof platter in 425° oven. Dip fish in mixture of egg whites and milk, then dip in cornmeal. Place on hot platter, and bake 25 minutes. Serves 4.

MINUTE FISH

1 pound fish filets   2 tablespoons chopped fresh
½ cup dry white wine   parsley
2 tablespoons chopped green   ½ teaspoon pepper
   onion

Arrange fish in shallow baking dish, and pour wine around fish. Sprinkle remaining ingredients over top and bake at 450° until top is browned and fish is cooked (about 15 minutes). Serve from baking dish. Serves 6.

FILET OF FLOUNDER

1 pound filets of flounder   2 medium onions, sliced thin
   (or codfish)   ½ cup skim milk
1 teaspoon paprika

Broil fish on one side until lightly browned. Turn fish over in pan. Sprinkle uncooked side with paprika. Layer on the onions, pour milk over top, return to broiler, and brown. Serves 4 to 6.

BROILED TUNA STEAKS
(or halibut or salmon*)

3 fresh tuna steaks
(approximately 2 pounds),
1½ inches thick
1 medium lemon

¼ cup vermouth
¼ teaspoon basil
Onion powder
Pepper

Rinse steaks under cold running water. Remove excess moisture with paper towels. Remove any clinging stomach lining. Sprinkle on both sides with the dry seasonings. Place steaks in shallow baking pan, no larger than necessary to accommodate fish. Sprinkle fish with juice of half of the lemon. Gently pour vermouth over fish. Let marinate 1 to 2 hours, spooning marinade over top occasionally and turning steaks once. Broil 6 inches from heating element. When lightly browned (10 to 15 minutes), turn steaks very carefully, using two pancake turners, one over and one under the steak. Baste with any excess marinade. Broil 10 to 15 minutes. Serve immediately and garnish with thin slices of the remaining half of the lemon. Any juice left in broiler pan makes a delicious sauce to pour over fish or rice, or to use as a dunk for bread. Serves 8.

TOMATOED TUNA OVER SPAGHETTI

4 ripe medium tomatoes
¼ teaspoon pepper
One 7-ounce can of tuna
½ cup **Cottage Cheese**
¼ cup evaporated skim milk

½ pound spaghetti *or* polenta,
cooked
1 cup finely grated **Fresh
Cheese**

---

*When cooking salmon, keep in mind that its delicate flavor is easily overwhelmed by excessive seasoning. Respect for its flavor demands moderation in the use of spices. It's hard to go wrong with a light sprinkling of the spices above; just don't gild the lily.

Dip tomatoes in boiling water for a few seconds. Remove and discard peel, and chop tomatoes into a saucepan. Add pepper, cover, and simmer in own juice 20 minutes (add small amount of water if necessary). Add tuna, cottage cheese, and skim milk, and stir. Place cooked spaghetti in baking dish, and pour tomato-tuna mixture over top. Top with grated cheese, and broil 10 minutes, 5 inches from cooking element. Serves 4.

TUNA VEGETABLE LOAF

Two 7-ounce cans of tuna
2 cups soft bread crumbs (no crusts)
¾ cup skim milk
½ cup chopped celery
½ cup grated carrot
¼ cup finely chopped onion
4 egg whites, beaten
1 tablespoon parsley flakes
1 tablespoon lemon juice

Drain and flake tuna. Combine bread and milk, and heat to just below boiling, stirring constantly. Remove from heat. Add tuna and all other ingredients and blend well in blender. Pour mixture into ungreased Pyrex meat loaf dish and bake at 350° until set (about 1 hour). Let stand 5 minutes before serving. Since dish is ungreased, serve with an ice cream scoop rather than slicing. Serves 6.

BRINY DEEP SALMON LOAF

One 7¾-ounce can of salmon, drained
3 cups soft bread crumbs
3 egg whites
½ cup skim milk
½ cup chopped onion
2 tablespoons parsley flakes
½ teaspoon tarragon
2½ cups **Curried Pea Sauce** (page 254)

Combine all ingredients except pea sauce, mixing and mashing well to distribute salmon, seasonings, and wet ingredients thoroughly in bread crumbs. Shape mixture in a 8″ × 8″ × 2″ Teflon pan. Bake 25 minutes at 400°. Pour hot curried pea sauce over entire surface of salmon loaf, and serve. Serves 4.

SALMON-STUFFED FISH FILET ROLLS

6 small fish filets, 2 ounces each (sole, scrod, flounder, etc.)	1 tablespoon lemon juice
	½ teaspoon tarragon
One 7¾-ounce can of salmon, drained and flaked	½ teaspoon paprika
	2½ cups **Curried Pea Sauce** (page 254)
2 tablespoons parsley flakes	
2 tablespoons chopped scallions	

Mix all ingredients except filets and pea sauce together, and spread this mixture on the filets, leaving a narrow border along the edges of each filet. Beginning with the tail end, roll up each filet and fasten with a toothpick. Place rolls in a shallow casserole dish, cover, and bake at 350° until fish flakes easily (about 20 minutes). Pour hot curried pea sauce over the filets and serve. Serves 6.

SALMON-STUFFED POTATOES

4 large potatoes	1⅓ cups crumbled leftover salmon steaks
2 cups **Cottage Cheese**	
1½ cups **Buttermilk**	Paprika

Bake potatoes at 425° until tender (about 1 hour). Make a "mock sour cream" mixture by combining all of the cottage cheese with 1 cup of the buttermilk (reserving the other ½ cup of buttermilk) in the blender and blending at high speed until very smooth. Cutting lengthwise, slice off one third of each potato, and scrape out as much of the pulp as possible without damaging the four large shells that will be restuffed. Mash pulp, then blend in about three quarters of the mock sour cream mixture, saving the rest for topping. Use a mixer to beat pulp and mock sour cream mixture to a consistency like stiff mashed potatoes. Add a little of the remaining buttermilk if necessary. Flake salmon and stir into mashed potato mixture. Restuff potato shells with this mixture, top with remaining mock sour cream and sprinkle with paprika. Bake 30 minutes at 400°. Or store uncooked in refrigerator until needed, and then bake 45 minutes at 400°. Serve hot. Serves 4.

NEPTUNE'S CHOWDER

2 pounds filets of firm-fleshed fish (e.g., halibut, red snapper, or sea bass)
3 large potatoes
1 medium onion, chopped
1 medium leek, chopped
1 stalk celery, chopped
1 clove garlic, minced finely
1 large carrot, diced

One 28-ounce can of tomatoes, chopped
1 cup **Tomato Sauce**
2 tablespoons parsley flakes
2 bay leaves
¾ teaspoon thyme
Dash of pepper
¾ cup sherry wine
1 medium lemon
3 tablespoons cornstarch

Cut fish into 1½-inch cubes and set aside. Boil potatoes until tender but not soft, then peel and dice. Place onion, leek, celery, and garlic in a large soup pot. Add ½ cup water, cover, and cook over medium heat until vegetables are tender and slightly yellow (about 15 minutes). Add carrot, tomatoes, tomato sauce, and spices, and simmer, covered, 30 minutes. Add wine, juice of the lemon, the cut-up fish, and the diced potatoes, and simmer 20 minutes more. Mix cornstarch with ⅓ cup cold water, stir into the simmering pot, and cook and stir until chowder thickens. Cook a few minutes more and serve. Serves 8.

MRS. MARSCH'S SQUID

4 small squid (hood about 6 inches long)
2 cups **Mrs. Marsch's Sauce for Squid** (page 251)

Clean squid. Remove tentacles and separate them from each other (you will have eight separate tentacles plus two arms). Cut hood into rings. If necessary, cut remainder of body into fork-size pieces. Bring sauce to a boil and add all parts of squid. Return to boil, cover, and simmer 45 minutes to an hour, or until squid is very tender. Serve on sourdough toast that has been rubbed with a freshly cut clove of garlic, or on spaghetti. Serves 4.

STUFFED SQUID

4 small squid (hood about 6 inches long)
1 chicken breast, skinned deboned, and coarsely ground
1 slice dry sourdough bread

2 egg whites
2 tablespoons parsley flakes
⅛ teaspoon garlic powder
⅛ teaspoon pepper
2 cups **Mrs. Marsch's Sauce for Squid** (page 251)

Clean squid, remove tentacles, and set hoods aside. Chop tentacles into small pieces. Combine tentacles with ground chicken and grind. Grind dry bread into chicken-squid mixture. Combine egg whites and spices, add to the chicken-squid-bread mixture, and blend with a fork. Stuff this mixture loosely into the four squid hoods, and skewer closed with a toothpick. Place squid in a small casserole dish, smother with squid sauce, cover, and bake 45 minutes at 350°. Uncover and place under broiler 3 or 4 minutes before serving. An elegant main dish for company, complemented well by spaghetti and a salad. Serves 4.

CHICKEN AND TURKEY DISHES

Chicken is one of the cook's very good friends. Roast chicken, stewed chicken, boiled chicken, fried chicken, or baked chicken —no matter how it's cooked, it's easy and good.

It is hard to believe that a three-pound chicken, under controlled conditions, will have eaten as little as eight pounds of grain during its entire lifetime. That's a truly phenomenal efficiency for creating meat from grain. Pound for pound, a young adult human will have consumed at least 1000 times as much in the way of foodstuffs as the lowly chicken. Maybe that is the reason why in 1932 the Republican party promised "a chicken in every pot." They probably thought it would be an easy promise to fulfill, given the chicken's proclivity for turning grain into living chicken.

In any event, in this section we present a number of taste-tempting chicken and turkey dishes. Trying them, one might wonder why one waits so long between cooking chicken dishes. A word of caution. Like fish and beef dishes, care must be exercised in the preparation of chicken dishes to make sure that each person's total daily consumption of meat (including all chicken, fish, and other meats) remains less than ¼ pound. This will insure a satisfactorily low intake of cholesterol.

Broilers, fryers, roasters, capons, fowls, stags, and *cocks* are all words referring to the same feathered creature. They differ in that they refer to specific sex, age, or size characteristics of the chicken in question. Young chickens of either sex are *broilers* if they weigh 2 to 2½ pounds, *fryers* if they weigh 2½ to 3½ pounds, and *roasters* if they weigh 3½ to 5 pounds. *Capons* are males that have been castrated and allowed to grow to a large size of 6 to 8 pounds. They resemble small turkeys when dressed and ready for sale at the market. *Fowl* is the euphemism used for a female of any size over ten months old. A *stag* or *cock* is an old male; not good eating, but excellent for the stock pot.

CHICKEN BREAST PAPRIKA

¾ pound of chicken breasts
½ cup **Buttermilk**
1 teaspoon paprika
1 cup flat or crinkly **noodles**
2 cups sliced mushrooms
¼ cup chopped onion
¼ cup chopped celery
2 tablespoons chopped green pepper
½ cup vermouth
2 cups **Sour Cream**
Chopped chives for garnish

Preheat oven to 450°. Remove skin and fat from chicken breasts. Cut the meat from the bones, into filets. Marinate 2 hours in buttermilk and paprika. Arrange in a single layer in a flat baking dish, smothered in marinade. (If desired, top with freshly ground pepper.) Bake 20 minutes. While chicken is baking, cook noodles. Meanwhile sauté vegetables in vermouth, in a covered pan. Boil off excess liquid. Add sour cream and heat gently until warm. Add the cooking juices from the chicken (which by now should be done) and mix. Serve chicken on bed of noodles topped with vegetable–sour cream mixture. Garnish with chopped chives. Serves 4.

CHICKEN CACCIATORE

4 small chicken breasts (total weight ¾ to 1 pound)
½ cup flour
2 tablespoons onion powder
½ teaspoon paprika

SAUCE:

1 cup chopped onion

2 cloves garlic, minced

One 28-ounce can of chopped tomatoes

1 teaspoon basil

½ teaspoon thyme

6 needles of dried rosemary (12 needles if fresh)

Dash of cayenne pepper

Remove skin and fat from chicken breasts. Place the flour, onion powder, and paprika in a broil-in-bag, and shake the chicken breasts in the bag in this mixture. Remove flour mixture from broil-in-bag, return chicken to the same bag, close with a twister seal, place two ½-inch slits in bag, and roast in 400° oven for 20 minutes, or until lightly browned. *To make sauce:* Cook onion and garlic until tender in juice from canned tomatoes. Add tomatoes, basil, thyme, rosemary, and cayenne pepper. Bring to a boil, and remove from heat. Remove chicken from browning bag, place in casserole dish, pour sauce over top, cover, and cook in oven 1 hour more. Serve in casserole dish. Use spaghetti as an accompaniment. Serves 4.

CHICKEN WITH YOGURT

¾ pound of chicken breast

1 medium onion, sliced

6 small carrots, cut lengthwise into flat strips

1 cup **Chicken Stock**

⅛ teaspoon celery seed

⅛ teaspoon thyme

⅛ teaspoon pepper

2 cups frozen cauliflower flowerets

1 cup frozen peas

¼ cup dry vermouth or other dry white wine

1 tablespoon rice flour

¾ cup **Yogurt**

1 tablespoon chopped fresh parsley

Remove skin, fat, and bones from chicken breast. Cut in half-inch cubes and Teflon-fry until white and separate. In large pot, combine onions, carrots, stock, celery seed, thyme, and pepper. Bring to boil, cover, and simmer 20 minutes, adding small amount of water if necessary. Add chicken, cauliflower, peas, and vermouth to pot. Simmer until vegetables are tender (about 15 minutes). Combine rice flour with 2 tablespoons of water or stock, and stir into pot. Boil for a minute or two to thicken, stirring constantly. Remove from heat. Stir in yogurt and serve topped with parsley. Serves 4.

CHICKEN-LACED MANICOTTI

¾ pound of chicken breast
4 manicotti shells, cooked *al dente* and cooled
1½ cups **Stuffing for Chicken Supreme** (p. 221)
¼ pound **Fresh Cheese,** cut into very thin slices
3 sprigs of fresh rosemary
2¼ cups **Mushroom Sauce**

Remove skin, bones, and fat from chicken, being careful to preserve the chicken meat in pieces that are as large as possible. Cut chicken into long strips 1 inch wide. Carefully fill manicotti shells with stuffing, and place stuffed shells in shallow baking dish, leaving ample space between. Wrap chicken strips diagonally around manicotti shells (about 2 strips per shell). Arrange cheese slices on top of manicotti shells, in between chicken strips. Place rosemary needles between manicotti shells, and pour sauce over all. Preheat oven to broil temperature. Insert casserole, and immediately reduce oven setting to 350°. Bake 30 minutes and serve. Serves 4.

STUFFED CHICKEN SUPREME

4 small chicken breasts
(weight of all 4 not to
exceed 1 pound)
1½ cups **Stuffing for Chicken
Supreme** (p. 221)

4 sprigs of fresh rosemary
¼ pound **Fresh Cheese,** sliced
very thin
2½ cups **Mushroom Sauce**
(page 253)

Remove skin and visible fat from chicken, but keep breast intact. Stuff the pocket of each breast with stuffing. Arrange breasts in round casserole, and place rosemary needles and any extra stuffing between breasts. Arrange thin slices of cheese on top of breasts, and pour sauce over all. Bake at 375° for 30 minutes or until chicken is done. Serves 4.

POACHED CHICKEN BREASTS

4 small chicken breasts
(combined weight less than
1 pound)
1 cup sliced fresh mushrooms
1 medium onion, chopped
1 cup **Chicken Stock**
¼ cup chopped pimiento

¼ teaspoon sage
2 teaspoons **Vegetable
Powder**
Freshly ground pepper
(½ cup white wine)
2 cups flat **noodles**

Remove skin and visible fat from chicken breasts. Sauté mushrooms and onions until tender in water or additional stock, using a skillet that can be covered. Add stock, pimiento, seasonings, and wine. Add chicken breasts, cover, and poach until cooked through (about 15–20 minutes). Cook noodles while chicken is poaching. When chicken is poached, retrieve from mushrooms and onions and place on a bed of cooked noodles on serving tray. Heap mushrooms and onions on top and serve. (If desired, mix 1 tablespoon cornstarch with ½ cup cold stock and add to cooking liquid after removing chicken. Cook until mixture thickens, then pour over chicken breasts and noodles.) Serves 4.

STUFFING FOR CHICKEN SUPREME

½ cup wild rice, rinsed
1 tablespoon regular nonfat dry milk
1 tablespoon parsley flakes
3 egg whites
⅛ teaspoon pepper
¾ cup finely diced **Fresh Cheese**

Place rice in small saucepan, add 2 cups water, cover, and simmer 35 minutes. Drain rice thoroughly. Combine dry milk, parsley flakes, egg whites, and pepper, crushing lumps of milk to make smooth. Stir in cheese and rice. Makes 1½ cups.

JUICY VEGETABLED CHICKEN

4 small chicken breasts (combined weight less than 1 pound)
2 cloves garlic, sliced
3 medium green peppers, sliced
2 cups thin onion slices
½ cup **Chicken Stock**
½ cup dry sherry wine
1 bay leaf
¼ teaspoon pepper
1 pound fresh mushrooms, sliced
2 medium tomatoes, cut in wedges
2 tablespoons cornstarch
¼ cup chopped fresh parsley
2 tablespoons chopped pimiento

Remove skin and fat from chicken and brown under the broiler. Place garlic slices in large skillet with 2 tablespoons water and cook over high heat for 2 minutes. Add browned chicken, green peppers, onion, stock, wine, bay leaf, and pepper. Cover, and cook 20 minutes over low heat, stirring occasionally. Add mushrooms and tomatoes and cook 10 minutes more. Remove bay leaf. Stir in a mixture of the cornstarch combined with 2 tablespoons of water, and cook and stir occasionally until thickened. Sprinkle with parsley and pimiento and serve. Serves 4.

JUICY TOMATO CHICKEN

4 small chicken breasts (combined weight under 1 pound), fat and skin removed
1 cup tomato juice

½ teaspoon basil
¼ teaspoon paprika
Pepper
1 sprig of fresh rosemary
Cooked brown rice

Combine tomato juice with basil, paprika, and pepper. Toss in rosemary. Pour over chicken breasts in shallow baking dish. Bake 45 minutes at 375° or until chicken is cooked through. Remove rosemary. Serve chicken and sauce over brown rice. Serves 4.

CHICKEN PARMESAN

3 chicken breasts, about ½ pound each
½ cup dry sherry wine
One 4-ounce jar of sliced mushrooms

2 large cloves garlic, minced
3 tablespoons flour
1 pound spaghetti
Grated green cheese (mock Parmesan cheese)

Place chicken breasts in 1 quart cold water and, using a low flame, slowly bring to a boil. Take from heat. Remove skin, fat, and bones, and break chicken into 1- to 2-inch chunks. Refrigerate cooking liquid until fat rises to surface. Skim fat away. Measure 2 cups of the cooking liquid and place into a large, heavy skillet. (Freeze the remainder for future use.) Add wine, and mushrooms, and garlic, bring to a boil, and reduce heat. Mix the flour with ¼ cup water, stir it into the skillet, and continue cooking and stirring until the skillet contents thicken. Add chicken, cover, and cook 25 minutes over very low heat. Cook spaghetti, place on warm platter, and pour chicken mixture over top. Sprinkle with grated green cheese and serve. Serves 6.

ARROZ CON POLLO
(Rice with chicken)

4 chicken legs with thigh, skinned and trimmed of visible fat
¼ cup vermouth
1 cup brown rice
1 cup sliced fresh mushrooms
1 cup chopped onion
2 cloves garlic, sliced

2½ cups **Chicken Stock**
One 28-ounce can of whole tomatoes
¼ cup chopped pimiento
2 tablespoons chopped fresh parsley
½ teaspoon pepper
Pinch of saffron

Moisten chicken with vermouth, and brown in broiler, 3 inches from element. With pastry brush baste frequently to prevent dryness, using cooking juices and water (or chicken broth). Remove chicken when lightly browned, and arrange in casserole dish. In separate pan, combine rice, mushrooms, onions, and garlic in ¼ cup stock and cook over moderate heat for 5 minutes. Add remaining stock, bring to a boil, cover, and simmer 20 minutes at very low heat. Add remaining ingredients, heat to boiling, and pour over chicken in casserole. Cover and bake at 350° for 50 minutes. Remove cover and cook 10 minutes more. Serves 4.

CHICKEN WITH CHERRIES

4 chicken breasts (combined weight less than 2 pounds)
1 cup water-packed canned cherries, drained
½ cup liquid from cherries
¼ cup dry red wine
½ cup **Chicken Stock**
4 teaspoons cornstarch

Remove skin and fat from chicken breasts. Cut meat off bones in pieces about 3 inches by 1 inch. Teflon-fry. Combine other ingredients, heat through, and add hot chicken. Serves 8.

CHICKEN IN MARINADE

½ frying chicken, disjointed and skinned, with visible fat removed
1 cup **Lemon-Dill Marinade** (page 268)

Marinate chicken 1 hour in marinade. Remove chicken from marinade (saving marinade), place in baking pan, and bake 45 minutes at 350°, basting with reserved marinade. Serves 3.

CHICKEN FRICASSEE WITH VEGETABLES AND DUMPLINGS

½ broiler-fryer chicken, cut up, with skin and fat removed
3⅓ cups **Chicken Stock**
1 medium onion, chopped
1 stalk celery, diced
1 bay leaf
½ teaspoon turmeric
1 small cabbage, cut in eighths
8 pearl onions
4 medium carrots, pared and cut in 2-inch pieces
1 cup frozen peas
¾ cup flour water (Blend 2 parts cold water with 1 part flour.)

DUMPLINGS:

2 cups flour
4 teaspoons baking powder
¾ cup plus 2 tablespoons skim milk
2 teaspoons finely minced fresh parsley

Place chicken in pot with stock, chopped onion, celery, bay leaf, and turmeric. Bring to a boil, cover, and simmer until chicken is almost tender (about 30 minutes). Add cabbage, pearl onions, and carrots, cover, and simmer 20 minutes more. Meanwhile, make up dumpling batter: sift together flour and baking powder. Then add milk and parsley and stir well to moisten all the dry ingredients. Back to the pot: add peas, allow simmering action to begin again, then stir in flour water, mixing well. Quickly add dumpling batter by teaspoonsful, spacing droppings apart. Cover tightly and allow to steam 10 minutes without lifting lid. Remove lid, and turn dumplings to moisten dry side. Serve with turmeric rice (rice made with ½ teaspoon turmeric per cup of raw rice). Serves 4.

TURKEY WITH BROCCOLI

¾ pound of turkey breast
1 teaspoon **Vegetable Powder**
¼ teaspoon pepper
3 cups sprigs of fresh broccoli (2- to 3-inch sprigs)

3 large mushrooms, sliced thin
¼ cup plus 2 tablespoons vermouth
1 tablespoon cornstarch

Remove skin and fat from turkey. Cut turkey into 1-inch cubes and Teflon-brown slightly. In saucepan combine turkey, vegetable powder, pepper, and 1 cup water. Cover and simmer until turkey is done (about 15 minutes). Add broccoli and mushrooms. Stir in a mixture of the vermouth and cornstarch. Continue cooking and stirring until thickened. Serve over brown rice. Serves 4.

TURKEY FRICASSEE

2 cups diced cooked turkey
2 cups **White Sauce**
1 teaspoon onion powder
Dash of garlic powder
Two 4-ounce cans of sliced
   mushrooms, packed in
   water

2 tablespoons **Mushroom
   Wine Stock** (page 75)
(Leftover cooked vegetables
   such as peas, corn, limas)
½ cup **Sour Cream**

Combine all ingredients except sour cream, and heat through. Fold in sour cream, and serve. Serves 4 to 6.

TURKEY-STUFFED CABBAGE ROLLS

1½ cups uncooked brown rice
1 medium head cabbage
2 cups cooked, ground
   turkey
½ cup chopped onion

¼ cup chopped celery
2 cloves garlic, minced
1 teaspoon basil
One 16-ounce can of tomatoes

Combine rice with 3¾ cups water, bring to a boil, cover, and simmer slowly 1 hour. Boil whole head of cabbage 25 minutes. Peal leaves from cabbage and place on a plate. Mix all ingredients except cabbage leaves and tomatoes. Put a large spoonful of this mixture on each leaf, tuck ends in, roll up, and place in a deep casserole dish. Chop leaves that are too small to roll and place them on top of the casserole. Chop tomatoes, and pour tomatoes and juice over all. Bake 50 minutes at 350°. Serves 6.

MEAT DISHES

In the English-language cooking literature, the word *meat* often means red meat only, and thus excludes fish, chicken, and so forth, which are white or brown, but not red. Even more specifically, it often refers only to the flesh of cattle, sheep, and hogs. That is a limited usage indeed. It does not refer to the flesh of fish or fowl, or even elephant; just cattle, sheep, and hogs. On the other hand, there is another common usage of the word *meat* that refers to the flesh of *any* creature in the animal kingdom that may be prepared for the table. Thus we are allowed to say "please pass a slice of white meat" when referring to the Thanksgiving turkey, and no one at the table corrects us for saying "meat" rather than "flesh."

In this book we use the word *meat* in its general sense, to mean the flesh of any creature in the animal kingdom prepared for the table. We call everything meat because the impact on our health from overindulging in meat is the same whether the meat is beef, lamb, tuna, chicken, or mountain lion. Excessive cholesterol and/or fat intake can be caused by eating fish and fowl just as easily as by eating beef and pork. The only difference among the meats is that some have so much cholesterol that they must be avoided altogether whereas others have so much fat that they must be avoided altogether. Thus, as we mentioned in chapter 2, shellfish, organ meat, fatty fowl, and animal skin must be avoided. All meats other than those mentioned in Chapter 2 are on an equal footing, and may be eaten in moderation (less than ¼ pound per person per day).

We have contradicted ourselves in one respect. We have entitled this section "Meat Dishes," even though it contains only "red meat" recipes. We have done this to keep in step with the way dishes are classified in virtually every other cookbook in the cooking literature. It will make it a little easier for the reader who is used to the existing cooking literature to locate recipes in this book.

The recipes in this section are mostly beef recipes. Many of them simply involve the use of leanest-grade hamburger. Some of them, however, call for special cuts: brisket, round steak, lamb leg, etc. Because there are so many kinds of special cuts (over 365 different cuts of "red meat" are in common use, one for every day of the year), it is easy to become confused as to what is what. Adding to the confusion is an overlaying system of grading meats (choice, prime, etc.) that is applied by the Department of Agriculture. The

BEEF CHART

Wholesale Cuts of Beef and Their Bone Structure

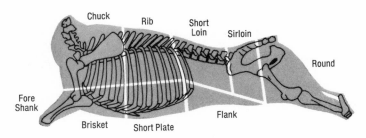

Chuck • Rib • Short Loin • Sirloin • Round • Fore Shank • Brisket • Short Plate • Flank

Retail Cuts of Beef and Where They Come From

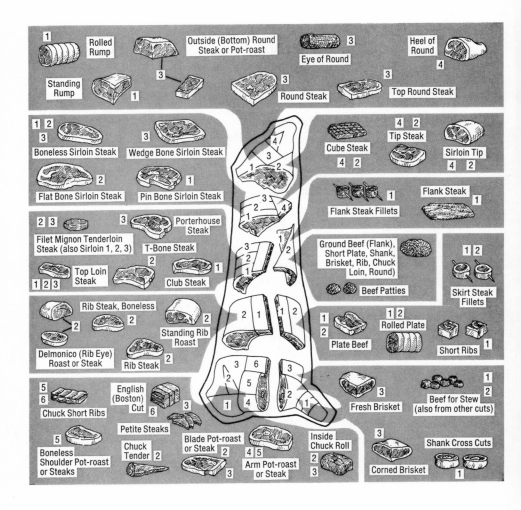

1 Rolled Rump

Outside (Bottom) Round Steak or Pot-roast

3 Eye of Round

Heel of Round 4

Standing Rump 1

3
1 Round Steak 3

3 Top Round Steak

1 2 3 Boneless Sirloin Steak

3 Wedge Bone Sirloin Steak

4 2 Tip Steak

Cube Steak 4 2

Sirloin Tip 4 2

2 Flat Bone Sirloin Steak

1 Pin Bone Sirloin Steak

1 Flank Steak 1

Flank Steak Fillets

2 3 Filet Mignon Tenderloin Steak (also Sirloin 1, 2, 3)

3 Porterhouse Steak

T-Bone Steak 2

Ground Beef (Flank), Short Plate, Shank, Brisket, Rib, Chuck Loin, Round)

1 2 Top Loin Steak 2 3 Club Steak

Beef Patties

1 2 Skirt Steak Fillets

Rib Steak, Boneless 2

2 Standing Rib Roast 2

1 2 Plate Beef

1 2 Rolled Plate

Delmonico (Rib Eye) Roast or Steak 2 Rib Steak

Short Ribs 1

5 6 Chuck Short Ribs

English (Boston) Cut 6

3

3 Fresh Brisket

1 2 Beef for Stew (also from other cuts)

Petite Steaks

5 Boneless Shoulder Pot-roast or Steaks

Chuck Tender 2

Blade Pot-roast or Steak 2

4 5 Arm Pot-roast or Steak 3

Inside Chuck Roll 2 3

3 Corned Brisket

Shank Cross Cuts 1

LAMB CHART

Wholesale Cuts of Lamb and Their Bone Structure

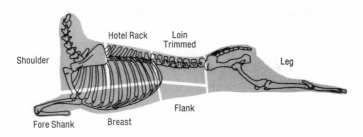

Shoulder · Hotel Rack · Loin Trimmed · Leg · Fore Shank · Breast · Flank

Retail Cuts of Lamb and Where They Come From

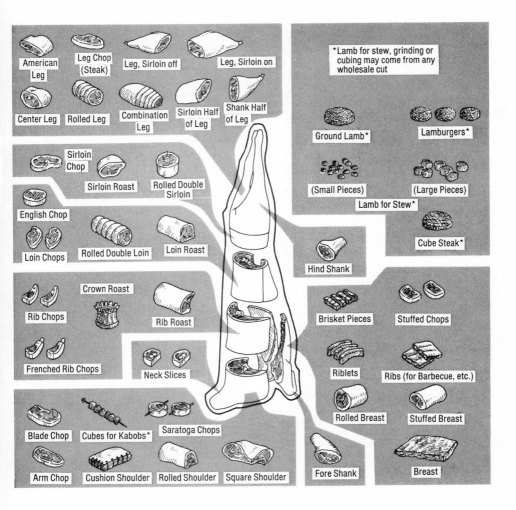

American Leg · Leg Chop (Steak) · Leg, Sirloin off · Leg, Sirloin on

Center Leg · Rolled Leg · Combination Leg · Sirloin Half of Leg · Shank Half of Leg

Sirloin Chop · Sirloin Roast · Rolled Double Sirloin

English Chop · Rolled Double Loin · Loin Roast

Loin Chops

Rib Chops · Crown Roast · Rib Roast

Frenched Rib Chops · Neck Slices

Blade Chop · Cubes for Kabobs* · Saratoga Chops

Arm Chop · Cushion Shoulder · Rolled Shoulder · Square Shoulder

*Lamb for stew, grinding or cubing may come from any wholesale cut

Ground Lamb* · Lamburgers*

(Small Pieces) · (Large Pieces)

Lamb for Stew*

Cube Steak*

Hind Shank

Brisket Pieces · Stuffed Chops

Riblets · Ribs (for Barbecue, etc.)

Rolled Breast · Stuffed Breast

Fore Shank · Breast

fact that terminology is not entirely uniform from place to place only makes matters worse. The words in the next few paragraphs may help to place some order and meaning on the many names and conventions used.

It is safe to say that all of the words, names, and conventions used in describing cuts of meat have only one purpose. That purpose is to provide information on the *quality* of the meat. Theoretically, when one hears a string of words such as *U.S. inspected, choice grade, yield 3, brisket of veal*, one can determine the quality of the meat and can, from this, determine the wisdom of making a purchase. In practice, it does not work out that way. There are too many loopholes in the system between the animal and the average consumer to let it happen. But in theory, that is what it's all about: the judging of quality.

Quality is determined by two things: tenderness and flavor. Tenderness is determined by: the animal's *age* (young animals are tenderer than mature animals), what *part of the body* the meat comes from (nonmoving parts, like the back, are tenderest), and the *amount of fat* in the lean (lean that is well marbled with fat is tenderest). Flavor is mostly determined by the animal's age (mature animals are generally more flavorsome).

Terms that are used to describe age are as follows:

Cattle
      Veal: 3 months or younger
      Calf: 3 to 8 months
      Beef: 8 months or older (usually 15 to 30 months)

Sheep
      Lamb: 12 months or younger
      Mutton: Older than 12 months

Hogs
      Pork: Any age (usually young hogs)

Terms that are used to describe parts of the body are shown in the pictures on the preceding pages. It can be seen that the cuts we recognize for implying tenderness (e.g., loin and sirloin) come from the animal's back.

Terms that describe the amount of fat that runs through the lean are:

Prime grade
Choice grade
Good grade
Standard grade

(Other terms are also used: commercial grade, utility grade, cull grade, cutter, and canner grade. These are used primarily for grading meats used in processed meat items like hot dogs.) These terms apply to veal, calf, beef, lamb, and mutton, but not pork. They are grades that are applied to meat by federal inspectors trained to judge overall meat quality for tenderness and flavor. For meat of similar age and from a similar location on the animal, these terms indicate the amount of fat that is marbled through the lean. Thus "prime" is fattier than "choice," which in turn is fattier than "good," etc.

How interesting it is that the highest meat grade, namely prime grade, has the fattiest lean. What this means is that tenderness, at least that derived from fat marbling, comes with a price. That price is more fat in the diet, and therefore more health problems caused by dietary fat. Thus, to get the ultimate "quality" in tenderness, one has to settle for a lower quality of health.

Because good and standard grades are much lower in fat content than prime or choice, we recommend sticking to them at the market. It is a little harder to successfully dry cook (roast, broil, sauté) these leaner cuts than their fattier counterparts, but they respond very well to slow cooking with moisture: pot roasting, stewing, etc. And while they may not be rendered fork tender quite so easily as the other grades, they are every bit as flavorsome and much more nutritious.

The recipes in this section require very little knowledge on the reader's part regarding cuts of meat and their various merits. Each recipe is self-explanatory and simple.

BEEF IN VEGETABLE SAUCE

½ pound round steak cut in
  strips ½" × 3"
¼ cup carrot juice

¼ cup **Tomato Sauce**
(½ cup **Yogurt**)
3 cups uncooked **noodles**

Brown strips of meat in Teflon pan. Add carrot juice, tomato sauce, and ½ cup water. Cover, simmer mixture until meat is very tender, then add yogurt and heat through. Meanwhile, cook noodles, drain, and arrange on hot platter. Pour meat mixture over top, and serve. Serves 4.

BEEF ROAST

Boneless beef roast (round,
  top round, or sirloin tip)
Freshly ground pepper
Garlic powder

Vegetable Powder
Cheesecloth
(Dry red wine)

Trim all visible fat, then reassemble roast if necessary. Sprinkle seasonings on all exterior meat surfaces, then wrap tightly in wet cheesecloth so that no part of roast has less than three layers of cheesecloth covering. When roast is wrapped, place directly on roasting pan and remoisten cloth with water mixed half-and-half with red wine. Roast in 500° oven for 15 minutes, then reduce heat to 300° and continue roasting, basting frequently with water and wine, until desired degree of doneness is achieved. (Allow 30 minutes per pound for medium doneness, 20 minutes for rare, and 40 minutes for well.) When roasting is completed, remove roast from oven and allow juices to set up for a few minutes. Remove cheesecloth and carve. For cutting thin sandwich slices, meat should be thoroughly chilled. Number of servings varies with size of roast. Remember to take care that each person receives no more than ¼ pound of meat per day.

BEEF AND CABBAGE

¼ pound top round steak
2 medium onions, coarsely chopped
⅓ cup tomato juice (or other vegetable juice)
6 dried juniper berries (find in spice section at supermarket)

¼ teaspoon pepper
⅛ teaspoon cayenne pepper
⅛ teaspoon whole anise seeds
⅛ teaspoon whole caraway seeds
1 medium head cabbage, cut into very thin wedges

Trim all visible fat from steak, and cut into ½-inch squares. Combine onions, tomato juice, and spices, bring to a boil, and add squares of round steak. Cover and simmer 1½ hours. Add cabbage, return to boil, cover, and simmer until meat and cabbage are tender (about 1½ hours more). Add more water if necessary at any time during cooking. Serves 4.

EASY STROGANOFF

3 cups uncooked **noodles** (or other pasta)
½ pound round steak, cut in ½-inch cubes
½ cup chopped onions

½ cup thinly sliced fresh mushrooms
⅓ cup **Beef Stock**
1 tablespoon cornstarch
½ cup **Yogurt**

Cook and drain noodles. Brown steak cubes over high heat in Teflon pan, being careful not to overcook (center of cubes should remain pink or red). In small covered saucepan sauté onions and mushrooms, using ¼ cup water. Remove cover and boil away most of liquid, stirring constantly. Blend stock with the cornstarch, and combine with the steak cubes and sautéed onions and mushrooms. Just before serving, heat this mixture until sauce boils and thickens. Add yogurt, and serve over the hot noodles. Serves 4.

SWISS STEAK

¾ pound top round or
    boneless round steak
1½ cups **Beef Stock**
One 8-ounce can of tomatoes
  1 cup sliced fresh mushrooms

1 medium onion, sliced
⅛ teaspoon sage
⅛ teaspoon pepper
¼ cup flour
3 cups mashed potatoes

Trim all visible fat from meat. Slowly Teflon-brown in a skillet with a tight-fitting lid. Pour over meat 1 cup of the beef stock, the tomatoes, mushrooms, onion, sage, and pepper. Bring to a boil, cover, and simmer 1½ to 2 hours, occasionally checking for adequate liquid and moving and turning meat to prevent sticking. In a small bowl, combine flour with remaining stock. When smooth, stir into Swiss steak mixture, and cook until thickened. Serve over mashed potatoes. Serves 4.

CHILI AND PEPPER STEAK

2 pounds round steak
1 medium green pepper,
    seeded and cut in strips
1 fresh California green chili,
    seeded and cut in strips
1 medium onion, chopped
2 stalks celery, diced

One 4-ounce can of sliced
    mushrooms
1 cup **Tomato Sauce**
1 teaspoon vinegar
½ teaspoon pepper
½ teaspoon garlic powder
3 tablespoons flour

Remove visible fat from steak, and tenderize by pounding if necessary. Brown both sides in Teflon skillet. Add all remaining ingredients except flour. Mix flour with 1 cup water, and add it also. Cover and simmer until meat is tender (about 25 minutes). Serves 10.

MEXICAN PEPPER STEAK

1 thin-sliced sirloin tip steak (about ¾ pound)	¾ cup sliced fresh mushrooms
¼ teaspoon black pepper	1 medium green pepper, chopped
¼ teaspoon garlic powder	1 clove garlic, sliced
½ medium onion, chopped	¼ cup **Green Taco Sauce**

Season steak with black pepper and garlic powder, and broil lightly on one side. Sauté all vegetables (including sliced garlic) in the sauce plus 2 tablespoons water. Turn steak over and heap on some of the vegetable mixture. Broil until done. Cut steak into 4 pieces, and serve each piece on a bed of rice topped with the rest of the vegetable mixture. Serves 4.

BEEF BURGUNDY

1 pound thick-sliced lean top sirloin of beef	½ cup **Beef Stock**
1 clove garlic	½ medium onion, sliced
Pepper	1 cup fresh mushroom slices
¾ cup dry red wine	1 tablespoon flour
	1 tablespoon cornstarch

Trim all visible fat from beef. Cut garlic in half and rub garlic well into meat. Sprinkle meat on both sides with pepper. Broil very close to heat to just barely brown, and set aside. Place wine, stock, onion, and mushrooms in pot. Slice and add the garlic halves. Bring to boil, cover, and simmer until onions and mushrooms are tender. Teflon-fry the flour until medium brown, shaking pan to prevent burning or sticking. Combine browned flour, cornstarch, and ¼ cup cold water. Add to pot, stir, and cook, uncovered, until clear and thickened. Slice beef diagonally, making slices thin and as large as possible. Pour sauce over top. Keep warm until ready to serve. Serves 6.

GREEN PEPPER STEAK

¾ pound thick-sliced top sirloin
1 cup chopped onion
1 clove of garlic, sliced
¼ teaspoon pepper

1 cup diced green pepper
¾ cup **Beef Stock**
One 8-ounce can of tomatoes
Flesh of one tamarind pod
1 tablespoon cornstarch

Trim all visible fat from steak. Slice into thin strips and Teflon-fry. Add all other ingredients except cornstarch. Cook until vegetables are tender. Remove tarmarind (may be reused). Mix the cornstarch with 2 tablespoons water, and stir into the pan with the other ingredients. Cook and stir until thickened. Serve over mashed potatoes. Serves 4.

TIP KABOBS

Tip Kabobs offer a real change of pace for dinnertime. Family and friends can make and cook their own and enjoy being together while they cook. Small children love them, and will ask again and again for another tip kabob dinner. They're terrific at dinner parties, offering guests an ideal opportunity to talk and get acquainted as they prepare and cook their own. Best of all, tip kabob ingredients can be made up in advance and simply set out at dinnertime. Use 1 pound of meat for each 6 people and marinate the meat in either marinade (not both) as instructed below. Skewer meat and other skewering ingredients, closely packed, on bamboo skewers

that have been soaked 24 hours in water to prevent their burning.
Broil on broiling rack or over hibachi.

MEAT:

Lean sirloin tip steak, cut into 1-inch cubes

WINE AND GARLIC MARINADE:

Use these amounts for each pound of meat, and marinate meat 3
to 6 hours.

2 cups dry white wine	2 cloves garlic, chopped fine
¼ cup vinegar (preferably champagne vinegar)	1 teaspoon garlic powder
	2 teaspoons onion powder
2 teaspoons lemon juice	¼ teaspoon pepper

VEGETABLE MARINADE:

Use these amounts for each pound of meat, and marinate meat
24 hours in refrigerator.

2 tablespoons lemon juice	2 teaspoons parsley flakes
1 cup vegetable juice	½ teaspoon whole celery seed
¼ cup cider vinegar	¼ teaspoon pepper
2 tablespoons vegetable flakes	

SKEWERING INGREDIENTS:

Place these items (or other tasty substitutions) in separate bowls,
for skewering.

Peeled and parboiled boiling onions	Eggplant cut in 1-inch cubes and marinated in vegetable marinade above
Green peppers cut in 1-inch squares	Chunks of fresh pineapple
Cherry tomatoes	(And, of course, marinated meat cubes)
Fresh mushroom caps	

EASY ORIENTAL DINNER

½ pound lean sirloin tip steak, trimmed of fat and cut in ribbons

1 package frozen Stir-Fry or Oriental-style vegetables (discard sauce packet)

1 tablespoon white vinegar

2 tablespoons **Mushroom Wine Stock**

2 tablespoons orange juice

2 tablespoons clear apple juice

1 tablespoon cornstarch

¼ teaspoon onion powder

Pinch of white pepper

3 cups cooked brown rice

In large Teflon skillet, brown meat and heat vegetables over high heat, stirring constantly with wooden spoon. Vegetables should be just barely tender, still slightly crisp. Combine vinegar, wine stock, juices, cornstarch, onion powder, and white pepper in small saucepan. Stir in ¾ cup of water and cook until thickened, stirring constantly. Add thickened sauce to meat and vegetables, and serve over rice. Serves 4.

BEEF ON RICE

2 pounds beef chuck

2 cups skim milk

2 tablespoons vegetable juice

½ cup orange juice

2 large onions, sliced

1 tablespoon grated orange rind

1 bay leaf, crushed

½ teaspoon pepper

½ teaspoon ginger

¼ teaspoon allspice

6 cups cooked rice

Trim all visible fat from beef. Cut into 1½-inch cubes and marinate 6 hours in milk. Brown beef in a large skillet, using the vegetable juice for cooking liquid. Place beef in saucepan. Sauté onions in same skillet, then add to the beef. Add all other ingredients except rice and simmer, covered, until beef is tender (1½ to 2 hours). Serve over rice. Serves 8 to 12.

BAG STEAK

1 pound flank steak
1 cup malt vinegar
1 cup cider vinegar

1 clove garlic, finely chopped
Pinch of pepper

Slice steak diagonally into very thin strips. Roll each strip and fasten closed by impaling with a toothpick. Combine all ingredients in a plastic bag, cinch up bag so that steak is fully covered by liquid, tie tightly, and let sit one hour. Remove steak and barbecue close to coals or under the broiler 3 minutes on each side, brushing with marinade. Serves 6.

CURRIED HAMBURGER

¾ pound leanest ground beef
1 teaspoon curry powder
⅓ cup chopped onion

Pepper
1 egg white
⅓ cup **Yogurt**

Brown beef in Teflon skillet. Remove beef. Brown curry powder in drippings. Add ¼ cup boiling water to residue in skillet, stir, and bring to a boil. Pour into a small jar, cool, and let fat rise to top. Remove fat. Pour remaining liquid into a saucepan, add onion and pepper, and cook until onion is tender. Add beef and heat through. In a bowl, beat egg white to soft peaks and blend in yogurt. Blend a small amount of meat and onion mixture into egg and yogurt mixture, then transfer all of egg and yogurt mixture to the saucepan. Stir and cook very slowly for 5 minutes. Serve over a generous helping of brown rice. Serves 4.

BRISKET AU JUS

3 pounds leanest beef
   brisket

1 teaspoon garlic juice
1½ cups **Onion Soup**

Remove and discard all visible fat from brisket. Rub garlic juice into surface of meat. Place brisket in roasting pan and pour soup over top. Cover tightly and bake 2 hours at 350°, checking occasionally for dryness. Add ¾ cup water if meat appears dry. Slice thinly across grain, and serve on warm platter with own juice. Serves 12.

HAMBURGER-CORN SKILLET DINNER

¾ pound leanest ground beef
1 cup soft bread crumbs
½ teaspoon pepper
One 10-ounce package of
   frozen whole-kernel corn

1 small onion, sliced
One 16-ounce can of tomatoes

Mix meat, crumbs, and pepper, and cook in skillet until meat is well browned. Drain fat. Add corn, onions, and tomatoes, cover, and simmer 25 minutes. Serves 4.

HAMBURGER-MACARONI SKILLET DINNER

1 pound leanest ground
   beef, broken up
1 medium onion, chopped
   fine
1 medium green pepper,
   minced

2 cups uncooked elbow
   macaroni
1½ cups **Lemon Mock Sour
   Cream**
One 16-ounce can of tomatoes
1 tablespoon chili powder

Combine ground beef, onion, and green pepper with 2 tablespoons water in skillet. Cover and cook 10 minutes over medium heat. Add remaining ingredients and bring to a boil. Reduce heat, cover, and simmer until meat and macaroni are done (about 30 minutes). Mix well. Serves 6.

HAMBURGER-ZUCCHINI SKILLET DINNER

¾ pound leanest ground beef
One 4-ounce can of
   mushrooms
2 teaspoons **Hot Sauce**
1 teaspoon onion powder

1 teaspoon garlic powder
2 medium zucchini, sliced
   in ¼-inch slices
1½ cups canned tomatoes
1 tablespoon vinegar

Place meat and mushrooms in skillet. Using fork to break up meat while it cooks, brown meat. Drain off rendered fat. Add hot sauce, onion powder, and garlic powder. Layer zucchini slices over meat, and pour tomatoes and vinegar over all. Cover and simmer 30 minutes. Serves 4.

BEEF AND TOMATO LOAF

1 pound leanest ground beef
1½ cups soft bread crumbs
1 small onion, chopped
1 small green pepper,
   chopped
½ cup skim milk

2 egg whites
1 teaspoon horseradish
½ teaspoon pepper
One 16-ounce can of tomatoes,
   chopped into quarters

Mix together all ingredients except tomatoes. Gently stir in tomatoes. Pack in loaf pan and bake 1½ hours at 300°. Drain off any rendered fat. Serves 6.

BAHIA RICE BED

2 cups uncooked rice
1 pound leanest ground beef, crumbled into small pieces
1 cup chopped onion
1 cup chopped green pepper
1 cup chopped celery
1 cup **Beef Stock** or water
1 teaspoon curry powder
1 canned California green chili, diced

Place rice in saucepan with 5 cups water, bring to boil, cover, and simmer 1 hour. Meanwhile, cook beef 15 minutes in large skillet over moderate heat. Drain and discard rendered fat. Add onion, pepper, and celery, and cook and stir 5 minutes. Add stock, curry powder, and green chili, cover, and simmer 30 minutes. Make a large bed of rice on each individual's plate, and fill center with meat and vegetable mixture. Serves 6.

MOUSSAKA
(Eggplant and ground beef is a Greek specialty)

1 large eggplant
½ pound leanest ground beef
1 medium onion, chopped
1 clove garlic, minced
1 cup **Tomato Sauce**
¼ cup dry red wine
2 tablespoons parsley flakes
½ teaspoon cinnamon
½ teaspoon nutmeg
1 egg white
1 tablespoon flour

Slice eggplant crosswise in pieces ½-inch thick. Lay on large, shallow, Teflon baking pan and bake at 435° until slightly browned. Turn slices to brown on both sides. Remove eggplant from oven, and reduce setting to 350°. Brown beef in a skillet. Add onion and garlic and continue cooking and stirring over moderate flame, until onion is tender. Add tomato sauce, red wine, parsley flakes, cinnamon, and nutmeg, and simmer 5 minutes. Add a mixture of the eggwhite, the flour, and 2 tablespoons water, and continue simmering and stirring until the contents thicken evenly. Layer contents evenly over eggplant slices closely crowded in baking dish, and bake until top is slightly browned and casserole looks a little dry at edges (about 30 minutes). Serves 4.

ITALIAN MEATBALLS

⅔ cup **Beef Stock**
1 clove garlic, finely chopped
1 bay leaf
10 seeds from mild red chilies (see page 263)
1 teaspoon lemon rind
⅛ teaspoon pepper
1 teaspoon parsley flakes

Dash of oregano
½ cup fresh bread cubes
2 slightly beaten egg whites
2 tablespoons skim milk
1 pouch PLUS-meat
½ pound leanest ground beef
1 tablespoon vermouth

Bring beef stock to boil in Teflon skillet. Add garlic and spices and simmer a few minutes. Remove bay leaf (may be reused). Pour into a bowl containing the bread crumbs, egg whites, and skim milk. Mash bread thoroughly. Add Plus-Meat, stir, and let stand 5 minutes. Add ground beef, stir, work with hands, then shape into 1-inch balls. Moisten residue in skillet with the vermouth and 1 tablespoon water. Heat to boiling. Teflon-fry meatballs in this skillet, a few at a time, shaking skillet with a circular motion to gently roll meatballs and brown on all surfaces. Bake 20 minutes at 300°. Makes about 25 meatballs.

SNOW PEAS AND BEEF

1 cup cooked, drained leanest ground beef
2 cups snow peas (about 50 pods)
1½ cups sliced mushrooms

¼ cup vermouth
4 teaspoons cornstarch
3 cups hot, freshly cooked rice

Place beef, peas, mushrooms, and vermouth in a Teflon pan. Add cornstarch blended with ½ cup water, and cook over medium heat, stirring constantly until thickened. Pour over rice and serve. Serves 4.

SCALLOPED POTATOES AND BEEF

3 medium potatoes
¼ pound leanest ground beef
2 tablespoons potato flour
½ cup evaporated skim milk
½ teaspoon **Vegetable Powder**
⅛ teaspoon pepper
1 tablespoon parsley flakes
¼ cup vermouth
¼ cup **Chicken Stock**
1 medium onion, sliced
¾ cup grated **Fresh Cheese**

Peel, slice, and partially cook potatoes. Brown beef and drain off fat. Combine flour and evaporated skim milk, then add vegetable powder, pepper, parsley flakes, vermouth, and chicken stock, and stir. Add onion, potatoes, and ground beef, and place in casserole dish. Top with cheese and bake 1 hour at 350°. Serves 4.

EVERYDAY MEAT LOAF

1 pound leanest ground beef
1 cup **Tomato Sauce**
3 egg whites
½ cup pearl barley
2 tablespoons parsley flakes
½ teaspoon garlic juice
½ teaspoon dill seed
¼ teaspoon pepper
¼ teaspoon oregano
¼ teaspoon rosemary
¼ teaspoon thyme
¼ teaspoon basil
¼ teaspoon celery seed
¼ teaspoon Herb Seasoning
¼ teaspoon dry mustard

Combine all ingredients, shape into a loaf, and bake 1 hour at 350°. Serves 6.

POTATO-FROSTED MEAT LOAF

1 pound leanest ground beef
1 small onion, chopped fine
½ cup minced celery
1 egg white
1 teaspoon basil
½ teaspoon garlic flakes
¼ teaspoon thyme
¼ teaspoon marjoram
¼ teaspoon pepper
4 slices fresh bread
3 cups fresh hot mashed potatoes

Mix all meat loaf ingredients together in loaf pan, except bread and mashed potatoes. Dip bread slices in fresh skim milk, squeeze out over the meat loaf mixture, tear into tiny pieces, and add to mixture. Bake 1¼ hours at 350°. Pour off rendered fat and place loaf on warm platter. Cover top and sides with fresh, hot mashed potatoes. Serves 6.

NADA'S BEEF CABBAGE ROLLS

A simple substitution in **Nada's Vegetarian Cabbage Rolls** (see page 181) makes the dish into a delicious, meaty-flavored beef dish. In place of the called-for 2 cups of beans, substitute 1 pound of leanest ground beef. Otherwise, follow the directions exactly. Serves 8.

STOVE-TOP STUFFED PEPPERS

6 large green peppers
1 cup tomato juice
2 cups cooked brown rice
½ pound leanest ground beef
2 egg whites, beaten
½ teaspoon celery seed
¼ teaspoon fresh ground pepper

Cut tops off peppers and remove seeds and ribbing. Mix ⅓ of the tomato juice with the remaining ingredients, and stuff peppers with this mixture. Stand peppers up in a saucepan and pour remaining tomato juice over top. Cover tightly and simmer until peppers are tender (45 minutes to 1 hour), adding liquid if necessary to prevent scorching. Serves 6.

CHILI-BEAN-AND-BEEF STUFFED PEPPERS

5 medium green peppers
3 ounces raw leanest ground beef
2 cups cooked kidney beans
3 cups cooked rice
1 cup whole-kernel corn
2 teaspoons chili powder
1 tablespoon **Chili Salsa**
1 cup **Tomato Sauce**

Wash peppers, cut tops off, and remove and discard seeds and pulp. Place in pot with cold water to cover, bring to boil, reduce heat, and simmer 5 minutes. Drain. Mix together beef, kidney beans, rice, corn, and chili powder. Fill peppers with mixture, crowd into small baking dish, and top with a mixture of chili salsa and tomato sauce. Cover, and bake 45 minutes at 350°. Uncover, and bake 15 minutes more. Serves 5.

STUFFED CABBAGE WITH APPLE JUICE

1 large head cabbage
1 pound leanest ground beef
1 cup uncooked brown rice
¼ teaspoon pepper
½ cup frozen apple juice concentrate
½ cup lemon juice
One 28-ounce can of tomatoes, chopped

Place whole cabbage in large pot, add 1 cup water, cover tightly, and steam until leaves can be separated (about 20 minutes). Separate and remove leaves one at a time, cut off tough part at bottom of leaf, and pile leaves on a plate. Chop the inside leaves that will be too small to stuff, and layer chopped portion over bottom of shallow baking dish. Mix together the ground beef, rice, and pepper. Place a large spoonful of this mixture onto each leaf, tuck ends in, roll up, and place in baking dish. Pour apple juice, lemon juice, and tomatoes (with their liquid) over top. Cover and bake 30 minutes at 325°. Uncover and bake 20 minutes more. Serves 6 to 8.

SLOPPY JOES IN PITA BREAD

1 medium green pepper	½ teaspoon cumin
1 pound leanest ground beef, broken up	⅛ teaspoon freshly ground pepper
1 tablespoon onion flakes	4 **Pitas**
1 cup **Tomato Sauce**	

Cut half the green pepper into rings, and put aside to use as a garnish. Mince remaining green pepper, and sauté with ground beef and onion flakes in 1 tablespoon water until beef is lightly brown and green pepper is tender. Drain fat. Add tomato sauce and spices, and cook until well heated (about 6 minutes). Cut pita rounds in half, open pockets in halves, and spoon in mixture. Serve Sloppy Joes on a platter, garnished with green pepper rings. Makes 8 Sloppy Joes.

ROAST LEG OF LAMB

Because of its high fat content, lamb is normally to be avoided. Leg of lamb, however, is usually as low or lower in fat than most cuts of beef. Choose "ungraded" or "good" grades rather than "choice" or "prime," because of their low fat content. Roast lamb fixed this way is delicious, and a welcome change of pace.

2-to-3-pound leg of lamb,
  preferably with a short
  shank
½ teaspoon onion powder
1½ tablespoons parsley flakes
  1 tablespoon mint flakes

½ teaspoon basil
½ teaspoon chervil
½ teaspoon dried rosemary
⅛ teaspoon fresh ground
  pepper
2 tablespoons vermouth

Remove all visible fat, then reassemble roast. Bone may be left in. Crumble together dried herbs and seasonings, and moisten with vermouth. If time permits, allow mixture to blend for a few minutes. Preheat oven to 550°. Massage lamb roast with seasoning mixture (it will be messy and pasty), working seasonings into all meat surfaces. Moisten and wring out a single layer of cheesecloth approximately 2′ × 3′, and wrap it around the roast. All roast surfaces should have two or three layers of cheesecloth covering when this has been done. Roast in large roasting pan, turning oven down to 325° when roast is put in. Baste with water or a half-and-half mixture of water and vermouth. Cheesecloth should remain moist at all times. Use bulb baster to baste roast with its own drippings, tipping pan and placing end of baster at bottom of liquid to avoid getting any fat that may have drained off roast. Allow 25 to 30 minutes per pound. Remove, discard cheesecloth, and serve.

LAMB CURRY

2 cups cubes of cooked lamb

CURRY SAUCE:
1 medium onion, chopped
1 medium green pepper,
  chopped
¾ cup chopped celery
1 clove garlic, chopped

2 tablespoons cornstarch
2 teaspoons curry powder
¼ cup **Sweet Lamb Stock**
1¾ cups skim milk

BEDDING:
3 cups cooked brown rice

RELISHES AND TOPPINGS:
½ cup **Ginger-Marinated**　　½ cup apple slices
Parsnips (page 69)　　　　½ cup pear cubes
½ cup chopped green onion　1½ cups **Sour Cream**
½ cup chopped, hard-
cooked egg whites

Make lamb cubes from leftover **Roast Leg of Lamb** (p. 247). (Remember to avoid cuts of lamb other than leg of lamb, because of their high fat content.) *To make curry sauce:* Cook chopped onion, green pepper, celery, and garlic in ½ cup water, covered, until tender. Mix together cornstarch, curry powder, and cold lamb stock, and stir until smooth. Add milk a little at a time, keeping mixture smooth. Combine with cooked vegetables and heat. Curry sauce is complete when mixture thickens. *To serve:* Add lamb to curry sauce, heat through, and serve over hot brown rice. Pass relishes and toppings in separate bowls, to sprinkle over top. Delete relishes or add others as desired. Serves 6.

CHAPTER 7

Sauces

For many recipes, it is the sauce that makes the dish. Some sauces are so delicious and versatile that they seem to work magic with everything they dress. Try these sauces as directed, and enjoy their impact on the dishes they accompany.

VERSATILITY SAUCE

This delicious sauce can really "make" a dish. Use it on **Green Bean Casserole** or over any pasta. Goes well on meats and other dishes too.

1 medium green pepper, chopped fine	2 tablespoons whole wheat flour
1 medium onion, chopped fine	1½ cups tomato juice
1 stalk celery, diced	½ teaspoon oregano flakes
1 clove garlic, minced	½ teaspoon basil

Sauté green pepper, onion, celery, and garlic in 2 tablespoons water, until tender (about 5 minutes). Sprinkle flour evenly over top, add tomato juice, oregano, and basil, and cook and stir over medium heat until sauce thickens. Makes 2 cups.

MEDITERRANEAN SAUCE

1 medium onion, chopped
1 medium green pepper, chopped
1 medium tomato, chopped
1 clove garlic, minced
1½ cups tomato juice

1 tablespoon paprika
1 teaspoon oregano
½ teaspoon cumin
Pinch of saffron
(Pepper)

Combine all ingredients, bring to a boil, and simmer 1 hour. Makes 2 cups.

RICHER MEDITERRANEAN SAUCE

In **Mediterranean Sauce,** above, substitute one 15-ounce can of tomatoes and one 6-ounce can of tomato paste for the tomato and tomato juice. Combine all ingredients, bring to a boil, and simmer 1 hour. Add water if necessary to prevent sticking. Makes 2 cups.

MRS. MARSCH'S SAUCE FOR SQUID

One 15-ounce can of tomatoes, cut up
¼ cup dry white wine
½ whole California green chili, canned
1 clove garlic, diced

2 tablespoons parsley flakes
2 tablespoons toasted onions
6 needles of rosemary
¼ teaspoon basil
⅛ teaspoon oregano
Pinch of cayenne pepper

Combine all ingredients and boil until odor of wine is largely dissipated. Cover and simmer 10 minutes. Makes 2 cups. Delicious with squid. (See **Mrs. Marsch's Squid.**)

STEAK SAUCE

10 tamarind pods, shelled
1 teaspoon vinegar
1 mushroom, sliced thin or chopped
2 tablespoons finely chopped onion
1 tablespoon tomato paste
1 tablespoon **Vegetable Powder**

1 teaspoon lemon juice
⅛ teaspoon curry powder
2 dashes of Angostura Bitters
⅛ teaspoon garlic powder
Dash of black pepper
Pinch of Cayenne pepper (not too much)
Pinch of turmeric

Bring tamarinds, vinegar, and 1¼ cups water to a boil. Cover and simmer 10 minutes. Remove tamarind seeds. Add remaining ingredients and simmer 10 minutes more. When cool, puree in blender. Keep in refrigerator or freeze in ice cube tray. Use on hamburgers and steaks. Makes 2 cups.

HAMBURGER SAUCE

¼ cup tomato paste
2 tablespoons cider vinegar
1 tablespoon apple juice
⅛ teaspoon garlic powder
½ teaspoon **Vegetable Powder**

¼ teaspoon onion powder
Generous pinch of turmeric
½ teaspoon mild paprika
¼ teaspoon tarragon
¼ teaspoon basil

Combine ingredients with 2 tablespoons water, and heat gently to combine flavors. Store in refrigerator until needed. Serve on hamburgers, meat loaf, or wherever catsup is normally used. Makes ½ cup.

MUSHROOM SAUCE

Simple as can be, this sauce is terrific as a base for tuna and other casseroles. Use also in **Stuffed Chicken Supreme.**

½ cup sliced fresh mushrooms
1 tablespoon garlic juice

2 tablespoons water
2 cups **White Sauce**

Sauté mushrooms in garlic juice and water. Combine with white sauce and heat. Makes 2¼ cups.

CHEESE SAUCE

1 cup **White Sauce**
¾ cup **Buttermilk Mock Sour Cream**
½ cup grated **Fresh Cheese**
(2 tablespoons Echtarharkäse cheese)

¼ cup dry vermouth (omit if white sauce contains vermouth)

To white sauce, add sour cream and cheeses. Cook slowly, stirring constantly until cheeses have melted and sauce is smooth. Add vermouth, stirring rapidly. Makes 2½ cups. Use promptly.

FRESH CHEESE SAUCE

1 cup grated **Fresh Cheese**
½ cup **Cottage Cheese**
½ cup skim milk

Combine ingredients in blender, and blend until very smooth. Makes 1¼ cups.

CURRIED PEA SAUCE

One 10-ounce package of
  frozen peas
1 cup skim milk
2 tablespoons chopped
  pimiento

1 tablespoon cornstarch
1 teaspoon curry powder

Place peas in saucepan, add ½ cup water, cover, and cook over medium heat until tender (5 to 8 minutes). Add milk and pimiento, and heat to just below boiling. Make paste of cornstarch, curry powder, and 2 tablespoons of water. Stir into peas and cook over low heat until thickened. Makes 2½ cups. Serve with **Briny Deep Salmon Loaf, Salmon-Stuffed Fish Filet Rolls,** or any other fish or chicken entree needing a sauce.

MISO

1¾ cups cooked and drained garbanzo beans
  2 tablespoons vinegar
  2 tablespoons beer

Combine ingredients in blender and puree. Store in the refrigerator, and use as a spice for soups. (See **Red Lentil Soup.**) Makes 2 cups.

BEAN-THICKENED GRAVY

1 cup dried black beans   3½ cups **Beef Stock**

Pick over and rinse beans. Cook beans in stock by either method below. Let beans cool enough to handle, then blend until fairly smooth in blender. Makes 1 quart.

Slow cooking method: Combine beans and stock and let sit overnight in refrigerator. Cover and cook until beans are tender (1 to 2 hours).

Pressure-cooking method: Combine beans and stock in pressure cooker and cook 35 minutes after regulator begins to rock, adjusting heat to maintain gently rocking action.

Storage: Freeze gravy in ice cube tray. Use cubes as needed.

Use: To add flavor, color, and texture to gravies, soups, stews, and casseroles.

TUNA MUSHROOM SAUCE

½ cup sliced fresh mushrooms
1 tablespoon vermouth
One 7-ounce can of tuna, undrained

1 cup **White Sauce**
½ teaspoon powdered mushroom
White pepper

Sauté mushrooms in vermouth and 1 tablespoon water. Combine all ingredients in saucepan and cook and stir to blend and thicken. Makes 2 cups.

SPAGHETTI SAUCE #1

Two 28-ounce cans of tomatoes
2 cups **Tomato Sauce**
1 large onion, chopped
½ cup dry burgundy wine
1 tablespoon grated green cheese

1½ tablespoons oregano flakes
1 teaspoon garlic powder
1 teaspoon basil

Blend tomatoes in blender, place in a saucepan, and cook and stir over high flame until cooked down to a thick consistency (about 45 minutes). Prepare and add remaining ingredients while tomatoes are cooking. Makes 2½ quarts.

SPAGHETTI SAUCE #2

One 28-ounce can of Italian plum tomatoes, finely chopped
1 clove garlic, finely minced
1 teaspoon oregano
1 teaspoon parsley flakes

Combine ingredients in saucepan and cook rapidly, uncovered, stirring occasionally, until thickened (about 15 minutes). If sauce becomes too thick, add ¼ cup water. Makes 3½ cups.

SPAGHETTI SAUCE #3

One 16-ounce can of tomatoes
One 6-ounce can of tomato paste
One 4-ounce can of mushrooms
1 clove garlic, sliced
4 tablespoons onion flakes
1 bay leaf
½ teaspoon basil
¼ teaspoon oregano
¼ teaspoon pepper
(2 ounces leanest ground beef)

Combine all ingredients (except ground beef) in a saucepan. Add 1½ cups water, and simmer 1 hour, removing bay leaf after 20 minutes. (Brown, drain, and add ground beef. Simmer 15 minutes more.) Makes 1 quart.

SPAGHETTI SAUCE #4

One 28-ounce can of Italian plum tomatoes
1 medium onion, finely chopped

1 clove garlic, finely minced ½ teaspoon basil
1 teaspoon parsley flakes ¼ teaspoon thyme

Bring ½ cup water to boil in skillet. Add onion and garlic and cook over moderate flame until tender (3 to 5 minutes). Add remaining ingredients and simmer slowly 20 minutes. Makes 1 quart.

SPAGHETTI SAUCE #5

¼ pound fresh mushrooms, sliced
1 large onion, chopped
3 tablespoons chopped green pepper
2 cups **Tomato Sauce**
Two 6-ounce cans of tomato paste
2 cloves garlic, minced
1 bay leaf
1 teaspoon pepper
½ teaspoon oregano

Sauté mushrooms, onions, and green pepper in ¼ cup water until tender (2 to 5 minutes). Add remaining ingredients and simmer 20 minutes. Remove bay leaf. Makes 1 quart.

SPAGHETTI SAUCE #6

Three 28-ounce cans of tomatoes, packed in puree
2 cups chopped fresh mushrooms
2 medium onions, chopped
1 medium green pepper, chopped
1 stalk celery, chopped
1 tablespoon garlic flakes
1 tablespoon parsley flakes
1 tablespoon oregano flakes
1 teaspoon pepper
1 teaspoon basil
1 teaspoon dried thyme leaves

Chop tomatoes briefly in blender. Combine all ingredients in a large saucepan, add ¼ cup water, cover, and simmer slowly 2 hours. Makes 3 quarts.

FLOUR WHITE SAUCE

This white sauce contains no butter. Therefore, it will lack the buttery taste typical of other flour-based white sauces. For this reason it won't stand alone as well as other white sauces. But it makes a very serviceable base for creamed vegetables and other recipes calling for a white sauce.

2 tablespoons flour	1 cup skim milk
2 tablespoons nonfat dry milk	(Dash of white pepper)
1 tablespoon cornstarch	(Dash of garlic powder)

In saucepan, combine flour, dry milk, and cornstarch with ¼ cup of the skim milk. When smooth, add remaining milk and mix well. Season and cook over moderate heat, stirring constantly. At first sign of thickening, reduce heat to very low, and continue stirring and cooking until sauce has thickened. Makes about 1¼ cups.

POTATO WHITE SAUCE

4 teaspoons potato flour	Onion powder
1 cup skim milk	White pepper
Dill weed	

Combine potato flour and milk. Cook until thickened, stirring constantly. Add seasonings to taste and heat through to blend flavors. Texture is like very thin, well-cooked mashed potatoes. Taste is bland potato. Use as a base for soups or casseroles. Makes 1 cup.

ARROWROOT WHITE SAUCE

This is a completely versatile white sauce; delicious and so easy to make.

1 cup skim milk   Dash of white pepper
1 tablespoon arrowroot flour   ½ tablespoon vermouth

Scald ¾ cup of the milk. Mix arrowroot flour and the rest of the milk in a separate container. Add to the scalded milk and cook over low-to-medium heat for about a minute, until almost properly thickened. Add pepper and vermouth and cool till completely thickened and vermouth odor is largely dissipated. Makes 1 cup.

RICE WHITE SAUCE

2 tablespoons rice flour   Onion powder
1¼ cups skim milk   **Vegetable Powder**

Combine rice flour and milk. Cook until thickened, stirring constantly. Season to taste with onion powder and vegetable powder and cook a few minutes more. Texture is very similar to butter and flour white sauce, but taste resembles a bland cooked rice cereal. Use as a base for soups or casseroles. Makes 1¼ cups.

COMPROMISE WHITE SAUCE

This white sauce is a compromise. It contains a tablespoon of butter. We have included it because, while it does contain fat (butter is nearly 100-percent fat), it matches in taste and texture the white sauces that are commonly used. However, 1 cup of this white sauce carries with it over 130 calories in fat. One would be well advised not to consume more than ½ cup daily.

1 tablespoon butter   Dash of white pepper
1 cup skim milk   ½ tablespoon vermouth
2 tablespoons flour

Combine butter and 1 tablespoon of the skim milk in a small sauce-pan. Heat and mix until butter melts and is evenly mixed with milk. Remove from heat, add flour, and mix. Begin cooking over low heat. Add small amounts of the remaining milk while cooking and stirring constantly. Use all milk. Cook slowly until thickening is nearly complete. Add pepper and vermouth and cook until fully thickened and vermouth has been cooked off (when the strongest part of the vermouth odor has vanished). Makes 1 cup.

The following four fruit sauces are delicious poured over skinned, broiled chicken breasts.

PINEAPPLE SAUCE

One 8-ounce can of crushed, unsweetened pineapple, with juice	1 tablespoon prepared mustard 2 tablespoons lemon juice

Combine in saucepan and cook and stir over low heat 5 to 7 minutes. Makes 1 cup.

ORANGE-BANANA SAUCE

4 underripe medium bananas, sliced	½ cup orange juice 1 tablespoon orange rind

Combine bananas, half of the orange juice, and the orange rind in a saucepan. Heat, stir, and add as much of the remaining orange juice as necessary to achieve desired thickness. Makes 1 cup.

SPICED APPLE AND ORANGE SAUCE

4 large, tart apples, peeled,   ⅛ teaspoon ground cloves
  cored, and cut into eighths
2 large oranges, peeled,
  sectioned, and seeded

Combine ingredients in saucepan with ½ cup water. Simmer 10 minutes. Makes 2 cups.

PEACHY TOPPING FOR CHICKEN

2 cups canned water-packed   1 teaspoon onion flakes
  unsweetened peaches, with   ¼ teaspoon paprika
  liquid   Dash of garlic flakes
¼ cup orange juice

Combine ingredients in blender and blend. Pour into saucepan and simmer 5 to 10 minutes. Makes 2 cups.

ABOUT CHILIES

Valued for their hot, delicious, spicy flavors, those marvelous plants we call chilies come in all sizes, colors, and degrees of hotness, and are called by a variety of names besides chilies. They are also called chili peppers, chile peppers, chilli peppers, chiles, or chillis. The most familiar chilies are the bell peppers and pimientos. That comes as a surprise to most of us, who don't even realize that bell peppers and pimientos are related, much less that they are both chilies.

Peppercorns, which are ground to make ordinary black (or white) pepper, are not part of the chili family. But cayenne pepper (red pepper) does come from the chili family. It is simply a blend of red chilies, dried and ground. Chili powder is also a mixture of chilies that have been dried and ground, often with spices like oregano and cumin added.

Chilies range in size from pea-sized to a foot long. Hotness varies from quite mild to quite painful (little chilies usually being hotter than large ones). Chili colorations depend not only on the chili's genes, but also on its age and whether it is fresh or dried. Immature chilies may be green, yellow, or white. As they mature they tend to darken into oranges, reds, or browns. Dried chilies are almost always a deep hue of red, orange, or brown.

The hot part of the chili is its seeds. The flesh and skin of the chili are normally mild. In making chili-based sauces, degree of hotness is determined by the quantity of seeds the sauce contains. The hotness of seeds varies greatly between different kinds of plant, and can even vary greatly between two chilies off the same vine. Therefore the only way to control hotness is to add seeds a few at a time while making the sauce, and taste for hotness as they are added.

Most of the chili-based recipes in this chapter call for fresh chilies. Fresh chilies may not be universally available, however. Often canned chilies, or fresh or canned chilies of another variety may be substituted with good results.

California Green Chilies: These chilies are usually mild and sweet. They average about 6 inches long, have a carrotlike shape, and are shiny green when fresh. They are widely available canned. We have seen them labeled and referred to as green chiles, diced chiles, and whole chiles. They are often referred to by the brand name Ortega Chilis. In this cookbook they are always referred to by their correct name, California green chilies. Outside this chapter, recipes usually call for them canned rather than fresh. In this chapter, we will have use for them primarily in their fresh form.

Jalapeño Chilies: These are the hot ones. Use them carefully; they can be painful as well as delicious. They are dark green, 2 or 3 inches long, and available canned (and in some places fresh), often under the name of hot peppers.

Yellow Chilies: A number of chilies are yellow, and they're all often referred to as simply yellow chilies. Commonly sold yellow chilies are: yellow wax, Armenian wax, caribe, and cascabel. They vary in size from 2 to 8 inches in length, and they can vary in hotness from mild to quite hot.

Mild Red Chilies: There are many mild red chilies available. Ancho, pasilla, and California greens are all mild, and all turn from their immature green to a red or brown as they mature or become dry. When a recipe calls for mild red chilies, any of these will do.

Tomatillos: These are sweet, green, golf ball–sized Mexican tomatoes. Tomatillos are used extensively in Mexican cooking, particularly in green taco sauce or green molé sauce. Sometimes they can be found fresh in markets that carry Mexican food specialty items. More often they are found canned. Of course, normal red tomatoes are small and green when immature. Unfortunately, immature red tomatoes cannot be substituted for tomatillos.

Cilantro: This is an herb widely used in the preparation of Mexican-oriented sauces and other dishes. It is also called coriander. Because it looks so much like parsley, it is also sometimes called Chinese parsley. If cilantro can't be located fresh at the market, it is usually available in the spice section under the name coriander.

CHILI SALSA

3 fresh jalapeño chilies	½ medium onion, chopped
3 fresh yellow chilies	1 stalk celery, chopped fine
2 fresh California green chilies	1 tablespoon vinegar
2 medium tomatoes, chopped	½ teaspoon coriander seeds (or ¼ cup finely chopped cilantro)
(4 tomatillos)	½ teaspoon garlic flakes

Seed the chilies, saving a teaspoon or so of the seeds to make the salsa hot. Chop the chilies, and combine all ingredients except the seeds in a saucepan. Add ½ cup water. Add seeds ⅛ teaspoon at a time, tasting for hotness at each addition. Stop at desired hotness. Cover and simmer 3 hours. Use on tacos, in beans, on refried beans, in burritos, or in any other dish to give a spicy Mexican flavor. Store in refrigerator or freezer. Makes 2 cups.

TACO SALSA

Use this salsa just like **Chili Salsa** (p. 263) to spice up any Mexican-style dish. It works better than chili salsa as a topping for tacos, burritos, and so forth, because it doesn't have the runny spots that chili salsa has.

One 28-ounce can of tomatoes in puree
5 fresh California green chilies, chopped, with seeds left in
5 fresh jalapeño chilies, seeded and chopped
5 fresh yellow chilies, seeded and chopped
(8 tomatillos)
1 medium onion, chopped
¼ cup chopped fresh cilantro (leaves and stems)
¼ teaspoon garlic flakes
1 tablespoon vinegar

Place tomatoes in blender and blend a second or two. Add remaining ingredients, ½ cup at a time, until a smooth blend of all ingredients is achieved. Add 2 tablespoons water, cover, and simmer 3 hours. Store in refrigerator or freeze for future use. Makes 1 quart.

GREEN TACO SAUCE

6 small unripe (green) ordinary tomatoes
(8 tomatillos)
1 medium onion, chopped

5 fresh California green chilies, chopped, with seeds left in

5 fresh jalapeño chilies, seeded and chopped

5 fresh yellow chilies, seeded and chopped

2 tablespoons chopped fresh cilantro

1 tablespoon vinegar

¼ teaspoon garlic flakes

Combine all ingredients with ⅔ cup water in blender, and chop. Pour into saucepan, cover, and simmer 3 hours. Cool, return to blender, and blend until smooth. Store in refrigerator or freezer. Makes 1 quart.

HOT SAUCE

2 cups **Chili Salsa**

Blend salsa in blender at high speed until smooth. Cook over medium heat, uncovered, until desired thickness is achieved. Use in place of commercial hot sauces. Store in refrigerator or freezer. Makes 1½ to 2 cups.

RED CHILI LIQUID

2 dried, mild red chilies (pasilla, ancho, or California)

1 cup boiling water

Toast chilies on cookie sheet in 400° oven for a few minutes only, until their aroma can be smelled. Be careful not to burn. Cool enough for easy handling. Remove seeds, stems, and pith. Rinse, and cover with boiling water. Let stand 2 hours. Store in refrigerator and use as needed. Remove chilies just before using. Makes 1 cup. (Flavor intensifies if chilies remain in their liquid.) Liquid may be frozen in small cubes for convenience.

GREEN MOLÉ SAUCE

8 fresh tomatillos (or one 10-ounce can of tomatillos)
1 small onion, chopped
2 tablespoons chopped fresh cilantro
2 tablespoons finely chopped canned California green chilies

(If tomatillos are fresh rather than canned, cook them, covered, in ½ cup water over medium heat about 15 minutes or until tender. Cool.) Chop and blend tomatillos in blender until fairly smooth. Sauté onion in ¼ cup water, then combine with tomatillos and other ingredients. Cover and simmer 15 minutes, stirring occasionally. Makes 1 cup. For convenience, freeze sauce in ice-cube tray. Use frozen cubes as needed. **Green Molé Sauce** is used as a Mexican-style sauce for turkey, beef, lamb, venison, and other meats. It is also used to make **Red Molé Sauce** (below).

RED MOLÉ SAUCE

½ cup **Green Molé Sauce** (above)
¼ cup **Red Chili Liquid** (p. 265)
(1 clove garlic, cut in half)
(Pinch of oregano)
(Pinch of pepper)
(Pinch of cumin)

Stir ingredients together and heat through. Remove garlic after heating, if cut garlic has been used. Makes 1 cup. Use as a Mexican-style sauce for turkey, beef, lamb, venison, and other meats.

RED MOLÉ SAUCE WITH TOMATO

1½ cups **Red Molé Sauce**   2 very ripe and red small
  (p. 266)   tomatoes

Quarter tomatoes, combine with red molé sauce, cover, and simmer 45 minutes. Makes 2 cups.

MILD PEPPER SAUCE

1 medium green pepper,   ½ medium onion, chopped
  chopped   1 tablespoon tomato paste
2 medium tomatoes,
  chopped

Combine ingredients with 1 cup water in a saucepan. Bring to boil, cover, and simmer 1 hour. Makes about 2½ cups.

ENCHILADA SAUCE

2½ cups **Mild Pepper Sauce**   ¼ teaspoon cumin
  (above)   ¼ teaspoon oregano
1 teaspoon chili powder

Combine ingredients, bring to boil, and simmer 15 minutes. Makes 2½ cups.

TOMATO SAUCE

Commercial tomato sauce almost always has added salt. Several brands of tomato juice and tomato paste, however, are available without added salt. A salt-free tomato sauce can be had simply by combining salt-free tomato juice and tomato paste.

1 cup tomato juice   (⅛ teaspoon basil)
2 tablespoons tomato paste   (⅛ teaspoon oregano)
(⅛ teaspoon onion powder)   (⅛ teaspoon thyme)
(⅛ teaspoon garlic powder)

Combine ingredients (using spices if desired) and heat through. Cool and store in refrigerator. Makes 1 cup.

LEMON-DILL MARINADE

½ cup water   ½ teaspoon dill weed
⅓ cup fresh lemon juice   ½ teaspoon pepper
2 tablespoons parsley flakes

Combine ingredients in small jar and shake well. Good as a marinade on green beans or other vegetables. Use also in **Chicken in Marinade.** Makes 1 cup.

BROWNED ONIONS

½ cup chopped fresh onions

Sprinkle 2 tablespoons of the onions into a heavy skillet. Cook dry over low heat. Stir when onions start to brown. When onions turn caramel brown, add 1 tablespoon water and remaining onions. Stir and cover for a few minutes. Onions are done when they become translucent. Use as a meat or vegetable garnish or whenever toasted onions are required. Makes ⅜ cup.

VEGETABLE POWDER

½ cup vegetable flakes   1 tablespoon onion flakes
1 tablespoon parsley flakes   ¼ teaspoon chervil

Pulverize all ingredients in blender. Store in airtight jar until needed. Use to enrich soups, stews, meats, and cooked vegetables. Makes ¼ cup.

CHAPTER 8

Breads

Is there anything in the world as pleasant as the smell of fresh baking bread? Certainly there is no air-freshener on the market that can cause the atmosphere of a house to be as inviting as bread in the oven. For at least 5000 years we humans have made bread, and the process hasn't changed much in all that time.

The making of bread all these years has been a partnership activity, the principals in the partnership being the cook on the one hand and a colony of yeast cells on the other. The cook provides a medium in which the yeast cells may rapidly multiply (namely, moist warm dough). The yeast colony, once established in the dough, reciprocates by manufacturing billions of tiny bubbles of carbon dioxide gas and other organic compounds. The gas bubbles cause the dough to expand, and the organic compounds give the dough wonderful flavors and odors. Oven heat then sets the gas-expanded dough into the light and airy texture for which bread is so famous.

Dough is simply a combination of flour and water. Any flour may be used to make an excellent dough for nurturing a yeast colony.

Wheat flour, cornmeal, rice flour, bean flour, and potato flour all make excellent yeast-supporting mediums. Despite the fact that all these flours are equally attractive to a yeast colony, wheat flour makes far and away the most superior bread. The reason for this is that wheat flour dough can be "worked" (mixed and kneaded) so as to develop a *gluten* dough. Gluten is a colloidal suspension of wheat proteins and water that arises only in wheat dough, and only when both moisture and agitation are present. The physical and chemical properties of gluten dough are perfect for getting the most *oomph* from the yeast colony, and as a result gluten doughs produce the lightest and best-textured breads.

Bread making begins with combining the yeast, water, and flour to make the dough. Unless a sourdough bread is being made, the yeast will be a commercial yeast, in the form of either a ⅔-ounce cake of compressed yeast or a ½-ounce envelope of dry yeast. Both forms contain a viable colony of living yeast cells, ready for action in the dough. Dissolve the yeast in whatever amount of liquid will be used in the dough. For the cake form, have the liquid at 85°. For the dry form, have the liquid lukewarm (105°). The yeast will dissolve in 5 to 10 minutes, without stirring. Add about half the flour that will be used in the dough, a little at a time, mixing with a spoon. Continue adding flour, mixing now by hand, until the dough begins to cling to itself rather than to the sides of the bowl. Turn out onto a lightly floured surface, cover with a cloth, and let stand 10 minutes.

Knead (about 10 minutes) in a constant, rhythmic fashion, until the dough has lost its stickiness and has developed a smooth, elastic surface. (Knead by folding the dough over on itself and pressing with palms. Turn dough a few degrees with each knead so that all parts of the dough receive equal treatment.) Optional: Grease the dough uniformly by placing the dough in a lightly greased bowl, then turning the dough over. Now let the action of the yeast in the dough work for a while to expand the dough. Cover the bowl with a damp towel, set in in a warm place (80° or so), and let the dough expand (rise) until it has doubled in size. This takes about 2 hours.

The dough is ready when an imprint of the fingertips is left when it is pressed.

Next, "punch down the dough" with the fist: press the fist deeply into the center of the dough, fold the edges of the dough into the center, and turn it over. Briefly knead again. (This may be done in the bowl.) Cover with a damp cloth, and let rise again, until not quite doubled. This takes about 1 hour.

Next, pinch the dough into the number of pieces called for, and shape each piece into a loaf shape. Place in a loaf pan, cover with a damp cloth, and let rise a third time, to not quite double in volume. This third rising takes about 1 hour. During rising, preheat oven to baking temperature called for, and bake for specified time.

The bread is done when it has pulled away from the sides of the loaf pan. Remove it from the pan and place it on a cake rack in a draft-free place to cool. Cool the bread thoroughly before wrapping in plastic for freezing or refrigerating.

Baking powders and baking soda are chemicals that are used to duplicate the rising action of the yeast colony. They work by liberating molecules of carbon dioxide when they come in contact with water. Thus, when one of these agents is mixed into a dough with flour and water, a chemical reaction takes place that produces bubbles of carbon dioxide that in turn cause the dough to expand just as with the yeast colony. Caution: because of the sodium content of baking powders and baking sodas, limit the amount used in baking. Cultivate recipes in which the amount of baking powder or baking soda is less than 1 teaspoon per cup of flour.

Commercial Breads. Very often one needn't worry about the salt that is used in making commercial breads. It is normally used in small amounts to regulate the action of the yeast and is of no health consequence. Sweeteners, shortenings, and additives, however, are not inconsequential in commerical breads. They are used in amounts that adversely affect health, and breads containing them should be avoided. In buying bread one should, first and foremost, read the ingredients label. If the ingredients label is missing, don't buy the bread. If the bread contains shortening or other fats, sugar or other sweeteners, or chemical additives, avoid it. If its only bad ingredient is salt, feel safe to use the taste buds in accepting or rejecting it. (Avoid obviously salty products like saltine crackers.) Sourdough breads and rolls, pita bread (sometimes called Bible bread or Armenian bread), Norwegian flatbread, and matzo crackers are examples of commercial breads that are usually free of sweeteners and fats.

WHITE BREAD

1 envelope active dry yeast   6 to 7 cups flour

Sprinkle yeast on ¼ cup lukewarm (105°) water and let soften a few minutes. Combine 2 cups warm (120°) water and 2 cups of the flour, add softened yeast, and beat with electric mixer for 3 minutes. Add remaining flour a cup at a time until dough can be handled. Turn out onto heavily floured board and knead until smooth and elastic (about 5 minutes). Let rise in warm place in smooth, floured bowl until double in bulk (about 30 minutes). Shape into two loaves. Place in Teflon baking pans and let rise again until double (1 or more hours). Bake for 1 hour at 400°. Makes 2 loaves.

DINNER ROLLS

1 envelop active dry yeast   4½ cups unbleached white
1 cup skim milk   flour
1 egg white

Sprinkle yeast onto surface of ¼ cup warm (110° to 115°) water. Scald milk, cool to lukewarm (105°), and pour into large bowl. Add dissolved yeast, egg white, and 2 cups flour. Beat until smooth, then mix in rest of flour. Turn out onto floured board, and knead until smooth and elastic (about 5 minutes). Place dough in lightly greased bowl, then turn dough in bowl, bringing bottom side up. Cover with towel wrung out in hot water, place in warm place (about 80°), and let rise until double in bulk (1 to 1½ hours). When doubled, punch down and place on floured board. Roll or pat dough until it is 1 inch thick. Cut with small drinking glass into biscuit shapes, place on Teflon pan, and let rise until doubled (about 45 minutes). Bake 20 to 25 minutes at 400°. Makes 10 to 15 rolls.

WATER BAGELS

1 envelope active dry yeast
1 cup lukewarm (105°) potato water (water in which peeled potatoes have been cooked)

2½ to 3 cups flour
1 egg white

Soften yeast 10 minutes in potato water. Stir in 1 cup flour, blending until very smooth, then stir in remaining flour until dough can be handled. Turn out onto floured board and knead 10 minutes or until smooth and elastic, adding flour while kneading to make a firm dough. Place dough in floured, nonstick casserole dish. Cover and let rise until double in bulk. Turn dough out, punch down, and knead until smooth. On floured surface, roll out dough and cut into 16 pieces. With hands, roll each piece into a 5-inch-long log. Shape log into donut, moistening ends to join. Let rise 15 minutes on well-floured board. Drop bagels into boiling water, a few at a time. Let each bagel boil for 1 minute, then turn and boil 3 minutes on other side. Remove bagels with slotted spoon and place on cookie sheet. Brush with a mixture of slightly beaten egg white and 1 tablespoon water. Bake at 425° until crusts are light brown and crisp (about 25 minutes). Great with **Cream Cheese.** Makes 16 bagels.

PITA BREAD

When pita bread is put into the oven, it is in the form of a round slab about the size of a slice of bread. This pita round bakes only a few minutes, and in that time it begins to puff up. Its surfaces puff apart, leaving a handy space inside the pita that is ideal for stuffing, sandwich-style. When a pita round has finished cooking, a slice may be made at its edge, gaining entry to the pocket inside. Or it may be snipped in two, making two stuffable pockets. Stuff it with leftover meat loaf, beans and cheese, taco stuffing, or any other sandwich makings desired. Use pita round also to make **Vegetable Pot Pies** or simply as a bread to serve at meals.

1 envelope active dry yeast
3 cups white flour
3 cups whole wheat flour

In a large bowl or pot, sprinkle yeast on 2 cups plus 2 tablespoons of lukewarm (105°) water. Let stand 10 minutes. Add whole wheat flour and stir in well. Add white flour, stir, then work with hands into a ball. On very lightly floured board (use 3 tablespoons flour for flouring board), knead dough about 5 minutes, or until smooth and elastic. Shape into a ball. Place in a flour-dusted bowl, cover with damp paper towel or cloth towel, and put in a warm place to rise. If necessary, remoisten towel. When dough has doubled, shape and stretch into a long roll. Cut in 16 pieces. Gently toss pieces in hands to round them into ball shapes, and place them on a clean, dry, flour-dusted cloth. Cover with dry paper towels, and let rise 30 minutes. Roll each ball into a flat circle no thicker than ¼ inch. Turn dough over, place on dry, flour-dusted towels, and let rise 30 minutes. Place each round, top side down, directly on oven rack or wire rack. Dough should not be sticky or wrinkled on rack. If necessary, flip dough several times on floured board to dry before placing on oven rack. Bake at 475° until pitas puff (usually less than 5 minutes). Immediately transfer to broiler and brown tops. Cool on cake racks, then store in plastic bag till needed. Makes 16 pitas.

CORN PITAS

1 envelope active dry yeast
4 cups flour

2 cups cornmeal (preferably
 fine-ground)

Prepare and cook corn pitas as in recipe for **Pita Bread** above. Expect corn pitas to take a little longer in the oven before they puff. Some may not puff at all. Those that don't puff won't have a pocket for stuffing, but make a fine corn bread. Recipe makes 16 corn pitas.

YEAST CORN MUFFINS

½ cup lukewarm (105°) water
1 envelope active dry yeast
½ cup flour

2 cups cornmeal
4 egg whites
½ cup skim milk

Let yeast soften in water 5 minutes. Add flour, and beat well with electric mixer. Add cornmeal, egg whites, and enough milk to make a batter consistency (like cake or muffin batter). Beat well again with electric mixer, and pour into muffin pans. When contents of muffin pans have doubled, bake at 375° for 25 minutes. Makes 8 to 12 muffins.

HERB BREAD

1 cup rye flour
½ cup white flour
2 cups whole wheat flour
¼ cup wheat germ
1 tablespoon parsley flakes
¼ teaspoon basil

⅛ teaspoon sage
1 teaspoon **Vegetable
 Powder**
1 medium potato
1 cup **Whey**
1 envelope active dry yeast

Combine rye, white, and wheat flours, wheat germ, and dried herbs. Blend well. Peel and cut up potato and cook in 1 cup water until tender enough to mash. Force hot potato and its liquid through a strainer. Stir, then combine with the whey. Mixture should be lukewarm. Heat or cool if necessary. Sprinkle yeast over surface of potato-whey mixture and allow yeast to soften 5 minutes. Add flour mixture, a large spoonful at a time, beating constantly with electric mixer until too thick to use mixer. Continue to stir in flour, mixing by hand, until dough can be worked. Turn out onto floured surface and knead well (about 10 minutes), working in as much flour as necessary for easy handling. Place kneaded dough in floured, smooth bowl, cover, and let rise in warm place until just barely double (about 1½ hours). Punch down, knead a few times, and shape into two loaves. Let rise in warm place in Teflon pans until double again (at least an hour, probably longer). Bake 40 minutes at 350°. When done, bread should sound hollow when thumped. Makes 2 loaves.

LEFSE

Try this delightful Norwegian bread as a breakfast bread or a dessert bread.

4 cups cut-up potatoes,
   cooked and drained
¼ cup evaporated skim milk

2 cups flour, plus additional
   flour for rolling out

Mash potatoes with milk. Cool thoroughly. Mix in 2 cups of flour, in half-cup measures. Continue to add flour just until dough can be handled. Dough will be very soft. Place dough in bowl in refrigerator and chill thoroughly (an hour or two). Pull off a handful at a time (about ½ cup each), leaving the rest of the dough in refrigerator. Use a well-floured, heavy pastry cloth and a well-floured, knit-covered rolling pin to roll out each piece into a circle.

For perfect shape, cut with a canister cover or pot lid, but do not rework scraps (Teflon-fry separately for samples, if desired). Drape each circle of dough onto the rolling pin (as for pie crust) and quickly transfer to a hot Teflon skillet. Teflon-fry a few minutes on each side. Cool on cloth-covered cookie rack. When cool, freeze in foil or in plastic bags, or store in plastic bags for immediate use. Lefse is best when very fresh and still slightly warm. Makes 16 small lefse (about 6 to 8 inches). Serve with a fruit sauce (see next chapter), or **Sour Cream** or both. Or use in place of flour tortillas.

MILK TOAST

Try this old American favorite for breakfast or as a late night snack.

3 cups **White Sauce**   6 slices dry toast

Dip slices of toast separately into fresh, hot white sauce until soft. Remove to serving platter, and pour sauce over all. Makes 6 slices milk toast.

ABOUT NOODLES

Many commercial noodles are made with whole eggs and so must be avoided because of the high cholesterol content of the egg yolk. Some commercial noodles are okay. Read the ingredients label to determine which brands to buy. Or make a batch of delicious homemade noodles instead.

HOMEMADE NOODLES

2 cups flour   4 egg whites

Place flour in bowl and make a well in the center. Pour egg whites into well, and mix into flour using a fork (and hands if necessary). Add water 1 tablespoon at a time, mixing thoroughly after each addition. Add only enough water (about 3 tablespoons in all to have dough form a ball. Dough will be very stiff. Turn onto a well-floured board and knead until smooth and elastic. Divide dough into four parts, and roll one part at a time until very thin, keeping other parts covered. Roll dough around rolling pin and transfer to freshly floured board. Cut into ⅛-inch strips, shake strips out, and lay on towel to dry (about 2 hours). Makes 6 to 8 cups dried noodles.

ABOUT SOURDOUGH BREADS

Sourdough breads are breads that develop their rising power from a soured dough mixture that is used in place of commercial yeast or baking powder or other rising agents. The sourdough mixture is actually a colony of microorganisms (yeast cells) that are living in the dough mixture, producing carbon dioxide (accounting for the rising power of the dough) and alcohol and other compounds (accounting for the odors and sour flavors of the dough). Any time a mixture of flour and water is made and kept warm, conditions are favorable for wild yeast cells, which ever populate the air, to take hold in the flour and water mixture, and to develop a thriving colony that will produce a usable sourdough mixture. That is why early frontiersmen were noted for making sourdough breads. Wild yeasts were always available in the air, whereas commercial yeasts and baking powders were not always available on the frontier. Actually, wild yeast strains vary greatly in the rising power and flavors that they are able to contribute to a sourdough. For this reason sourdoughs made from wild yeasts are not always excellent substitutions for commercial yeasts and rising agents. When our frontier ancestors encountered a strain with superior cooking qualities, it was highly prized. The dough might be kept active for many years, mother passing to daughter and close friends a sourdough starter from the original colony so that new colonies of the same superior strain would be established in other kitchens. (Some sourdough colonies in Europe have reputedly been kept active, in various kitchens, for centuries.)

The dough mixture that houses the colony of yeast cells is usually called a sourdough starter. To keep the sourdough starter active indefinitely, one need only keep it refrigerated, and every month or so rework and divide it. Rework it by removing from refrigerator, letting stand 1 hour, then adding 1 cup of sifted flour and 1 cup 85° water for each cup starter. Beat until smooth, let sit 3 hours, then divide it into two or more clean containers and refrigerate. Pass a container to a friend from time to time, so that if the original colony goes bad, a good offspring colony exists somewhere that can restart it. Discard starter if abnormal coloration develops.

The cook who can obtain from a friend a sourdough starter that is known to have superior cooking qualities is ready to make sourdough bread. The cook who cannot obtain a good starter must make one from scratch. The recipe below uses a commercial yeast, known to be of high quality, to make the starter. For the adventurous cook who wants to capture and try a wild yeast strain, substitute ½ teaspoon salt and ½ teaspoon sugar for the commercial yeast, and let starter develop 48 hours at 90° rather than 24 hours at 75° to 85°.

SOURDOUGH STARTER

1 cup lukewarm (105°) water
1 envelope active dry yeast
1 cup flour

Place ¼ cup of the water into a bowl. Gently stir in yeast. Let stand 5 minutes, then add remaining water. Gradually add flour until mixture is the consistency of thin pancake batter. Cover with cloth and let stand 24 hours at 75° to 85°. Store in refrigerator in tightly closed crock until used or reworked.

SOURDOUGH BREAD

1 cup **Sourdough Starter** (p. 280)
1 cup whole wheat flour
3 to 6 cups unbleached white flour

Set out starter to warm to room temperature (about 1 hour). Scrape all of starter into a very large pan or bowl. Add 1 cup whole wheat flour, 1 cup unbleached white flour, and 1 cup room-temperature water. Continue to add water until mixture (or "sponge") resembles pancake batter. Cover loosely and allow sponge to remain at warm room temperature (80°) for 15 to 36 hours, depending on degree of sourness desired. (This bread contains no salt. The sourer the bread, the less the salt is missed. For really sour bread, let sponge sit as long as 36 hours.) Stir sponge, and RETURN ONE CUP OF SPONGE TO STARTER POT. To remaining sponge, add unbleached white flour, ¼ cup at a time, stirring constantly, until dough becomes too thick to stir and can be handled. Turn out onto well-floured surface and knead rapidly with well-floured hands. Knead thoroughly, working in a minimum of flour. When fully kneaded, dough will be smooth and elastic. Allow dough to rest for 5 minutes on well-floured surface. Divide dough in half and gently but quickly shape into two loaves. Place each loaf seam side down in nonstick loaf pan. Let loaves rise at warm room temperature until 2½ times original size (3 to 4 hours). Bake at 425° until crust is deep brown (about 50 minutes). Turn loaves out to cool on their sides on wire racks. Makes 2 loaves.

SOURDOUGH BISCUITS

½ cup **Sourdough Starter** (p. 280)
1 cup skim milk
1 cup flour

Mix above ingredients in large bowl, cover, and leave at room temperature overnight. Next day add 1 cup flour to mixture and turn mixture out onto a floured bread board. Then combine:

½ cup flour
1 teaspoon baking powder
½ teaspoon baking soda

and sift over the dough. Knead lightly, then roll out to 1-inch thickness and cut into biscuits. Place in baking pan and let stand in warm place 30 minutes. Bake 30 minutes at 375°. Makes 10 to 15 biscuits.

CHAPTER 9

Desserts and Toppings

There is no question that the sugars and fats in cakes and cookies, pies, pastries, and other desserts contribute heavily to prevailing ill health and premature death in all Western cultures. For this reason we can expect long and healthy lives for ourselves and our children only if we wisely choose to avoid the vast array of sugary, fatty temptations to which we have become so accustomed. It would be nice if there were some way that our customary desserts could be created minus the gremlins that inhabit them. But alas, there is no earthly way this can be done. Fortunately, there are a number of delicious dessert dishes that don't rely on sugar and fat for their taste, and in this chapter we present recipes for some of them.

One caution: by and large, the recipes in this chapter use fruits and fruit juices to supply the sweetness needed in the desserts. The problem is that fruits, especially in their mashed, cooked, dried, and juiced forms, have an effect on blood fats that is similar to the effect created by ordinary sugars. Thus, even though safe, as desserts go, they should be used in limited amounts.

FRESH FRUIT DESSERT

½ watermelon (cut
   lengthwise)
1 cantaloupe
½ pound seedless grapes
4 bananas, sliced

4 peaches, sliced
½ fresh pineapple, cut in
   chunks
6 sprigs fresh mint

Remove inside of watermelon with a melon scoop. Sawtooth the edge of the melon. Cut and clean the cantaloupe and use a melon scoop to get as much of the fruit as possible. Toss all fruit (except bananas) gently in watermelon shell and chill. When ready to serve, add bananas and toss lightly. Garnish with mint sprigs. Serves 6 to 10.

BUTTERMILK CHIFFON CHEESECAKE

FILLING:

4½ cups **Cottage Cheese**
1 cup **Buttermilk**
One 6-ounce can of frozen
   apple juice concentrate
2 tablespoons unflavored
   gelatin

One 8-ounce can of
   unsweetened crushed
   pineapple
1 teaspoon vanilla
3 egg whites, beaten to
   stiffness

CRUST:
Grape-Nuts

TOPPING (optional):
One 20-ounce package of
   frozen strawberries

1 tablespoon cornstarch

Make filling: Loosely crumble cottage cheese into blender. Add buttermilk and blend until very smooth. Thoroughly dissolve the can of frozen apple juice in 2 cans water. If contents of blender appear too dry, add a few tablespoons of the apple juice to blender and blend. Combine gelatin and pineapple in large bowl and mix well. Heat 1 cup of the apple juice to boiling, pour over gelatin and pineapple mixture, and stir to dissolve gelatin. Set aside to cool. Beat egg whites to stiffness. Add vanilla and the contents of the blender to the cooled pineapple-gelatin mixture, then fold in egg whites.

Make crust: Dampen enough Grape-Nuts with apple juice to cover bottom and sides of two 9-inch pie pans.

Make Topping (optional): Place strawberries in saucepan. Blend cornstarch with 2 tablespoons apple juice, combine with remaining apple juice (should be about ¾ to ⅞ cup), and add to saucepan. Bring to boil, reduce heat to medium-low, and cook until thickened.

Assemble cheesecakes: Pour filling into pie pan, spooning some over middle to make nice rounded form. Spread on topping and refrigerate until firm (about 1 hour). Makes 2 cheesecakes.

REFRIGERATOR CHEESE PIE

½ cup dry bread crumbs
2 tablespoons orange juice (or apple juice)
One 16-ounce can of crushed pineapple in unsweetened juice
1 tablespoon unflavored gelatin
1⅔ cups **Cottage Cheese**
½ teaspoon vanilla

Toss bread crumbs with orange juice. Sprinkle into pie plate and press onto bottom and partway up sides. Brown in broiler for a minute. Pour ½ cup of the juice from the pineapple into a saucepan. Sprinkle gelatin on top to soften, then heat to dissolve gelatin. Place pineapple and remaining juice in blender and add cottage cheese and vanilla. Blend until mixture is *very* smooth. Combine cottage cheese mixture and gelatin mixture and pour into cooled pie shell. Refrigerate until set. Serve with sliced bananas and **Sour Cream** spread over top, or topped with a **fruit sauce.** Makes 1 pie.

JUNKET

1 Junket rennet tablet
½ cup regular (definitely not instant) nonfat dry milk

2 cups skim milk
½ teaspoon vanilla

Dissolve junket tablet in 1 tablespoon water and set aside. In saucepan, thoroughly mix together dry milk and ½ cup of the skim milk. (This is difficult. Use the blender.) Add remaining skim milk and vanilla. Heat slowly to 110° or until a few drops on the inside of the wrist feel comfortably warm. Add junket tablet dissolved in water, stir no more than a few seconds, and immediately pour into custard cups. Let stand undisturbed on counter for 10 minutes, then chill. Top with **fruit sauce** and serve. Makes four ½-cup servings.

Note: Did it curdle, or fail to set? The worst thing one can do to junket is to overheat the milk. Remember that 110° is only a little higher than a bad fever. If the milk gets too hot, let it cool back to a comfortable 110° before adding the junket tablet.

RICE MOLD

1 tablespoon unflavored gelatin
½ cup pineapple juice
½ cup crushed pineapple
½ cup strawberries

1 cup **Yogurt**
½ teaspoon vanilla
¼ teaspoon almond extract
1 cup cooked rice

Sprinkle gelatin over pineapple juice in saucepan. Heat until dissolved. Blend all ingredients except rice in blender. Combine with rice, pour into mold, and refrigerate until set. Serves 6.

RICE PUDDING

½ cup white rice
1½ cups skim milk
2 tablespoons dry nonfat
  milk
2 egg whites, slightly beaten

¼ cup raisins
½ teaspoon vanilla
Cinnamon
Nutmeg

Bring rice and 1 cup water to a boil. Cover and simmer 15 minutes. Combine skim milk, dry nonfat milk, egg whites, raisins, and vanilla. Add to cooked rice and pour into casserole dish. Sprinkle top with cinnamon and nutmeg and bake 1 hour uncovered at 300°. Serves 4.

NOODLE PUDDING SUPREME

1 pound **Cottage Cheese**
1 cup **Yogurt**
2 cups cooked **noodles**
2 apples, peeled and sliced
2 egg whites, stiffly beaten

¼ cup raisins
1 teaspoon cinnamon
1 teaspoon vanilla
(½ cup Grape-Nuts)

Blend cottage cheese and yogurt in blender until smooth. Combine with remaining ingredients (except Grape-Nuts) and bake in Teflon baking pan 1 hour at 350°. Serve hot or cold. For additional crunch, sprinkle grape-nuts over top before serving. Serve 6.

DOG BONE COOKIES

1 cup finely chopped
  Jerusalem artichokes
3 egg whites
½ teaspoon baking powder

1 teaspoon grated lemon peel
½ teaspoon almond extract *or*
  1 teaspoon vanilla
1 cup flour

Teflon-toast Jerusalem artichokes until first signs of browning or burning appear. Beat egg whites to soft peaks. Beat in baking powder, lemon peel, and almond extract. Stir in Jerusalem artichokes and flour. Combine thoroughly. Dough will be very stiff. With floured hands, shape tablespoon-sized dough lumps into dog-biscuit-shaped cookies. Place on nonstick cookie sheet and bake at 375° for 10 to 12 minutes or until dry and lightly browned. Cool on racks, and store in closed container or plastic bag. Makes one dozen small bones.

GRACIE'S BEET BARS

1 cup diced or grated raw
  beets
1 ice cube

½ cup papaya pineapple
  nectar
(Fresh strawberries)

Combine beets, ice cube, and nectar in blender until smooth. Pour into ice pop molds or 3-ounce paper cups. Place a few small strawberries or cut-up strawberry pieces in each cup. Insert popsicle sticks and chill until very firm. Makes four to six 3-ounce bars.

ICE CREAM PIE

¾ cup apple juice
¾ cup nonfat dry milk
2 bananas, sliced

2 cups frozen blueberries
2 cups frozen strawberries
2½ cups Grape-Nuts

Combine apple juice and dry milk, and beat with electric mixer until whipped (works faster if bowl, beater, and ingredients are icy cold). Pour half of whipped mixture into blender, and blend with fruit, a little at a time, until thick and of an even consistency. Add to remaining half of whipped mixture and mix well. Add 1½ cups of the Grape-Nuts and mix well again. Moisten remaining Grape-Nuts and flatten into a layer on the bottom of 2 pie pans. Pour pie mixture into pans and freeze (about 2 hours). Makes 2 pies.

APPLE PIE

½ cup uncooked rolled oats
6 cups thin-sliced apples
⅔ cup pineapple juice

2 tablespoons raisins
½ teaspoon cinnamon
Grape-Nuts

Layer oats onto bottom of 8-inch-square Teflon pan. Add apples, pour pineapple juice over top, and sprinkle evenly with raisins and cinnamon. Cover with foil and bake 1 hour at 350°. Remove foil, cover with Grape-Nuts, and bake 15 minutes more. Makes 1 pie.

BERNICE'S FRUIT PIE

2 cups boysenberries
2 cups sliced apples
1 cup unsweetened
   pineapple, crushed

1 cup apple juice
1 tablespoon cornstarch
½ cup uncooked rolled oats
Grape-Nuts

Place boysenberries, apples, pineapple, and apple juice in saucepan, cover, and simmer 15 minutes. Stir in a paste made of the cornstarch and 2 tablespoons water. Cook and stir until thickened. Layer oats onto bottom of Teflon sheet pan. Spread thickened fruit mixture over top. Bake 15 minutes at 400°. Sprinkle Grape-Nuts over top and bake 5 minutes more. Makes 1 pie.

HAWAIIAN AMBROSIA

1 cup canned crushed pineapple, thoroughly drained

½ cup **Sour Cream** or other very smooth mock sour cream

½ cup grated **Fresh Cheese**

1 ripe papaya, cubed* (if unavailable, substitute fresh or canned apricots or peaches, diced)

2 bananas, sliced

Combine pineapple and sour cream. Fold cheese, papaya, and bananas into sour cream mixture. Serves 6.

GRAPE GELATIN

Try this on the kids. We think they'll love it. Ours did.

1 tablespoon unflavored gelatin

1½ cups grape juice

Pour ¼ cup of cold grape juice into flat-bottomed bowl. Sprinkle gelatin on top, to soften. Add ½ cup boiling water and stir thoroughly, until all gelatin has dissolved. Add remaining cold grape juice, stir well, and chill until set. Makes 4 half-cup servings.

WHIPPED FRUIT MOLD

Two 8-ounce cans of juice-packed pineapple chunks or tidbits

2 tablespoons regular nonfat dry milk

¾ cup skim milk

---

*Suggestion for cubing papaya: Cut in half, then remove seeds with spoon. Cut papaya halves into a number of lengthwise slices. Skin by slipping a paring knife along each slice just under the skin. Cut each skinned slice into ½-inch cubes.

1 tablespoon unflavored
   gelatin
1 banana

1½ cups watermelon cubes
   (¾-inch cubes)

Pour juice from canned pineapple (slightly over ½ cup) into flat-bottomed bowl. Sprinkle gelatin on juice and let soften 5 minutes. Meanwhile, in blender, combine banana, dry milk, and skim milk. Blend until very smooth. Add ½ cup boiling water to softened gelatin and stir until dissolved. Add banana mixture and stir. Chill until slightly thickened. Remove from refrigerator and beat until foamy. Fold in watermelon and pineapple. Pour into mold if desired. Chill until set. Garnish, if desired, with parsley or brightly colored fruit. Serves 6 to 8.

Variations: Additional banana slices or other fresh fruit (except pineapple) may be added with watermelon and pineapple. Unsweetened canned fruit cocktail, drained, may also be added.

ORANGE FLUFF

1 tablespoon unflavored
   gelatin
½ cup frozen orange juice
   concentrate

2 fresh egg whites
1 cup canned mandarin
   oranges, water-packed

Sprinkle gelatin on top of ¼ cup cold water in flat-bottomed bowl. Add ½ cup boiling water and stir until all gelatin is dissolved. Add orange juice concentrate and ½ cup cold water, stir well, and refrigerate. When gelatin has slightly thickened, beat it to a froth at high speed with electric mixer. Beat chilled egg whites until bowl can be turned sideways without spilling. Immediately fold egg whites into gelatin and beat again. Pour into serving bowl or individual serving cups. Refrigerate. When thoroughly set, decorate with well-drained mandarin orange slices. Serves 6.

ORANGE GEL

¾ cup cold tap water
1 tablespoon unflavored
   gelatin
One 6-ounce can of frozen
   orange juice concentrate
   (do not thaw)

½ cup ice water

Place cold tap water in saucepan. Sprinkle gelatin over top, and heat slowly, stirring constantly, until gelatin dissolves (about 3 minutes). Remove from heat. Add frozen juice, stir until melted, then add ice water. Pour into champagne glasses and chill until set. Serves 4.

ORANGE SHERBET

One 6-ounce can of frozen
   orange juice concentrate
1½ cups skim milk

⅔ cup nonfat dry milk
3 drops vanilla

Combine all ingredients in blender and blend until well mixed. Place in freezer until firm. Serve topped with fresh fruit and Grape-Nuts for crunch. Makes 1½ pints sherbet.

STRAWBERRY YOGURT

2 cups sliced strawberries   2 cups **Yogurt**

Stir strawberries into yogurt, crushing a few of the strawberry slices so as to make the yogurt pink. Refrigerate until served. Serves 4.

STRAWBERRY CREPES

1 recipe **Yogurt Crepes** (page 314)

2 cups **Strawberry Sauce** (page 294)

3 cups **Sour Cream** or other mock sour cream

As each hot yogurt crepe comes off the skillet, flip onto warm plate. Spread generously with sour cream, roll up, and top with strawberry sauce and another dollop of sour cream. Makes 16 strawberry crepes.

STEWED FRUIT SAUCE

The whole family will love this stewed fruit sauce. Use it by itself, on pancakes, or on rice pudding.

1 teaspoon cornstarch
¼ cup apple juice
¾ cup sliced strawberries
¼ cup vermouth
1 medium apple, pared and sliced

2 tablespoons raisins
Pinch of cardamom
4 canned apricot halves
¼ cup frozen blueberries

Combine cornstarch and apple juice. Mash ¼ cup of the strawberries. Add mashed berries and vermouth to cornstarch and apple juice mixture. Cook, stirring constantly, until thickened. Add ¼ cup water, the sliced apple, the raisins, and the cardamom, and simmer until raisins puff and apples are tender and can be cut with the side of a wooden spoon (about 10 minutes). Add remaining strawberry slices, apricots, and blueberries and warm through, stirring enough to prevent sticking. Makes 2 cups.

APPLE BAKE

4 cups fresh apple slices	1 teaspoon cornstarch
2 tablespoons raisins	½ teaspoon cinnamon
1 tablespoon lemon juice	(½ cup rolled oats)
¼ cup apple juice	(½ cup Grape-Nuts)

Toss apple slices with raisins, lemon juice, and 1 tablespoon water. Set aside. Combine apple juice, cornstarch, and cinnamon with ½ cup water and cook, stirring constantly, until clear and slightly thickened. Spread rolled oats evenly over bottom of baking dish. Combine thickened sauce and apples and pour over oats. Top with Grape-Nuts and bake at 300° until apples are very tender (about 40 minutes). The oats and Grape-Nuts give the dish a delightful crust-and-crumb-pie effect, but may be omitted. When omitted, this dish may still be served by itself, or it may be served over pancakes. Serves 8.

SPICED APPLESAUCE

One 15-ounce can of unsweetened applesauce	½ teaspoon cinnamon
	1 tablespoon unprocessed bran flakes
One 15-ounce can of unsweetened sliced apples	1 tablespoon quick-cooking rolled oats
1 tablespoon cornstarch	

Combine ¼ cup water with all ingredients except bran and oatmeal and heat to boiling. Spoon into 6 custard cups. Mix together bran flakes and oatmeal and sprinkle lightly over top. Bake 40 minutes at 350°. Serves 6.

STRAWBERRY SAUCE

1 cup apple juice	1 cup mashed strawberries
2 teaspoons cornstarch	½ cup sliced strawberries

In a small saucepan, combine apple juice and cornstarch until lump-free. Add mashed berries, and cook over low-to-moderate heat, stirring constantly, until thickened, red, and bubbly. Add sliced berries just before serving over pancakes. Makes 2 cups.

YAM AND APPLE PUDDING

3 medium yams
3 medium apples, pared and sliced
Half of a 6-ounce can of frozen orange juice concentrate

Boil yams in jackets until partially done (about 20 minutes). Cool, peel, and slice into a casserole dish. Add apples and orange juice concentrate, cover, and bake at 350° until tender (about 1 hour). Serves 4.

BLUEBERRY SAUCE

1 cup clear apple juice
2 teaspoons cornstarch

1 cup frozen whole blueberries

Mix apple juice and cornstarch in small saucepan until lump-free. Add berries and cook, stirring constantly, over moderate heat until sauce clears and thickens, mashing berries while stirring. Serve hot over pancakes. Makes 1½ cups.

Optional: When sauce is ready to serve, stir in an additional ½ cup of frozen berries. Use this cooled sauce over pancakes or reheat slightly, stirring gently to avoid crushing berries.

WILD BLUEBERRY SAUCE

One 15-ounce can of wild blueberries

1 tablespoon cornstarch

Drain berries, saving all juice. Combine juice and cornstarch in saucepan and cook until sauce clears and thickens. Add berries and heat through. Makes 2 cups.

TART CHERRY SAUCE

1 cup canned water-packed cherries

½ cup juice from cherries

2 tablespoons red grape juice

1 tablespoon cornstarch

Place ¼ cup water in small saucepan, add all ingredients except cherries, and cook and stir until thickened and clear. Add cherries and heat through. Serve over pancakes, with yogurt, or over rice cakes. Makes 1½ cups.

CHAPTER 10

Beverages

Since caffeinated, sweetened, and oiled beverages are verboten in longevity cookery, one needs to become familiar with beverages that are free of such gremlins.

If soda pop, coffee, and milk shakes are out, what is *in*, one might ask? Plenty. For starters, try herb teas, vegetable juices, fruit juices, skim milk, decaffeinated coffees, and some of the lemonades and other beverages in this chapter. Try also mixing orange juice, pineapple juice, and other fruit juices with **Buttermilk.** There are untold thousands of herbs, fruits, vegetables, and combinations of these things from which delicious beverages can be made. Be experimental and discover them. Use the beverages in this chapter as *ideas for beverages*, rather than as the final word on longevity beverages.

A word of caution: don't overdo it on fruit juices. As we mentioned earlier, excessive amounts of fruit juices can increase blood fats and the attendant health problems that high levels of fat create. And much as we hate to be party poopers, it is important to avoid alcoholic beverages, even beer and wine. The reason? A single ounce of alcohol has an immediate and long-lasting effect on blood levels. Blood fats increase to as much as three times normal levels, and stay elevated as long as 72 hours. Ah, how we hate to say *that!* (Wines used in the recipes in this book don't count. The alcohol content is cooked off before the dish is served.)

ICED CAMOMILE TEA

In the storybook Peter Rabbit drinks camomile tea to mend his distressed body after his narrow escape from Mr. McGregor's garden. How rejuvenating camomile tea can be, if it is made from herbs that have not yet lost their taste and fragrance. Tea that is sold in a carton or in cellophane may not be airtight and may have lost its punch. The resulting beverage can be disappointing. Shop for airtight containers and avoid tea that has obviously sat a long time on the supermarket shelf.

2 tablespoons camomile tea
Leaves or sprigs of fresh mint
Lemon wedges

Place tea in a 6-cup teapot, add boiling water, and let steep 5 minutes. Pour through tea strainer and chill. Serve over ice, in tall glass, trimmed with floating fresh mint leaf and a lemon wedge on side of glass. Makes 6 cups.

ZIPPY TOM

Hot as you like it, Zippy Tom is a real waker-upper.

1 quart tomato juice
4 lemons
1 teaspoon chili powder
Pepper

Garlic powder
French's Herb Seasoning
4 celery stalk tips, with leaves

Combine tomato juice, the juice of the lemons, and the chili powder. Season to taste with pepper, garlic powder, and herb seasoning. Serve with stalk of celery in each glass. Makes four 8-ounce servings.

HALF-WHEY ORANGEADE

2 cups orange juice
2 cups **Whey**

Combine, chill, and serve. Believe it or not, it's delicious. Makes 1 quart.

PINEAPPLE-ORANGE WHEY

This marvelous pick-me-up tastes half orange and half pineapple. Try adding a little lemon juice for extra tartness.

4 cups orange juice
1 cup pineapple juice
3 cups **Whey**

Combine ingredients, chill, and serve. Makes 2 quarts.

PINK LEMONLESS ADE

This mock pink lemonade is another favorite for hot summer days.

2 cups **Whey**
1 cup grape juice
1 cup apple juice

Combine ingredients and serve over ice. Makes 1 quart.

WHEY LEMONADE

The children go for this mock lemonade in a big way on hot summer days. For sweeter lemonade, increase the apple juice or the pineapple juice, or use sweeter Whey.

2 lemons	2 cups pineapple juice
2 cups **Whey**	(½ cup apple juice)

Juice the lemons, and grate the rind to get ½ teaspoon lemon rind. Combine lemon juice, grated rind, and remaining ingredients. Chill and serve. Makes 5 cups.

HOT ALFALFA TEA

The unique taste and smell of alfalfa are definitely evident in this tea. It's hard to be a fence sitter with alfalfa tea. One either likes it a lot or doesn't like it at all.

½ cup alfalfa seeds	1 quart cold water

Bring seeds and water to boil, cool, and strain, producing a liquid tea extract. Use extract fresh, or freeze in ice cube tray. Add ¾ cup boiling water to ¼ cup fresh extract, and serve. Use frozen cubes of extract to float in **Iced Camomile Tea** or mint tea. Makes 1 quart alfalfa tea extract.

APRICOT COOLER

4 canned apricot halves, water- or juice-packed	2 ice cubes
	½ cup skim milk

Place all ingredients in blender, blender-chop to break up ice cubes, then blender-mix for about 30 seconds. Pour into glass, removing undissolved ice. Garnish with fresh mint, if desired. Makes 1 glass.

APPLE MILK

Mix skim milk and apple juice in equal proportion. Serve immediately, topped with nutmeg and cinnamon.

BANANA SHAKE

1 very ripe banana   3 ice cubes
1 cup skim milk
1 tablespoon regular nonfat
  dry milk

Chop and mix in blender until ice dissolves. Makes 1 shake.

CHAPTER 11

Breakfast Makings

For a delicious stick-to-the-ribs breakfast or an elegant weekend brunch, try any of the dishes in this chapter. For quick and easy breakfasts, try some of the acceptable commercial hot cereals: Wheat Hearts, Cream of Wheat, Roman Meal, Ralston, Quaker Oats, etc. Serve with fresh fruit, skim milk, toast, juice, or decaffeinated coffee. Try serving a plate of bite-size pieces of fruit (pineapple, orange wedges, apple slices, etc.) with slices of hard-cooked egg white. Try acceptable cold cereals (Grape-Nuts, Shredded Wheat) with fruit and skim milk. Or serve any of the above as an accompaniment to the dishes presented in this chapter. Above all, enjoy the fact that delicious breakfasts such as these will add a freshness and vigor to each new day that cannot be matched by the sugary, fatty breakfasts that are so common in Western culture.

DOROTHY'S SPANISH OMELETTE

½ cup chopped green pepper   2 teaspoons chopped

¼ cup chopped onion
1 tablespoon garlic juice
1 canned California green
  chili, chopped
½ small tomato, squeezed of
  juice and chopped

pimiento
6 egg whites
Pinch of saffron
½ cup grated **Fresh Cheese**
(**Chili Salsa**)

In skillet, sauté green pepper and onion in garlic juice and 2 tablespoons water. Add chopped chili, tomato, and pimiento, and boil off remaining liquid. Combine egg whites and saffron and beat to soft peaks. Fold cheese into egg whites, followed by the contents of the skillet. Return to skillet and fry until eggs are set, turning to avoid scorching. Pour off any water rendered during cooking. Serve topped with chili salsa if desired. Serves 4.

SCRAMBLE

8 cubic inches of tofu
½ cup **Cottage Cheese**
6 egg whites
Pinch of saffron

¼ cup **Buttermilk**
Pepper
Onion powder

Crumble tofu into cottage cheese and stir to combine thoroughly. Add saffron to egg white, stir, then add to tofu mixture. Stir in buttermilk. Add spices to taste. Pour into preheated Teflon frying pan, allow to congeal slightly, then stir with wooden spoon or turn with pancake turner, depending on texture desired (fluffy or solid). As soon as egg has congealed, serve with **Chili Salsa**. Serves 4.

EGGS À LA BUCKINGHAM

This recipe first appeared in the cooking literature in *Fannie Farmer's Boston Cookbook* in 1896. It is as good today as it was more than fourscore years ago.

10 egg whites   Pinch of saffron
½ cup milk   6 slices **Milk Toast**
⅛ teaspoon pepper   ⅓ cup grated **Fresh Cheese**

Beat egg whites slightly with fork, add milk, pepper, and saffron, and place in a Teflon skillet. Cook and stir mixture until eggs are in slightly underdone condition. Arrange pieces of milk toast on ovenproof platter. Pour eggs over toast, sprinkle with cheese, and bake at 325° until cheese melts or browns slightly and eggs finish cooking (about 15 minutes). Serves 6.

FRIED EGGS

Teflon-fry a batch of eggs "over medium" or "over hard." As each 3 or 4 eggs are fried, quickly slit the membrane that holds the yolk in the egg, and scoop out yolk. It is hot, tricky business, but not too hard to get the knack of. Keep the yolkless fried eggs warm in the oven while the rest are being fried. The platter of fried eggs that results very much resembles ordinary eggs fried over hard or over medium. Serve them with **Hamburger Sauce,** pepper, other spices, or by themselves. ("Over-easy" eggs and "sunny-side-up" eggs can't be fixed in this manner, because the yolk plays a much more important role in the look and texture of the egg, and can't simply be spooned out and discarded.)

BREAKFAST BAGELS

Use those bagels in the freezer for a quick, popular breakfast.

6 **Bagels**
½ pound **Fresh Cheese**
2 medium-to-large tomatoes

Split each bagel into 2 circular half-bagels. Lay bagel halves, cut face up, on broiler pan. Slice cheese thinly, and cover each bagel with cheese slices. Slice each tomato into 6 slices, and lay one slice on each bagel. Broil until cheese melts. Serves 6.

BAGELS WITH SALMON

4 **Bagels**	¼ cup **Sour Cream**
One 7¾-ounce can of salmon	½ cup **Cottage Cheese**

Split each bagel into 2 circular half-bagels. Lay bagels on broiler pan, cut side up. Combine salmon and sour cream, and spread over each half-bagel. Top each with a thin layer of crumbled cottage cheese. Broil 5 minutes 4 inches from heating element in pre-heated broiler. Serves 4.

BROILED BREAKFAST

8 cherry tomatoes, cut in half	4 ounces **Fresh Cheese,** sliced
4 slices **Sourdough Bread**	thinly
Slivers of rare roast beef *or*	Paprika
raw lean steak *or* fish filets	Fresh parsley sprigs

On attractive broiling tray, arrange tomato halves, bread, and beef or fish tidbits. Cover bread with cheese slices and broil until cheese has melted. Sprinkle paprika over cheese slices and decorate tray with parsley sprigs. Serves 4.

STEEL-CUT OATMEAL

Oatmeal can be prepared in a variety of ways, and they're all good. This recipe uses long, slow cooking and steel-cut oats (each individual oat cut into about 3 pieces by blade-fitted steel rollers) to get a delightful creamy-style oatmeal.

⅔ cup steel-cut oats	Freshly ground nutmeg
2 cups boiling water	Skim milk
Cinnamon	

Add oats to boiling water, cover, and simmer 40 minutes over very low heat. Top with cinnamon and nutmeg. Serve with skim milk. Serves 4.

COUNTRY-STYLE OATS

Fast and easy, this breakfast meal will stick to the ribs all through the morning, whether physical labor or sedentary work is called for. Delicious.

2 cups whole rolled oats	Bananas, sliced
2 cups boiling water	Skim milk

Stir oats into boiling water and cook and stir 2 or 3 minutes. Cover, remove from heat, and let stand 10 to 15 minutes. Serve with banana slices and milk over top. Serves 4.

BERRY WHEATENA

¾ cup Wheatena	Skim milk
1 cup frozen berries (blueberries, boysenberries, strawberries, etc.)	

Bring 3 cups water and Wheatena to a boil. Simmer 4 to 5 minutes, stirring occasionally. Add berries (still frozen), cover, and cook one minute more, over very low heat. Serve with skim milk. Serves 4.

TOASTED RICE CEREAL ·

1 cup short-grain brown rice   Nutmeg
2 cups water   Cinnamon
Skim milk

Toast rice in Teflon pan over moderate-to-high heat until rice spins, pops, and begins to turn brown. Remove from heat immediately. In covered saucepan, combine rice and water, bring to a boil, and simmer 15 minutes. Stir to fluff, and serve with skim milk, adding nutmeg and cinnamon to taste. Serves 4.

TOASTED WHEAT BERRY CEREAL

1 cup wheat berries (whole   2 cups water
   dried wheat kernels)   Skim milk

Toast wheat berries in Teflon skillet over moderate-to-high heat until berries spin, pop, and begin to brown. Combine with water in saucepan, cover, and simmer 45 minutes. Serve with skim milk. Serves 4.

WHEAT BERRY CEREAL

1 cup wheat berries (whole   Dash of allspice
   dried wheat kernels)   Fresh strawberries, sliced
½ teaspoon cinnamon   Skim milk
Dash of nutmeg

Add wheat berries to 2 cups boiling water, cover, and simmer ½ hour. Add spices and cook 5 minutes more. Drain, top with sliced strawberries and skim milk, and serve. Serves 4.

HOT SHREDDED WHEAT

This is the way Grandma used to serve shredded wheat down on the farm. We all loved it, especially on those winter mornings that were dark and cold. It's just as easy for 1 person as for many. For each person use:

2 biscuits shredded wheat
2 tablespoons unprocessed bran flakes
(1 teaspoon defatted wheat germ)

Fresh fruit *or* hot **fruit sauce**
Cold skim milk

Place shredded wheat biscuits in individual serving bowl. Pour boiling water over biscuits and drain immediately. Top with bran flakes, wheat germ, and fruit or sauce. Add milk and serve immediately.

PANCAKES

Cooking time, temperature, and technique are far more critical in the pancake recipes that follow than in the foolproof chemical commercial mixes. Good results are possible, but expect a few failures.

SOURDOUGH PANCAKES

Batches of batter need to be kept small when making these sourdough pancakes. To double or triple the number of pancakes, make 2 or 3 separate batches of batter, frying up the pancakes as soon as each batch of batter is mixed. This recipe uses **Sourdough Starter.** One generally keeps only about a cup of starter on hand, so the starter needs to be multiplied the night before so that the pancakes can be made in the morning, and the starter pot replenished as well. To do this, the night before, bring 1 cup starter to room temperature. Add 2 cups whole wheat flour and enough water to achieve a consistency like pancake batter. Let sit out all night. By morning, entire mixture will have converted to 3 cups of **Sourdough Starter,** enough to make 2 batches of sourdough pancakes and still return 1 cup of starter to refrigerator.

2 egg whites	¼ cup skim milk
1 cup **Sourdough Starter**	¼ cup white flour

Beat egg whites until stiff. Gently fold in starter, milk, and white flour. Teflon-fry over low to moderate heat. Makes 6 medium pancakes.

VELVETY PANCAKES

½ teaspoon baking powder	2 egg whites
1 cup flour	1½ cups evaporated skim milk

Combine baking powder and flour. Beat egg whites to soft peaks, then add milk and beat again. Combine wet and dry mixtures and stir lightly. Teflon-fry pancakes on both sides. Top with a **fruit sauce.** Makes 12 to 14 pancakes.

ETHEREAL PANCAKES

2 or 3 egg whites	⅓ cup skim milk
½ cup flour	

Beat egg whites until stiff. Fold in flour, then milk, beating mixture a few seconds after adding milk. Pour batter onto hot Teflon skillet and fry slowly. Turn when first side is brown and fry second side. Usual tests for doneness don't work. Peek to check for brownness. Use all batter as soon as possible. Makes 6 pancakes. For more pancakes, make a second recipe.

POTATO PANCAKES

2 medium potatoes, cooked and peeled
4 egg whites
½ cup **Yogurt** *or* **Sour Cream**
¼ cup grated onion
2 tablespoons finely chopped fresh parsley

1 tablespoon whole wheat flour
1 teaspoon **Vegetable Powder**
Pepper to taste

Grate potatoes into egg whites. Add remaining ingredients and stir well. Drop mixture on hot Teflon skillet, forming pancakes. Brown on both sides and serve with additional sour cream. Makes 16 small pancakes.

CORN PANCAKES

8 egg whites
½ cup cold evaporated skim milk

2 cups cornmeal

Beat egg whites stiff, then beat in milk just to combine. Stir in cornmeal. Spread mixture in rounds in Teflon skillet, and fry both sides. Serve with **fruit sauce.** Makes 10 to 15 pancakes.

YOGURT PANCAKES

8 egg whites
½ cup flour

½ cup **Yogurt** *or* **Sour Cream**

Beat the egg whites to soft peaks. Combine half the egg whites with flour and yogurt and mix well. Fold in remaining egg whites. Drop by spoonfuls onto hot Teflon skillet and cook until golden on both sides. Serve with a **fruit sauce.** Makes 16 small pancakes.

GRANDINI BREAKFAST

1 cup grandini style pasta, or other tiny pasta
2 egg whites

⅓ cup **Buttermilk**
⅓ cup skim milk

Add grandini to 2 cups boiling water. Cook until thick, like oatmeal. Stir in egg whites, buttermilk, and skim milk. (Milks will form curd, and eggs will set.) Continue to stir and boil to desired serving consistency. Top with fruit and skim milk. Serves 4.

BREAKFAST SPAGHETTI

1 cup whole wheat spaghetti broken into 1-inch pieces
1 cup cooked brown rice or wheat berries
4 egg whites
¼ cup dry nonfat milk

½ cup **Buttermilk**
2 tablespoons lemon juice
½ cup **Cottage Cheese**
Sliced strawberries
(Freshly ground nutmeg)

Cook and drain spaghetti, then combine in saucepan with cooked rice. Blend egg whites, dry milk, buttermilk, and lemon juice with electric mixer. Add this mixture to cooked spaghetti and rice, and stir rapidly to coat. Add cottage cheese, continue rapid stirring, and cook slowly to coagulate egg white. Top with strawberries and nutmeg, and serve. Skim milk may be poured over at the table. Serves 4.

YOGURT CREPES

3 egg whites
½ cup **Yogurt**

¾ cup skim milk
¾ cup flour

Beat egg whites and yogurt until foamy. Beat in milk, then flour. Spoon onto hot Teflon griddle, spreading out into thin pancakes. Turn as soon as spatula will slide under pancake without sticking. Makes 16 crepes.

POLENTA

½ cup cornmeal

¼ teaspoon dill weed

Soak cornmeal 20 minutes in ½ cup cold water. Bring 1⅓ cups water to a boil, and stir in cornmeal mixture. Simmer 20 minutes, stirring constantly. Add dill weed a few minutes before cornmeal is finished cooking. Pour into small rectangular dish and let cool and solidify. Cut into cubes or thick slices and Teflon-fry. Serve with **Yogurt** or **Sour Cream** as a breakfast accompaniment. May also be served topped with spaghetti sauce like a pasta. Serves 4.

BREAKFAST FRUIT COCKTAIL

One 8-ounce can of
   juice-packed pineapple
2 bananas

1 papaya
Lime

Cut fruit into bite-size pieces. Combine all ingredients, including juice from canned pineapple. Serve in stemmed glasses garnished with lime wedge. Serves 4.

FRENCH TOAST

6 egg whites
½ cup evaporated skim milk

Cinnamon
6 slices bread

Combine egg whites and skim milk. Sprinkle with cinnamon. Soak bread slices on each side in egg mixture, then Teflon-fry over low heat on both sides. Serve plain or topped with a **fruit sauce.**

BEEF SAUSAGE

1 pound leanest ground beef
¼ cup ice water
1 teaspoon to 1 tablespoon Ralston cereal
1 teaspoon **Vegetable Powder**
¼ teaspoon pepper
¼ teaspoon paprika
¼ teaspoon basil

¼ teaspoon caraway seed
¼ teaspoon dill weed
¼ teaspoon onion powder
⅛ teaspoon garlic powder
⅛ teaspoon cayenne pepper
⅛ teaspoon celery seed
20 dill seeds
Dash of thyme

Combine all ingredients and refrigerate overnight. Shape into 16 patties, and Teflon-fry just until cooked through. Since 1 patty equals 1 ounce, keeping track of meat consumption will be easy. Makes sixteen 1-ounce patties.

MOCK PORK SAUSAGE

1 cup ground chicken breast
1 cup leanest ground beef
¼ cup cold water
¼ teaspoon pepper
⅛ teaspoon garlic powder

⅛ teaspoon sage
⅛ teaspoon savory
10 needles of dried rosemary, crumbled

Combine all ingredients. Shape into 16 patties and store in freezer until needed. Each patty will contain about 1 ounce meat, making meat consumption easy to keep track of. When ready to use, Teflon-fry frozen patties under pot lid at low to moderate heat until cooked through. Makes sixteen 1-ounce patties.

CHAPTER 12

Sandwich Makings and Spreads

Place any kind of food between two slices of bread and—*voilà!*—one has a sandwich. How could a concept so simple have escaped discovery before John Montague (the 4th Earl of Sandwich) introduced it in the 1700s? In fact, how did the world get along without sandwiches before the earl did his thing? Maybe sandwiches have been around as long as bread, but without a name. Perhaps, being nameless, the poor sandwich drifted through the centuries unrecognized as an entity on its own, never seen as anything more than a random intermingling of bread with other foods. Then in a stroke, the popular Earl of Sandwich gave the concept a name and a place in history.

Any breads acceptable to longevity cookery are fair game for making sandwiches. Lefse, sourdough bread or biscuits, tortillas, and especially pitas—all make unique, interesting sandwiches. Use the sandwich ideas in this chapter, and experiment with other breads and foods as well.

LEFSE ROLLS

¼ pound leanest ground beef
½ cup cooked brown rice
¼ cup **Beef Stock**
¼ cup chopped onion
¼ medium tomato, chopped
2 fresh mushrooms, chopped
2 tablespoons chopped green
   pepper

2 tablespoons Plus-Meat in
   ¼ cup water
1 tablespoon flour
Dash of thyme
4 **Lefse**

Brown ground beef in Teflon skillet, and drain off any rendered fat. Add remaining ingredients except lefse, cover, and simmer until onions and peppers are tender (about 15 minutes). Place several spoonsful of this mixture on each lefse, and roll up burrito-style. Eat with fingers or with knife and fork. Makes a filling lunch for 4.

MEATBALL SANDWICHES

Sauce ingredients:
½ medium green pepper,
   chopped
½ medium onion, chopped
1 clove garlic, minced
1½ cups tomato juice
2 tablespoons tomato paste

½ teaspoon basil
¼ teaspoon oregano
20 seeds from mild red
   pepper (see page 263)
Sandwich ingredients:
1 recipe **Sourdough Biscuits**
1 recipe **Italian Meatballs**

Place green pepper, onion, and garlic in ½ cup water, and simmer until tender. Add remaining sauce ingredients and bring to boil. Add meatballs and heat through. Cut biscuits in half, place half a meatball on each biscuit half, top with sauce, and eat sandwich-style or with knife and fork. Makes 15 small sandwiches.

GARBANZO BURGERS

1 cup well-cooked and
   drained garbanzo beans
1 cup leanest ground beef
¼ cup ice water

¼ cup chopped onion
Pepper
Pinch of fenugreek

Chop beans and beef together in meat grinder. Stir in water and onion, and season to taste. Blend with hands and shape into burgers. Teflon-fry and serve with **Hamburger Sauce** on **Sourdough Bread.** Makes 6 to 8 burgers.

SOFT TACOS

1 cup cooked and drained
   leanest ground beef
1 cup grated **Fresh Cheese**
6 corn tortillas

⅓ cup **Enchilada Sauce** *or*
   Chili Salsa
1 cup shredded lettuce

Cook beef and cheese in Teflon skillet over low heat until cheese softens. Lay tortillas out on a hot griddle, and spoon a sixth of meat and cheese mixture into center of each tortilla. Top each tortilla with enchilada sauce and lettuce, roll tortilla up (fastening with toothpick if desired), and serve. Makes 6 soft tacos.

CHALUPAS DE LAREDO

½ cup **Red Molé Sauce**
2 cups **Refried Beans**
12 corn tortillas

2 cups grated **Fresh Cheese**
4 cups shredded lettuce
3 cups chopped tomato

Warm molé sauce. Reheat beans and combine beans and molé sauce. Spread on tortillas to the edges, then cover with grated cheese. Bake on cookie sheet at 450° until cheese softens (about 10 minutes). Top with lettuce and tomato and serve. Makes 12 chalupas, serving 4 to 6.

L.A. CHALUPAS

1 cup **L.A. Bean Dip**
6 corn tortillas
1 medium tomato, chopped

1 canned California green
    chili, chopped
2 cups shredded lettuce

Spread bean dip over tortillas, arrange tomatoes and chilies over top, and bake at 450° until tortillas become crisp (about 10 minutes). Top with lettuce and serve. Makes 6 chalupas.

PITA SANDWICHES

The rest of the sandwiches in this chapter are all pita bread sandwiches. The pita bread shell, because of its unique ability to containerize nearly any kind of stuffing, makes an ideal and versatile sandwich bread. Try some of the pita sandwiches below and become convinced of pita's superiority in sandwich making.

EMPANADA DE MAÍZ
(Stuffed pie of corn)

Stuff pitas with leftover chili corn pie for a delicious sandwich-style corn-pie treat.

6 **Corn Pitas** *or* regular **Pitas**   1 cup shredded lettuce
3 cups leftover **Chili Corn Pie**

Slice each pita in half to form two stuffable pockets. Stuff pockets with chili corn pie and shredded lettuce. Makes 12 stuffed sandwiches.

PITA BURRITOS

6 **Pitas**
2 cups hot **Refried Beans**
1 cup grated **Fresh Cheese**
½ cup chopped onions

¼ cup finely chopped canned California green chilies
½ cup **Chili Salsa**

Cut each pita into 2 stuffable pockets. Mix hot beans with cheese, and stuff each pocket with some of mixture. Top each with onions, chilies, and salsa, and serve. Eat sandwich-style. Makes 12 pocket-style burritos.

SISTER'S ZUCCHINI BURRITOS

4 egg whites, stiffly beaten
½ cup flour (approximate)
2 cups diced zucchini
1 cup grated **Fresh Cheese**
1 tablespoon chopped canned California green chili
¼ teaspoon garlic powder

⅛ teaspoon pepper
Pita Bread (2 large or 3 small)
Lettuce, shredded
Tomatoes, chopped
Green onions, chopped
(Chili Salsa)

To stiffly beaten egg whites, add sufficient flour to make a consistency like thick pancake batter. Add zucchini, cheese, green chili, garlic powder, and pepper. Teflon-fry until brown on one side.

Turn, reduce heat, and continue cooking until eggs are done and zucchini is still somewhat crisp. Cut pitas in half, forming pita pockets, and stuff with the egg and zucchini mixture. Top with lettuce, tomatoes, and onions. If desired, dress with chili salsa. Delicious! Makes 4 to 6 stuffed pitas.

PITA MEAT LOAF BURGER

Pitas   **Sour Cream**
Leftover **Everyday Meat Loaf**   (Tomatoes, chopped)
Chopped lettuce   (Onion, chopped)

Cut each pita into 2 stuffable pockets. Stuff each pocket with left-over meat loaf. Heat 20 minutes in 400° oven, or 1 minute in microwave oven. Top with lettuce and sour cream (and tomatoes and onion if desired). Makes an excellent sandwich to take to the office if a microwave oven is available. Also makes a marvelous cold meat loaf sandwich.

PITA GRILLED CHEESE AND TOMATO

Pitas   Very thin slices of **Fresh Cheese**
Tomato slices

Slice each pita into 2 stuffable pockets. Place 2 tomato slices and 2 cheese slices in each pocket. Bake at 400° for 20 minutes or cook 2 minutes in microwave oven. Great for the office.

PITA JOES

Pitas   Shredded lettuce
Chili con carne

Slice pita bread in half to make 2 envelopes. Fill each envelope with chili con carne and overstuff with shredded lettuce. Allow 2 to 3 half sandwiches per person. Ideal for sailing, picnicking, or parties.

SUMMER SANDWICH

Pitas
Fresh Cheese, grated
Roast Beef, thinly sliced
Cucumber slices
Lettuce, shredded

Cut pitas in half, making pairs of stuffable pockets. Fill pockets with grated cheese, roast beef slices, and cucumber slices. Overstuff with shredded lettuce. Makes an ideal sandwich for that hot summer day.

PITA PIZZAS

6 **Pitas**
2 cups tomato topping (equal parts tomato paste and water)
2 cups grated **Fresh Cheese**
One 4-ounce can of mushrooms, drained
Other toppings desired (chopped onion, green pepper, etc.)
Garlic powder
Oregano
Basil

Split pitas to form 12 rounds. Spread rough side of rounds with tomato topping, then layer on cheese, mushrooms, and other toppings. Sprinkle evenly with spices. Arrange pizzas on cake rack on cookie sheet and bake at 450° until cheese has softened (about 15 minutes). Makes 12 pizzas.

SQUASH PITAS

2 cups **Mashed Squash**   Fenugreek
1 cup tiny cantaloupe cubes   5 **Pitas**
Nutmeg

Combine squash and cantaloupe. Season to taste with nutmeg and fenugreek. Cut pitas into stuffable pita pockets, and stuff with squash and melon mixture. Makes 10 sandwiches.

TUNA SALAD SANDWICHES

3 **Pitas**   2 cups **Tuna Salad**

Cut pitas into 6 stuffable pockets and stuff with tuna salad mixture. Makes 6 sandwiches.

SPREADS

The four spreads below can help dress up an otherwise bland sandwich. Use also **Hamburger Sauce** or **Sour Cream.**

GARBANZO SPREAD

1 cup cooked garbanzo beans (chick-peas)
1 cup **Sour Cream**
¼ cup cooking liquid from beans
½ clove garlic, minced
1 tablespoon lemon juice
1 tablespoon chopped fresh parsley
¼ teaspoon crushed coriander seed
¼ teaspoon cumin
Dash of cayenne pepper

Combine all ingredients in blender, adding more liquid if necessary. Spread on matzos, pitas, or bread. Makes 2½ cups.

TUNA SALAD SPREAD

¾ cup **Garbanzo Spread**
  (above)

½ cup **Sour Cream**
½ cup canned tuna

Combine ingredients. Makes an ideal canapé spread. Makes 1½ cups.

MOCK CREAM CHEESE

1½ cups **Cottage Cheese**
¼ cup **Buttermilk**

¼ cup skim milk

Combine all ingredients in blender and blend until very smooth. Refrigerate. Mixture will thicken to a cream cheese consistency. Makes 2 cups.

HORSERADISH DRESSING

¼ cup **Sour Cream**
¼ teaspoon dried Japanese
  horseradish

Combine ingredients and refrigerate 3 or 4 hours. Makes ¼ cup.

CHAPTER 13

Cheeses

Cheese has been a part of human food-fare for a long, long time. According to the eminent cheesemaker Don Radke,* there are *written* records of cheesemaking that date back 6000 years. Who knows how many years cheese was made and used prior to written records? For thousands of years cheesemaking was a family affair. Cheeses were made in small batches in small kitchens by families wanting to convert the family cow's milk to a product that wouldn't go bad so quickly. Today cheese is mass-produced outside the family kitchen, and all the family knows about cheese is what it sees in the supermarket.

Cheeses are important in this book. Cheese is often used as a critical ingredient in a recipe to add texture, consistency, or flavor. The trouble is, it is hard to find cheeses at the supermarket that don't have fat contents so high as to make them totally unacceptable in longevity cookery. Therefore, the serious longevity cook will need cheese recipes that do not suffer from this drawback. In this chapter we present recipes for very low-fat cheeses.

*Don Radke, *Cheese Making at Home: The Complete Illustrated Guide* (Garden City, N.Y.: Doubleday & Company, Inc. 1974).

It is sad but true that many of the commercial cheeses with which we are most familiar have a fat content in excess of 50 percent and cannot be made with a lower fat content without sacrificing their familiar flavors and textures. Thus Cheddar, Romano, long horn, and Swiss exclude themselves from longevity cookery (and this chapter) because of their fat content.

Generally speaking the "cured" cheeses, those that need to be aged for some period of time before they are eaten, cannot be made successfully with a low fat content. This is not the case for the uncured, or "fresh," cheeses that may be eaten as soon as they are made. Many are possible to make with a low fat content, and can often be found at the supermarket. Dry curd cottage cheese, farmer's cheese, and hoop cheese are uncured cheeses in this category. Of course it is also possible to make these and other uncured cheeses with a high fat content. The reader is advised to read the nutrition information on a cheese before buying. If the fat content exceeds 8 percent on a *dry weight* basis, the cheese should be avoided. Unfortunately, the nutrition information available on a cheese label rarely states the fat content in terms of dry weight. If it states some fat content information but doesn't *say* this information refers to dry weight, one can be sure it doesn't refer to dry weight. In that case, the stated fat content will have been computed on the basis of the fully moisturized cheese. This changes the figures drastically: the cheese should be used only if the label clearly states that its butterfat content is less than 1.5 percent. If the label doesn't state its fat content at all, don't buy it.

The cheeses in this chapter are all uncured cheeses, including cream cheese, cottage cheese, ricotta cheese, sour cream, hoop cheese, and mozzarella-style fresh cheese. Unless kept frozen, these cheeses need to be eaten within a few days for best results. Their high moisture content and low salt content effectively preempt a long shelf-life.

The basic process of cheesemaking is simple. All cheesemaking begins with milk that is allowed to sour. The soured milk is then allowed to coagulate into a gelatinous mass (either slowly, of its own accord, or more quickly with the addition of a *rennet* enzyme tablet). The gelatinous mass is then cut with a knife into many small pieces (called *curds*), and heat is slowly applied, driving the liquid (called *whey*) from each curd, and causing each curd to shrink in size and increase in firmness. The whey is then drawn off and the curds are compacted together to form a solid body of cheese. The cheese is either eaten fresh in this form, or cured by allowing it to sit on a shelf for some period of time. That's all there is to cheesemaking. In summary the process is:

1. Allowing the milk to sour
2. Allowing, or assisting, the milk to coagulate
3. Driving out the whey by cutting and heating the curds
4. Compacting the curds into a solid body of cheese
5. Aging, or curing, the cheese

Since we're not concerned with cured cheese, we'll simply omit step number 5. Let's now look at each step in the process in a little more detail in order to highlight some of the factors that are important in making good cheese.

In the process of souring, the acidity of the milk increases greatly. An elevated acid content is necessary for the effective and timely release of the whey from the curds. The acid is produced in the souring milk by living microorganisms that create it as a part of their life cycle. *Raw* milk, since it is not pasteurized, already contains organisms that can do the job of creating the desired acidity. All one must do is warm the milk, let it sit while the natural organisms within it multiply, and—presto!—properly soured milk emerges. Pasteurized milk does not contain the living organisms required for proper souring. So the organisms must be introduced into the milk. The addition of a little **Buttermilk** or **Yogurt,** or commercial *cultured* buttermilk or yogurt,[1] will supply those necessary little organisms, and the milk will sour nicely.

---

1. For tastiest results, use a commercial yogurt made from the organism *Lactobacillus bulgaricus*. Health food stores often carry brands that indicate on their label the strain from which they are made. With a buttermilk starter, best results are achieved when the buttermilk, whether homemade or commercial, is as fresh as possible.

In the process of coagulation, the protein in the milk is being broken down into smaller protein fragments by enzymatic action of the same organisms. These protein fragments then aggregate into billions of small particles. These particles form what is known as a *colloidal suspension:* particulate matter (the protein) floating in a liquid (the whey). As the particles increase in size and number, the whole solution finally stiffens into a gel, and one giant curd is formed. Coagulation is complete when a knife blade inserted between the curd and pot can pull the curd in one mass cleanly away from the sides of the pot. It is to hasten the formation of this coagulum that rennet is added to the soured milk. Rennet is an enzyme extracted from a calf's stomach that speeds up both the breakdown of the milk protein and the formation of the gel. Rennet can be found in most supermarkets under the brand name Junket-rennet.

The whey will eventually begin to ooze from the surface of the single giant curd, after the milk has coagulated. By cutting this large curd into many, many smaller curds,[2] a great increase is achieved in the surface area from which the whey may ooze. This greatly facilitates the driving out of the whey from the curds. Slow, gentle heating and careful agitation achieve the complete separation of curd and whey, and the whey may then be drained away.

Finally, the curd is compacted into a solid body of cheese. This is done by wrapping the curd in cheesecloth and squeezing, or by putting the cheese into a cheese press and exerting pressure. In cottage cheese, no compacting is needed. The curds are eaten just as they are.

---

2. The curd should be cut into uniformly sized pieces to insure a uniform separation of curd from whey throughout the cheese. This helps produce a consistently good cheese. An easy way to cut the curd into uniformly sized cubes is as follows. First draw the knife through the curd and make evenly spaced slices across the pot from edge to edge and clear to the bottom. Then cut again in the same uniform fashion, but crosswise to the first slices. Now the top surface of the curd looks like a checkerboard of uniform squares, and the curd itself has been cut into square columns. To cut the columns into cubes, slice again, in both directions, and *along the same lines* as the first slicing, but tilt the knife 45° from the vertical while slicing. This will slice the columns into cubes.

WHEY

In the process of making any cheese, whey is produced, lots and lots of it. Should the whey be discarded once it is drained away from the curd? Absolutely not. While the curd has captured the lion's share of the milk's protein, the whey has captured most of the milk's carbohydrate. Whey is a marvelously nutritious liquid that is in no way inferior to the curd. Whey can be used in beverages, general cooking, or in making other cheeses. See, for instance, **Whey Lemonade, A Whey to Cook Rice,** and **Ricotta Cheese.** Whey can be sweet, as when **Fresh Cheese** is made, or sour, as when **Small-Curd Cottage Cheese** is made. So when storing whey away, be sure to taste it, and label it according to its sweetness or sourness.

FRESH CHEESE[3]

Fresh cheeses are sliceable mozzarella-style cheeses that combine well with nearly all other ingredients in casseroles, pizzas, lasagna dishes, etc. Because they contain so little butterfat, they have less taste than commercial fresh cheeses. The reader may wish to add spices at the appropriate place in the fresh cheese recipes to add a little extra zip. Experimentation is called for to find spices, herbs, and peppers that produce best-liked flavors.

The two fresh cheese recipes that follow differ in their sourness and the ease with which they melt. Rennet fresh cheese is a sweet cheese that melts with difficulty. Use it in casseroles and other dishes in which a little sweetness will be an asset and in which long, hot cooking is called for. (Long hot cooking will insure that the cheese will melt sufficiently.) Buttermilk fresh cheese is slightly sourer than rennet fresh cheese, but melts easily. Use it in cas-

---

3. The term "fresh cheese" is often used as a generic name for *any* uncured cheese that may be eaten immediately, without an intervening curing or aging process. But in this book we mean only one or the other of our two particular fresh cheeses when we say fresh cheese.

seroles and other dishes that could use a slight touch of sourness, and which have a shorter cooking time in which to melt the cheese.

RENNET FRESH CHEESE

4 quarts skim milk
1 cup nonfat dry milk
½ cup **Yogurt** or a commercial yogurt (see footnote 1 above)

2 cups **Buttermilk**
2 rennet tablets

Combine dry milk with 2 cups of the liquid milk in the blender. Add to remaining milk and warm to 96°. Blend yogurt and buttermilk in blender, then add to warmed milk. Let sit 1 hour. Add rennet dissolved in ¼ cup cold water and stir 2 minutes. Remove all utensils and allow coagulation to occur (about 30 minutes). Place over very low heat and begin breaking up curd with hands. Repeatedly squeeze curds into ever smaller pieces as temperature gradually rises. Curd will separate from whey and shrink in size. Use hands to prevent curd from matting into aggregates. When the temperature of the whey rises to 90°, dip curd from whey with hands or a tea strainer and place into a cheesecloth-lined colander. Immediately catch curd up in cheesecloth. (Save whey for **Ricotta Cheese.**) Curd may be quickly seasoned at this point if desired, with garlic powder, bits of canned California green chili pepper, etc. Draw cheesecloth up to form a bag, twist bag tightly to drain off residual whey, and cheese is ready to use almost immediately. Makes about 1 pound.

BUTTERMILK FRESH CHEESE

½ gallon raw skim milk (Raw milk is a must. Pasteurized milk won't work.)

2 cups **Buttermilk** *or* a nonfat commercial *cultured* buttermilk

Heat skim milk to 90°. Add buttermilk and stir well. Let sit in a warm place (80°) until coagulated (about 5 hours). Stir once or twice gently to break curd up slightly, then heat slowly over lowest heat until temperature again rises to 90°. Dip curds out with hands or tea strainer and place into cheesecloth-lined collander to drain. Curds may be quickly seasoned at this point if desired. Bag up curds, and press with a large can of something to squeeze out remaining whey (10 minutes to 1 hour). Ready to use almost immediately. Makes about ½ pound.

COTTAGE CHEESE

Nonfat cottage cheeses can often be found at the supermarket. Look for brands that specifically state that the fat content is less than 1½ percent. Brands labeled "Dry Curd Cottage Cheese" usually have very low fat contents, sometimes less than ½ percent. Even though nonfat cottage cheeses are readily available at the market, they are so easy and so much fun to make at home that we have included recipes for them below. An added bonus to making them at home is that homemade versions taste better than commercial versions.

Use these cottage cheeses in recipes calling for a cottage cheese, or serve them as separate dishes. Spice with sage, caraway seeds, or chives. Allow 2 or 3 hours for flavors to blend.

LARGE-CURD COTTAGE CHEESE

1 gallon skim milk	1 rennet tablet
¼ cup **Buttermilk**	

Place skim milk in pot and heat slowly to 75°. Heat on an asbestos pad in order to slow down the temperature rise. Combine skim milk and buttermilk, and stir in rennet tablet dissolved in 1 table-spoon water. Cover, and let sit undisturbed in a warm place (about 75°) until coagulated (about 16 hours). Cut curd into ½-inch cubes, and place over low heat. Allow temperature to rise slowly to 115° (about 45 minutes), gently stirring occasionally to maintain a uniform temperature throughout the curds and whey. Test curd for firmness,* allowing temperature to rise to 120° if necessary. When properly firmed, pour off or dip out most of whey, then pour contents of pot into cheesecloth-lined colander. Allow remaining whey to drain through, and bag curd up in cheesecloth. Rinse curd thoroughly by dipping and working cheesecloth bag in large kettle of ice water. Set bag of curd in colander, and let drain well (1 to 2 hours). Cottage cheese is now ready to serve. Makes 1 quart.

SMALL-CURD COTTAGE CHEESE

Small-curd cottage cheese is prepared in a manner much like that of large-curd. Small-curd differs from large-curd in the size and firmness of the curd and in the addition of a slight, pleasant sourness. Because of its slightly greater sourness, the curd takes longer to expel its whey and achieve proper firmness during the heating process. The time needed for it to coagulate is also longer, since rennet is not added. (This longer time to coagulate is responsible for the increased sourness.)

1 gallon skim milk ¼ cup **Buttermilk**

Heat skim milk slowly to 75°. Combine ingredients, cover, and let sit undisturbed in a warm place (about 75°) until coagulated (about 22 hours). Cut curd into ¼-inch cubes, and place over low heat. Allow temperature to rise slowly to 115° (about 45 minutes), gently stirring occasionally to keep a uniform temperature throughout the curds and whey. Hold at 115° until curd firms properly (about 25

*Squeeze curd with fingers; should be firm, but not hard.

minutes), gently stirring occasionally. Allow temperatures to rise to 120° if necessary to achieve desired firmness. When firm, pour curds and whey into cheesecloth-lined colander. Allow whey to drain through, and bag the curds up into the cheesecloth. Rinse curds thoroughly by dipping cheesecloth bag repeatedly into a large pot of ice water. Set bag of curds into colander to drain (1 to 2 hours). Cottage cheese is then ready to serve. Makes 1 quart.

GRANDMA'S COTTAGE CHEESE

½ cup regular nonfat dry   1 gallon skim milk
  milk   1½ cups **Yogurt**

Blend dry milk with 2 cups of the skim milk. Stir blended milk into remainder of skim milk. Add yogurt, cover, and let sit undisturbed in a warm place until coagulated (about 24 hours). Cook over lowest heat until curds have firmed (about 1 hour). (Stir occasionally in order to keep temperature constant. Try not to break up curd excessively in this process.) Pour contents of pot into cheesecloth-lined colander. Let whey drain through, and bag up the curds in the cheesecloth. Rinse thoroughly by dipping bag of curds repeatedly into a large kettle of cold water. Set bag of curds in colander, place a large can (of something) on top of the bag, and let drain 2 hours. Refrigerate curd, crumble to uniform size, and serve. Makes 1 quart.

HOMEMADE HOOP CHEESE

Hoop cheese is nothing more than nonfat small-curd cottage cheese that has been compressed into a block. Because it is crumbly, it is only barely sliceable. What it does best is crumble back into a cottage cheese. To make it at home use:

1 pound **Small-Curd Cottage Cheese** (p. 331)
1 clean, empty tin can with bottom intact
1 round block of wood that fits snugly into can

Grind cottage cheese in meat grinder, using finest grinding disk. Repeat twice more. Spoon ground cottage cheese into tin can, and cover with round block of wood. Compress cheese by forcing block of wood hard into tin can. Use a short segment of broomstick and a lot of arm muscle to accomplish this compression. Refrigerate. To remove cheese, open can from other end and push cheese out. Makes 1 pound.

INSTANT CHEESE

¼ cup powdered buttermilk   2 cups skim milk

Combine ingredients and, stirring constantly, cook over medium heat until curds begin to form. Stir and force curds together with spoon until all curds have been matted into a ball. Remove ball, knead several times, then press flat. May be used immediately for snacks or diced up in salads. Store in refrigerator. Makes a little less than ½ cup.

RICOTTA CHEESE

Ever wonder what to do with all that leftover whey? Some of it can be used to make delicious ricotta cheese, which in turn can be used in Italian lasagna and manicotti dishes.

3 quarts sweet whey,*   1½ cups skim milk
   freshly made   1 quart sour whey*

*Sweet whey tastes sweet and milky. Sour whey is sour and lemonlike. **Rennet Fresh Cheese** makes sweet whey (about 3 quarts for 1 recipe). **Small-Curd Cottage Cheese** makes sour whey (about 2¾ quarts for 1 recipe).

Combine sweet whey and skim milk and quickly heat to just below boiling. Heat sour whey to 110° and add 1 cup of it to sweet whey mixture. A curdlike material will form and rise to the surface. This is ricotta. Skim it off as it rises and place it into a cheesecloth-lined colander. When no more ricotta rises to the top, add another cup of sour whey, and the ricotta will begin forming and rising again to be skimmed off. Keep adding sour whey, a cup at a time, until ricotta ceases rising altogether. Cool cheese to lukewarm and stir. It is now ready to use. (If cheese is too dry, add 2 tablespoons **Sour Cream** or **Buttermilk**.) Makes 1 cup.

SOUR CHEESE

½ gallon raw skim milk
2 cups commercial churned nonfat buttermilk
1 rennet tablet

Combine milks, heat to 90°, and let stand at room temperature 24 hours. Add rennet tablet dissolved in ¼ cup cool water, and let sit until coagulated (30 minutes). Pour into a cheesecloth-lined colander and bag curd up in cheesecloth. Drain 3 hours. Makes 2 cups.

SOUR CREAM

This recipe makes a *mock* sour cream. No real cream at all is used, yet it is truly delicious. It tastes much like real sour cream, and may be used wherever real sour cream is used. Use it on baked potatoes, in salads, on pancakes, as a dip, etc.

½ gallon skim milk
¼ cup **Buttermilk** *or* commercial cultured nonfat buttermilk

Combine ingredients and heat slowly to 95°, stirring constantly. Cover, remove from heat, and let stand in a warm place until coagulated (1 or 2 days). Turn curd into colander lined with 4 layers of cheesecloth. Let drain 20 minutes. Then place colander into a large pot, supported up off the bottom of the pot by a good 4 inches. (This 4-inch clearance will insure that as the curd continues to drain, the waterline of the draining whey will not rise up so high as to soak the curd and prevent further draining.) Place this whole draining assembly into a plastic bag, tie bag closed, and put in refrigerator for 1 or 2 days. Turn curd into a bowl and stir until smooth. Makes 2 cups.

CREAM CHEESE

2 cups **Sour Cream**

Cut 4 squares of cheesecloth, each large enough to envelop ½ cup of the sour cream. Place ½ cup of sour cream on each cheesecloth square, and bag it up in the cheesecloth, fastening each bag with a wire tie. Place bags on a cake rack over a pan to drain. Place this draining assembly in a plastic bag, tie bag closed, place in refrigerator, and let drain 1 or 2 days. Makes 1½ cups.

JUNKET CHEESE

1 Junket rennet tablet
¼ cup regular nonfat dry milk
2 cups skim milk

Dissolve rennet tablet in 1 tablespoon cool water. Combine dry milk with small amount of the skim milk. If necessary, beat with mixer or egg beater to dissolve powder. Stir in remaining milk.

Heat to lukewarm (110°), stirring constantly. Remove from heat, add dissolved rennet tablet, and stir for no more than 30 seconds. Let stand undisturbed until curd forms. Cut curd into 1-inch cubes, and cook in double boiler over hot water (20 minutes for a soft-curd cheese and 60 minutes for a sweet dry-curd cottage cheese). Drain in a cheesecloth-lined colander for several hours. Use as an ingredient in blintzes, crepes, and casseroles. Or spread generously on a **Lefse,** roll lefse up, and smother with a **fruit sauce** and **Sour Cream.** Makes ¾ cup.

BUTTERMILK

It is easy to make buttermilk with a very low fat content. In fact, many commercial buttermilks have fat contents as low as 1-percent fat by *dry weight.* That would put the fat content of the undried product so low, about $1/10$ of 1 percent, as to be totally negligible. Here's the recipe.

1 quart raw skim milk
1 cup **Buttermilk** *or* commercial *cultured* buttermilk*

Warm raw skim milk to 90°, add buttermilk, and stir well. Cover, and let sit in a warm place (80°) 3 to 5 hours. At some point after the first 3 hours of sitting, the buttermilk will be ready. If it *tastes* like buttermilk, it's ready. Pour into a jar and refrigerate. If it sits out for too long after the buttermilk taste has developed, the curd and whey will separate, and the nice uniform buttermilk we want will have been lost. If the buttermilk *does* happen to separate, do not despair. Make **Buttermilk Fresh Cheese** from it, use it as a fine starter, or simply use it as a "separated" kind of buttermilk. Makes 5 cups of delicious sweet buttermilk.

*Use nonfat brands if possible. Otherwise filter out butterfat particles by pouring through several layers of cheesecloth. Realize that repeatedly making **Buttermilk** from already made **Buttermilk** plus skim milk will gradually reduce any initial fat content (created by using a commercial buttermilk) to nearly zero.

YOGURT

Add a little yogurt to a lot of milk, keep the milk lukewarm (100°) for 10 hours, and like magic you have converted all that milk to yogurt. The easiest way to maintain a constant temperature for the required length of time is with a yogurt maker. Lacking a yogurt maker, try this: heat the milk to 100°, pour it into a warmed thermos bottle, add the yogurt, cap the bottle, wrap it in towels, and place it in a warm, draft-free place. Or mix the yogurt and milk, pour into small containers, nestle the containers around a heating pad set at medium, and cover everything up with towels. In any event, here's the recipe:

¼ cup regular nonfat dry milk
1 quart skim milk
3 tablespoons **Yogurt** *or* any commercial yogurt

Combine dry milk with ½ cup of the liquid milk and stir to make a smooth paste. Stir paste into remaining milk and add yogurt. Maintain at a temperature of 100° for 10 hours, refrigerate, and serve. Makes 1 quart.

Glossary

al dente	Pasta cooked *al dente* is pasta that is slightly undercooked.
Armenian pita	Another name for *pita bread*.
au jus	Cooked in its natural juices.
bake	To cook food in an oven. More generally, to dry-cook food.
baste	To occasionally moisten a food with liquid during the cooking process.
beat	To briskly mix until smooth, or to add air by brisk mixing (as in beating egg whites).
Bible bread	Another name for *pita bread*.
blanch	To pour boiling water briefly over food so as to achieve an effect on the outer surface of the food without affecting the inside of the food. Blanching does different things to different foods. It can seal flavors in, drain color away, make colors fast, or loosen outer skins, depending on the food being blanched.
blend	To mix two or more ingredients until they form a smooth, homogeneous mixture.
broil	To cook by direct exposure to radiant heat: cooking by direct flame as opposed to oven cooking that is accomplished by exposure to heated air.
broiler chicken	A young chicken of either sex weighing between 2 and 2½ pounds. See also page 216.

burrito	A Mexican style dish made by rolling up beans, meat, or other stuffing material in a tortilla.
capon	A castrated male chicken, allowed to grow to a large size: 8 to 10 pounds.
chop	To cut into many pieces.
coagulate	This is the name for what happens when a liquid thickens into a single, cohesive mass. Examples are the curdling of milk and the clotting of blood.
cock	An old male chicken. Not good eating, but great for the stock pot.
colloidal suspension	A mixture of a powder and a liquid, in which the powder does not dissolve in the liquid, but rather is suspended as tiny solid particles within the liquid. Chili powder and water make a colloidal suspension when mixed. Curdled milk is a colloidal suspension of protein fragments in liquid whey.
curd	After soured milk coagulates, it will separate into two components: a liquid component and a more or less solid (cheesy) component. The solid, or cheesy, component is called the curd. The liquid component is called whey.
dash	About $^1/_{16}$ teaspoon.
dice	To cut a food into small, uniformly sized cubes.
dredge	To coat by sprinkling, as with flour.
Echtarharkäse *(cheese)*	A soft, commercial skim milk cheese, often found in the imported cheese portion of the deli section at the supermarket.
empanada	Mexican turnover-style pies.

filet	A slice of boneless meat or fish. To filet something is to cut it into filets.
flake	To gently break into small pieces, as to flake canned salmon.
fold	Suppose one has beaten a mixture until it is light and fluffy (like egg whites and milk). How does one add new ingredients to such a fluff and make sure to get the ingredients uniformly distributed throughout? One does this by a process called *folding*. Add ingredients, then, with a spoon, cut down through the mixture, across the bottom of the bowl, and up and over through the top surface of the mixture.
food gremlin	Food ingredients known to be causally related to the degenerative diseases: heart disease, diabetes, high blood pressure, atherosclerosis, and stroke. Food gremlins are fat, sugar, salt, caffeine, and cholesterol.
French-cut	French-cut green beans are green beans that are cut on the bias instead of straight across. That's all. French-cut tomatoes are tomatoes sliced vertically from top to bottom rather than through the equator of the tomato. That's all.
fryer chicken	A young chicken of either sex weighing between 2½ and 3½ pounds.
gremlin	See *food gremlin*, above.
hors d'oeuvre	A French term meaning literally "outside the main works." Hors d'oeuvres are appetizers that (outside this book) are served to moderate the adverse effects of before-dinner drinking of alcoholic beverages.

jicama	A large root-vegetable. Looks something like a turnip, but can be much larger, often a foot in diameter. Jicama has a thin, light brown skin that looks aged and unappetizing. But the potato-like flesh underneath is sweet and juicy, reminiscent of the taste of water chestnuts. It is excellent sliced into fresh salads. Look for it in markets specializing in foreign foods.
julienne	A soup containing julienne vegetables (vegetables cut into long strips).
kelp	Seaweed. Find it in the foreign foods section of the supermarket.
knead	To work dough with the palms of the hands. See page 271.
longevity cookery	*Gremlin*-free cooking.
marinade	Any spicy liquid in which foods are soaked to enrich their flavors.
marinate	To soak in a *marinade*.
mince	To chop into extremely small bits.
parboil	To partially cook by boiling.
parfait glass	A stemmed glass for holding frozen custards and other cold or frozen desserts.
pasta	Macaroni, spaghetti, noodles, or any other food consisting of shaped and dried dough.
pinch	An amount of dry ingredient that can be held between the thumb and the tip of the index finger. (This means a single layer of the ingredient. One is not allowed to stack a mound of material between the index finger and thumb and call it a pinch. That's too much.) A pinch is less than a dash.
pita bread	Pancake-shaped bread with a hollow in-

terior suitable for stuffing. Same as Armenian pita or Bible bread.

puree A paste made by rubbing cooked vegetables through a sieve. To puree a vegetable means to make a puree out of it.

ramekin An attractive casserole dish of individual size. Food is cooked in the ramekin and eaten directly from it. Spaghetti in an Italian restaurant is usually served in a ramekin.

regular nonfat dry milk Doesn't mix as well as instant nonfat dry milk, but tastes a lot better.

roast Means the same as bake, but is used exclusively when talking about baking meats.

roaster chicken A young chicken of either sex weighing between 3½ and 5 pounds.

sauté General usage has *sauté* meaning to cook rapidly in fat. Longevity cooking has *sauté* meaning to cook rapidly in small amount of *nonfat* liquid (usually garlic juice and water). Sautéed vegetables are much more flavorsome when sautéed in water and garlic juice than when sautéed in fat.

scald To heat to just below boiling.

scallop To bake food that is immersed in liquid.

shred To cut into long, thin, narrow strips.

simmer To cook in water over low heat, at a temperature between 135° and 160°.

soft peaks As egg whites are beaten, more and more air is incorporated into the eggs and the egg mixture becomes stiffer and stiffer, until there comes a time when, if the beater is withdrawn from the mixture, it will pull up a peak of egg white with it. *Soft peaks* fall over easily and fluidly. Further beating will produce *stiff peaks*, which hold their shape.

stiff peaks   See *soft peaks*, above.

Teflon   A material with which cooking utensils may be coated during manufacture so as to render their cooking surfaces nonstick.

tofu   A soybean product resembling fresh cheese. Find it in the deli section of the market under foreign foods.

tortilla   A thin unleavened Mexican-style pancake made from corn or flour and baked on a very hot surface. Used widely in Mexican restaurants to roll up beans, cheese, and meat. Burritos and enchiladas are Mexican dishes made from rolled-up, stuffed tortillas.

toss   To mix lightly.

trivet   A metal stand with short feet for use under a hot dish at table.

whey   After soured milk coagulates, it will separate into two components: a more or less solid (cheesy) component, and a liquid component. The liquid component is called *whey*. The solid component is called the *curd*.

whip   To beat rapidly so as to incorporate a large amount of air.

wilt   To plunge leafy foods briefly in boiling water so as to cause the freshness of the leaves to be lost.

VEGETABLE COOKING AND SPICING CHART

VEGETABLE	PRECOOKING PREPARATION	COOKING PROCEDURE	SPICES TO ADD	COOKING TIME
Artichokes	Wash well, cut off stems, and square off bottoms with knife. Slice off cluster of pointy leaves at top, and snip off pointy ends of other leaves. Dip in lightly vinegared water to prevent discoloration.	Place 3 or 4 artichokes in ½ cup boiling water, bottoms down. Cover tightly and simmer over low heat. When done, turn upside down to drain.	Sprinkle each artichoke lightly with thyme before cooking. Or, as is most common, use no spice at all.	30 to 40 minutes
Asparagus	Wash. Snap off butts (will snap where tender part begins). Line asparagus up and slice into ½-inch pieces, leaving top 3 inches of the spear unsliced.	Add the ½-inch pieces to ½ cup boiling water. Cover tightly and simmer a few minutes. Add spears, and continue simmering (tightly covered) until tender.	Add marjoram and perhaps a dash of tarragon or parsley when the spears are added.	15 minutes
Beans, Dried (pinto, navy, red, kidney, etc.)	Wash in cold water. Discard beans that float and any pebbles masquerading as beans.	Bring large amount of water (2 quarts per pound of beans) to a hopping boil. Add beans (so slowly that boiling action is not lessened). Reduce heat and simmer until tender.	If desired, add chopped onions and an **Herb Bundle** after adding beans. Remove bundle, and spice to taste with pepper and oregano about 15 minutes before cooking is finished.	1 to 2 hours

Vegetable	Preparation	Cooking	Seasoning	Time
Beans, Fresh (limas)	Shell and rinse.	Combine beans with water (½ cup water per 3 cups shelled limas) and bring to boil. Reduce heat, simmer until tender.	Lightly add rosemary and sage before cooking.	20 to 30 minutes
(green beans: snap beans, string beans, or wax beans)	Wash, snap off ends, and cut into 1-inch pieces if desired (or cook whole).	Add beans to boiling water (1 cup per 3 pounds beans), cover tightly, and simmer until tender.	Sprinkle in marjoram and oregano when cooking begins.	15 to 20 minutes
Other fresh beans	Shell and rinse.	Combine beans with water (1 cup water per 3 cups shelled beans) and bring to boil. Reduce heat and simmer until tender.	Toss in rosemary and sage before cooking.	45 minutes to 1 hour
Beets	Whole: slice off greens and root. Scrub, but don't pare.	Cover with water and bring to boil. Reduce heat and simmer until tender. Drain, cool, and pare.	Throw in bay leaf at beginning of cooking. Dash in Angostura Bitters or tarragon during last 15 minutes.	45 minutes to 1 hour
	Sliced or diced: pare and slice or dice.	Combine with water (½ cup per 2 cups beets), bring to boil, and simmer tightly covered until tender.	Sprinkle with tarragon or Angostura Bitters.	30 to 45 minutes

VEGETABLE COOKING AND SPICING CHART

VEGETABLE	PRECOOKING PREPARATION	COOKING PROCEDURE	SPICES TO ADD	COOKING TIME
Broccoli	Remove leaves and cut off the hard, inedible part of stem. Wash well. Break broccoli into flowerets, splitting or chopping stem.	Place in vegetable steaming rack, in bottom of pot. Add water (to bottom of rack), cover tightly, and steam until tender.	Sprinkle with thyme and nutmeg before steaming.	20 minutes
Brussels Sprouts	Remove stems and outer leaves. Wash.	Place in pot with 2 tablespoons water. Heat tightly covered a minute or two over medium heat (until steam begins to loosen lid). Reduce to low heat and cook without lifting lid.	Dash sparingly with sage or marjoram at beginning of cooking.	15 minutes
Cabbage	Remove wilted outer leaves. Wash.	Place in pot with ¼ cup water. Cover tightly and cook over medium heat until steam begins to loosen lid. Reduce to low heat and cook tightly covered without lifting lid.	Sprinkle with marjoram at the beginning of cooking.	15 minutes
Carrots	Wash. Mature carrots: cut up. Young carrots: leave whole.	Place in pot with a few tablespoons water. Cover	Sprinkle with parsley just before serving.	20 minutes

	Preparation	Cooking Method	Seasoning	Time
		tightly and cook over medium heat until steam loosens lid (30 seconds). Reduce to low heat and cook tightly covered until done.		
Cauliflower	Remove leaves and some of woody stem. Wash. Separate into flowerets or leave whole.	Place in vegetable steaming rack in bottom of pot. Add water to level of rack bottom, cover tightly, and steam until tender.	Add thyme and savory before cooking.	15 to 20 minutes, whole, 10 to 15 minutes, flowerets
Corn	Remove husks and silk, and wash well. Leave kernels on cob. or Slice kernels off, cutting shallowly toget only top half of kernels. Gather remaining juices and hearts of kernels off cob by scraping cob with back of knife blade.	Drop into boiling water and boil until tender. Cover with water and boil until tender.	Toss in rosemary or marjoram before cooking. Add marjoram before cooking.	10 minutes 5 minutes
Eggplant	Pare and dice.	Cover with small amount of water or tomato juice and simmer until tender.	Sprinkle with basil, onion flakes, and pepper halfway through cooking.	45 minutes to 1 hour

VEGETABLE COOKING AND SPICING CHART

VEGETABLE	PRECOOKING PREPARATION	COOKING PROCEDURE	SPICES TO ADD	COOKING TIME
Lentils	Wash.	Simmer, covered, in 2½ cups water per cup lentils, until tender.	Season with oregano in last 30 minutes of cooking.	2½ hours
Peas (green)	Shell and wash.	Combine with a few tablespoons water, cover tightly, and cook over medium heat until steam loosens lid (30 seconds or so). Reduce heat to low, and cook tightly covered without lifting lid.	Before cooking begins, dash in savory and thyme. Or sprinkle lightly with rosemary.	10 to 15 minutes
Potatoes Young	Wash well. Do not peel.	Cover with water and boil until tender. Drain and peel if desired.	Season with fresh ground pepper before serving.	15 to 20 minutes
Mature	Wash well. Cook either: peeled and sliced;	Cover with small amount water and boil until tender. Drain.	Season with pepper and parsley flakes before serving.	10 to 15 minutes
	or whole.	Cover with water and boil until tender. Drain and peel.	Season with pepper and parsley flakes before serving.	30 to 40 minutes
		or Bake at 350° until tender.	Season with sour cream and chives.	About 1 hour

Rice	Use non-instantized brown rice.	Combine rice with water or stock (2½ cups liquid for each cup rice). Bring to boil, cover, and simmer until tender. Fluff with fork before serving.	Sprinkle with thyme and season liberally with parsley before fluffing and serving.	1 hour
Spinach	Rinse well, and chop.	Use no water when cooking except the water remaining on leaves after washing. Place in pan, cover tightly, and cook over medium heat until steam is generated to loosen the lid. Reduce heat to low and cook tightly covered until tender.	Sprinkle on fresh nutmeg before serving.	8 minutes
Squash Summer squash (zucchini, cymling, yellow, crookneck, etc.)	Wash well, and slice, with or without paring.	Fry, a cup at a time, in 2 tablespoons water over high heat, holding lid tightly in place with hand and shaking pan occasionally. Do not overcook. Should be somewhat crisp.	Dash in thyme, savory, or nutmeg before serving. Dash in fresh ground pepper also, if desired.	3 or 4 minutes

VEGETABLE COOKING AND SPICING CHART

VEGETABLE	PRECOOKING PREPARATION	COOKING PROCEDURE	SPICES TO ADD	COOKING TIME
Winter squash (acorn, Hubbard, turban, banana, butternut, etc.)	Cube the flesh of the squash, discarding rind and seeds. *or* Cut into serving pieces. Do not pare.	Place 1 inch water in large saucepan. Heat to boiling, add squash, cover, and simmer until tender. Bake at 350° until tender.	Add basil before cooking. Sprinkle on cinnamon before serving. Sprinkle with cinnamon before serving.	20 minutes 1 to 1½ hours
Sweet Potatoes or Yams	Scrub. Do not pare.	Cover with water and boil until tender. Drain, peel, and serve. *or* Bake at 450° until fork-tender.	Dash on Angostura Bitters before serving. Allow guests to split yams and season with fresh ground pepper at table.	30 to 45 minutes 1 hour
Tomatoes	Peel; plunge briefly in boiling water, then remove loosened skin. Chop, saving juice.	Place in saucepan with chopped onions and chopped green peppers. Simmer slowly in own juice (nothing more) covered.	Season with pepper and parsley flakes before serving.	10 to 25 minutes

MEASUREMENT EQUIVALENTS

Dash . . . . $1/16$ Teaspoon
1 Tablespoon . . . . .3 Teaspoons
2 Tablespoons . . . . .1 fluid Ounce
4 Tablespoons . . . . .¼ Cup
5 Tablespoons plus 1 Teaspoon . . . . .⅓ Cup
8 Tablespoons . . . . .½ Cup

1 Ounce[1] . . . . .2 Tablespoons
2 Ounces[1] . . . . .¼ Cup
4 Ounces[1] . . . . .½ Cup
6 Ounces[1] . . . . .¾ Cup
8 Ounces[1] . . . . .1 Cup

For water (or substances with density of water):
1 Fluid Ounce . . . . .1 Weight Ounce
2 Cups . . . . .1 Pound
1 Pint ("A pint's a pound the world around.") . . . . .1 Pound

16 Ounces[1] . . . . .1 Pint
16 Ounces[2] . . . . .1 Pound
2 Cups . . . . .1 Pint
4 Cups . . . . .1 Quart
2 Pints . . . . .1 Quart
4 Quarts . . . . .1 Gallon
8 Pints . . . . .1 Gallon

1. fluid ounce
2. weight ounce

CAN-SIZE EQUIVALENTS

8-Ounce . . . . .1 Cup
Buffet . . . . .1 Cup
Picnic . . . . .1¼ Cups
No. 300 . . . . .1¾ Cups
No. 1 Tall . . . . .2 Cups
No. 303 . . . . .2 Cups
No. 2 . . . . .2½ Cups
No. 2½ . . . . .3½ Cups
No. 3 Cylinder or 46-Ounce . . . . .5¾ Cups
No. 10 . . . . .12 to 13 Cups

HOW MUCH BEFORE AND HOW MUCH AFTER
Before and After Purchase
Before and After Cooking

FOOD	AS PURCHASED→IN KITCHEN to	BEFORE COOKING→AFTER COOKING to
Apples	1 pound → 3 cups, sliced	——
Asparagus	1 pound ———————————→	1 cup cooked tips, +1 cup chopped cooked stems
Beans,[1] dried	1 pound → 2½ cups	1 cup → 2⅓ cups
Beets	1 pound ———————————→	2 cups, diced cooked
Black-eyed peas, dried	1 pound → 2⅔ cups	1 cup → 4½ cups
Broccoli	1 pound ———————————→	1 cup cooked flowerets, +½ cup chopped cooked stems
Cabbage	1 pound → 4 cups, shredded	——
Carrots	1 pound → 2½ cups, diced	——

1. See separate headings for black-eyed peas, green beans, kidney beans, lentils, lima beans, and peas.

Ingredient	Conversion	
Cauliflower	1 pound → 3 cups pieces	1 cup pieces → 2/3 cup pieces
Celery	1 small bunch (1/2 pound → 2 cups diced)	
Cheese	1 pound → 5 cups freshly grated	
Corn	1 medium ear (6 ounces) → 2/3 cup kernels	1 cup → 3/4 cup
Cornmeal	1 pound → 3 cups	1 cup → 4 cups
Cottage cheese	1 pound → 3 cups	
Flour, white	1 pound → 4 cups	
Flour, whole wheat	1 pound → 3 3/4 cups	
Green beans	1 pound → 3 1/2 cups, sliced & cooked	
Green peppers	1 pound → 2 1/2 cups	
Hamburger	1 pound → 2 cups	
Kidney beans, dried	1 pound → 1 1/2 cups	1 cup → 6 cups
Lentils	1 pound → 2 2/3 cups	1 cup → 3 cups

HOW MUCH BEFORE AND HOW MUCH AFTER

Before and After Purchase
Before and After Cooking

FOOD	AS PURCHASED → (to) IN KITCHEN	BEFORE COOKING → (to) AFTER COOKING
Lima beans, dried	1 pound → 2⅓ cups	1 cup → 1½ cups
Lima beans, pods	1 pound → ¾ cup, shelled	1 cup → 1¼ cups
Macaroni	1 pound → 5 cups	1 cup → 2 cups
Milk, nonfat dry	1 pound → 4 cups	——
Mushrooms	1 pound → 5 cups, sliced	——
Noodles	1 pound → 6 cups	1 cup → 1¾ cups
Oats, rolled	1 pound → 5 cups	1 cup → 1¾ cups
Onions	1 medium (⅓ pound) → ½ cup chopped	——
Peas, in pod	1 pound ————	→ 1 cup shelled & cooked

Peas, split	1 pound → 2 cups	1 cup → 2½ cups
Potatoes	1 pound (3 medium) —————→ 2½ cups diced cooked, or 2 cups mashed	
Rice[2]	1 pound → 2¼ cups	1 cup → 3½ cups
Spaghetti	1 pound → 5 cups, broken	1 cup → 2 cups
Spinach	1 pound → 4 cups raw, chopped	4 cups (chopped) → 1½ cups
Sweet potatoes	1 pound (3 medium) —————→ 2 cups mashed, cooked	
Tomatoes	1 pound → 2 cups, chopped	———
Wild rice	1 pound → 2⅔ cups	1 cup → 4½ cups

2. See separate heading for wild rice.

GENERAL INDEX

The items and recipes in boldface constitute a vegetarian index. The authors have included recipes that call for gelatin, rennet and junket, but would like to point out that nonanimal alternatives to these items are available at Health Food Stores.

RECIPE TITLE INDEX

NOTES

NOTES

NOTES

NOTES

NOTES

NOTES

NOTES

NOTES

NOTES

NOTES